Memories
of World War II
AND ITS AFTERMATH

By a Little Girl Growing up in Berlin

Memories
of World War II
AND ITS AFTERMATH

1 9 4 0 - 1 9 5 4

By a Little Girl Growing up in Berlin

AN AUTOBIOGRAPHY
Inge E. Stanneck Gross
VOLUME ONE

Island In the Sky Publishing Co.
Eastsound, Washington
www.MemoriesOfWWII.com

ABOUT THE PHOTOGRAPHS, MAPS AND ILLUSTRATIONS
The vast majority of photographs in this book were taken by the author or her family members and are used by permission. Every effort has been made by the author and publisher to locate and secure permission from the copyright owners of historical photographs, maps and illustrations from the World War II era that may be still protected under copyright. A few such images from the author's scrapbook are used pursuant to the fair use doctrine or because they are apparently now in the public domain. However, if any reader is able to provide further information on the origin of any of these images, the author would appreciate being contacted through the Publisher at the offices listed below.

Published by Island In The Sky Publishing Co.
P.O. Box 139, Eastsound, Washington 98245-0139
www.MemoriesOfWWII.com

Publisher's Cataloging-in-Publication Data

Gross, Inge Erika.
    Memories of World War II and its aftermath : by a little girl growing up in Berlin   1940 to 1954 : an autobiography volume one / Inge E. Stanneck Gross.

    p. cm.
    ISBN-13: 978-0-97603-286-1
    ISBN-10: 0-9760328-6-4

    1. Gross, Inge Erika. 2. World War, 1939–1945—Personal narratives. 3. German-Americans–Biography. 4. Berlin (Germany)—History. 5. Berlin (Germany)—History—Blockade, 1948–1949. 6. Russians—Germany (East). I. Title.

D811.5 G7 2005
921—dd22   2004110582

Jacket design by Linda Griffith, Portland, Oregon
Printed in the United States of America by Patterson Printing Co.

Contents

Foreword

I have read many books by those who were associated with Berlin during and after World War II but none that expresses so well the human dimension over such a span of time. Inge brilliantly covers the war years, years after the war, being under the Soviet thumb for eighteen months, the Airlift experience, and the period leading up to her immigration to America. This exceptional work is wrapped up in a blanket of gratitude born of terrible sacrifice. All the above is a first–hand, on–the–scene account.

It is a must reference document for educational institutions and community libraries, historical organizations, German American clubs and similar organizations. It is also an excellent read for inquisitive minds searching for the meaning of life and the power of determination.

My first flight to Berlin was early in July 1948. I turned the wings of my heavily laden C-54 Skymaster over the bleak ruins of that once magnificent city and headed for Tempelhof Central Airport. I couldn't imagine how over two million West Berliners could survive in that moonscape. I had 20,000 pounds of flour in the back end. That would help some, but it would take a lot more. Stalin had cut off all means of livelihood for the West Berliners—coal, food, electricity, everything! We were called on short notice to feed our former enemy. At first I didn't feel too good about that. Those were faceless people until I got to know some of them. Most were women and children. They had to have food or starve, but they wanted freedom more than flour. We had both. Their exceptional gratitude melted barriers between former antagonists.

West Berlin children told me, "We don't have to have enough to eat. Just give us a little. Someday we will have enough to eat, but if we loose our freedom we will never get it back." *American* style freedom was their dream—Hitler's past and Stalin's future, their nightmare.

I didn't know it at the time, but some of the bricks under my wings were all that was left of the apartment that once housed a little girl of six. I was destined to meet her years later. She with her family had fled in only their night clothes down one of those streets the night of 1 March 1943. One hundred barrels of gasoline near their apartment were about to explode. Buildings all about them were aflame. You will feel the heat of the fires. Her account will place you beside her in the apartment cellar; often her only refuge during the almost nightly bombings. You will feel the dread of a little girl going to school each morning, wondering which of her friends would not be there; wondering when her time would come—not *if*, but when.

This incredible book is an absolutely riveting story of survival against all odds, and describes what freedom means in language one can fully understand. Inge is the little girl, now an author and proud to be an American citizen. Her description of events and people during the war, afterward, the Airlift, and her difficult path to America is unique. There are very few people alive who were so deeply immersed in each phase, and fewer yet with her mastery of the English language. Her beautiful descriptions put you there in person, and almost a hundred pictures from that period help the reader visualize what she is describing.

The story of her mother's love is woven through the fabric of her life like a golden thread. Her father was captured at Stalingrad and was one of the very few who survived. He returned on foot to Berlin in 1945, seven months after the war was over, starved, barely alive, and not recognizable. Inge describes in her grandmother's words the emotional reunion after he finally convinced her that he was her son.

Her mother engineered the family's escape from Berlin on 3 March 1943, without permission, to the little country town of Straupitz. It was here in 1945 that the town was overrun by Soviet troops. You feel the anxious concern of her mother and Inge, now a tall ten–year–old. There was rape, stealing and a fight to survive. Totally innocent, Inge did not realize the danger she was in. Her description of the steps her mother took to protect her without telling her "why" are beautiful and humorous. For almost eighteen months she lived under Communist rule. Kind actions by some Russians, especially to the children, were not enough to dim her drive for freedom. She wanted no part of Communism.

In November 1946 they had to navigate the Communist checkpoints to move back to West Berlin. You feel the tension as they arrive at their final checkpoint, five hours after their Russian permit to leave the Russian Occupation Zone had expired, and they wondered if they would be turned back.

The years after the war were equally hard and the family barely survived. The time of the Blockade was especially difficult. Inge since age eight had the total responsibility of handling the family's precious ration cards. She stood in grocery lines for hours at a time to get food before supplies ran out. She would often faint from hunger. Many starved during this period.

I began dropping handkerchief parachutes, laden with candy and gum to the children of West Berlin starting in July 1948. Sometime between then and the New Year I dropped a load of these goodies and almost hit Inge's brother, Peter, but he didn't get one. Inge's account of his description of what happened is special.

I first met Inge in 1998 in Washington DC at a Berlin Airlift Veterans Association (BAVA) annual meeting. All of a sudden this beautiful woman comes up to me, threw her arms around my neck, gave me a big hug. There were tears streaming down her face. She was there to say "thank you" to all the veterans for their part, almost fifty years ago, in saving her life and the lives of 2.2 million other Berliners during the Berlin Blockade. She won the hearts of all the Airlift veterans at the meeting. Inge has become a member of BAVA. She attends all of our meetings to express her gratitude. I quickly presented Inge with her "Hershey" candy bar since she had not caught one in 1948-1949.

In my view, the real civilian heroes of the Berlin Airlift were the West Berliners. They slept in bombed–out buildings with little or no heat, little food, and very little electricity. They said they would never give in to the Russians. Inge epitomizes that spirit and the reason the Airlift succeeded.

Inge immigrated to America in 1954 but visited West Berlin again in 1962. One night she had no way of knowing that two of her East Berlin cousins were on their stomachs with their only possessions being the clothes on their backs, a shovel, and some barbed–wire cutters, headed to the canal that separated them from freedom in West Berlin. So many before had bartered all they had, including their lives, for a chance to be free—and had lost. Miraculously the cousins made it through. Three days later they related to Inge each challenge they faced in the process. You will relive each of these life and death challenges because Inge immediately recorded their words in a long letter to her husband which she has included in this book.

This is a wonderful account of very difficult times. Yet as you read Inge's words you will find a person with a wonderful, positive outlook on life; someone who wanted no part of Communism, and truly is proud to be a citizen of this great country.

We are proud to have her as an active member of BAVA. She is a constant reminder to all the aircrews and all the ground personnel of Britain, France and the United States of why we were there.

You will learn, laugh, be edified and enjoy each exciting chapter. More significantly, you will better appreciate and understand the importance of the right to choose ones own destiny. This inherent implant resides in the soul of every human being, irrespective of borders or frontiers. This precious commodity does not come free. We recognize it as *freedom,* conceived by our founding fathers on the axiom, "In God We Trust." Inge's book speaks to this inherent need.

Gail S. Halvorsen, Col USAF (Ret)
The Berlin Candy Bomber

Known to Inge and the children of Berlin as
Uncle Wiggly Wings and *The Chocolate Pilot*

Preface

The birth of my first grandchild—Meagen Moser—thirteen years ago prompted me to recognize that neither of my children, and to a lesser extent my husband—Mal—really knew what my life was like as a child growing up in wartime Berlin. Yes, they knew the broad outline—and we had visited Berlin—but I had never really wanted to talk about some of my childhood experiences—they were in my past, and some were experiences that are perhaps best left in the past.

Just before Meagen's birth I decided I would try to write about my early childhood in Berlin. I was almost six years old when my father was drafted, and I became aware that Berlin was being bombed. It was difficult for me to transpose my mind back into that of a six–year–old, trying to remember what it felt like, and what my emotions were, which I had for so long tried to forget. I found that I could not just sit down and remember—I had to be alone without interruptions. I would remember a tiny piece of some event and by working hard at it, gradually transpose myself back in time to that era. One memory tag led to another, and over time I was able to recall many events that I had totally forgotten about.

It was both a painful and a therapeutic process—painful because of the memories of horrible things that happened, and therapeutic because reliving the experiences helped to erase some of the pain that had been bottled up within me for more than half a century.

What started out as an effort to write down some of my early memories for just my family has turned into a far more ambitious project. I shared parts of the manuscript with a number of friends during the intervening years, and all have encouraged me to continue and to expand it. They pointed out that as time goes by there are fewer and fewer people left from that era, and even fewer still who have written about those times. It is my hope that these pages will not only add to my children and grandchildren's knowledge, but will contribute to the history of that time.

Originally I had intended to cover only the war years (1940 to 1945), but I quickly realized that the years after the war had been even more difficult, and that this story, too, needed to be recorded. I immigrated to the United States on the M.S. Italia from Hamburg in May 1954, and this book ends at that point.

In fact, I did not stop writing but continued. A second book covering the period 1954 to 2004 is also being published at this time, describing my experiences as a new immigrant to this wonderful country, and providing a fairly detailed account of my life—and adventures.

I have included an epilogue in this book with a brief outline of my life over the past fifty years for the reader who may wonder what happened to me after I immigrated. I have also included several detailed excerpts from this second book that relate to the infamous Berlin Wall and the Cold War because they had their origin in World War II and in many ways are a continuation of the story I am telling here.

I thank my husband, Malvern Gross, for his encouragement and support, as well as his technical help in laying out the book in an electronic document that my printer could use. My book coach, Joyce Griffith, and my design artist, Linda Griffith, both provided invaluable help in making these books happen. Special recognition goes to Sylvia Cole of Tricor Press for her unselfish assistance in providing her insights as well as editing skills.

This book has also allowed me to acknowledge the contributions many people have made in my life without whom I would not be here today. More than any other person, my mother, Johanna Stanneck, has been the guiding light in my life. Her legacy lives on in my brother Peter and me.

Inge E. Stanneck Gross
Eastsound, WA
February 2005

Dedicated to the Memory of
Our Mother

Johanna M. Stanneck

Peter and I would not be here today
but for her unselfish devotion, common sense,
innate intuition, and the ability to find humor
in the most bleak of circumstances.

PART I

THE WAR YEARS

1

Fall 1940
The End of my Childhood Innocence
Age Six

Berlin Deutschland

Memories of my First Air Raid

August 25, 1940. I was nearly six years old and knew nothing about war. Not until that night anyway. Peter, my little brother, was just two. It was not customary to get a baby sitter for young children. When the parents went out for an evening, the keys to the apartment were left with neighbors who would occasionally look in on the sleeping kids, or listen for anyone crying.

Mom told me she was going to accompany Papa to the railroad station. He had been drafted by the army to report for active duty and was leaving that evening. If the real reason for Papa's departure was explained to me, I did not understand the significance of it. Mom gave me instructions that if Peter started to cry and did not stop, I could give him the bottle which had been set on the kitchen table. I don't know how many hours Mom was away, but it seemed like forever because I was scared. One of those frequent violent thunderstorms had awakened me, and unlike other times I remembered, it lasted for a much longer time. I have always been afraid of thunderstorms, and that night I was alone and had to worry about the baby waking up and crying. I kept hoping he would not because I was too scared to go into the kitchen to fetch the bottle.

There seemed to be much more lightning than I had seen during other thunderstorms, and the thunder sounded different somehow. I spent a good part of the time hiding underneath my featherbed praying that the baby would not cry and that Mom would return soon. Peter was a good little boy, he slept right through it all. But why was Mom not returning? The railroad station was not that far away, even though I thought it was a long ways each time we had to walk there to catch the train when we went to Grandma's.

What I did not know was that Papa had to leave from Berlin's central railroad station *Anhalter Bahnhof* on a long distance train, and that the departure of that train as well as Mom's return were delayed by the first major air raid on Berlin. There had been other more minor air raids during which the people in our area mostly stayed in their apartments. We lived near the southwestern edge of the city with no targets nearby that were of importance. During this particular air raid the center of the city had been bombed, and Mom and Papa had to take cover in an air raid shelter. They were worried sick about us. Meanwhile, our good neighbors decided not to wake us after checking and hearing no crying. They spent the whole time sitting on the steps outside our apartment. When Mom returned I told her how afraid I was of the terrible thunderstorm. She comforted me and said she had heard it, too, and let it go at that.

The rude Awakening

The next day I played with a boy who was a year older than I was, and he knew.

When I told him about the most terrible thunderstorm the night before, he told me that what had happened during the night was called an "air raid." Airplanes fly over the city and drop bombs which will make our houses explode. He also told me that from an airplane the houses look as small as match boxes. I found that fascinating. After all, to a small child an apartment house in Berlin is about the biggest thing there is. For a house to look as small as a match box was unimaginable—fantastic—awesome—like magic! The wonder of that fact blocked out any fear about future air raids and the possibility that we and our house might be blown to bits.

The question as to why "somebody" was trying to do this to us, and why those somebodies hated us so much was to come up time and again during the many subsequent air raids. Reinhard, the boy who had told me about air raids did not know, and for the moment it was not as important as the wonder of an airplane that flies high up in the sky where the clouds are and makes big houses look little, like match boxes. Wouldn't it be wonderful to go up in an airplane and see those match boxes! I did not know until now as I am writing this that man's inherent dream to fly and to see what a bird sees surfaced in me at that time. I remember exactly the awe I felt at the moment the boy told me about the match boxes, and how I wished I could see them, even though that dream seemed too unreal to come true. Many years later I would pilot an airplane myself and think of that moment of awe. The impression never left me. To this day, when I see an old–fashioned match box I think of big houses seen from airplanes, and when I look out of an airplane window and see houses, I think of match boxes.

Bombs and Ration Cards

After that memorable day those fantastic airplanes became frequent nightly visitors, and the terror they brought made their magic fade into the background. Oh, at first the air raids seemed exciting. We could get up in the middle of the night, get dressed and go to the big house by the street and visit with Tante Hilda and Onkel Rudolf and all the other neighbors. We sat in the damp, spooky cellar that had little stables with neat stuff stored in them. The house was quite old. There were dirt floors and no electric light down in the cellar, and we had to use candles. I loved candlelight. It was like Christmas. Everyone had moved some chairs into the cellar so we could sit down. But after a few times the visiting wasn't much fun because the people were tired—and cold— and scared, especially when the noise outside was like big thunderclaps, and close by. Then it seemed as if the bombs were falling right on top of us. The house shook with every nearby explosion; bits of mortar loosened and fell from the brick walls and bits of plaster from the ceiling. Some old people started to pray, and others moaned or let out little yells. All this was frightening me.

A couple of times after air raids had done damage in the part of the city in which we lived, Onkel Heinz, my friend Alice's father, took Alice and me to look at the bombed buildings. We thought it was rather neat how a whole wall of a house and parts of the rooms could be blasted away, and we could see the people's furniture in what was left of the rooms. We also saw some burned–out houses. At that time the explosive bombs were fairly small, and fire bombs were most commonly sent down on us. Onkel Heinz also helped us look for bomb fragments which Alice and I started collecting. This was a fad with our playmates at the time. War was still somewhat exciting for us then. We had not yet come into contact with the horrors of it.

We still had enough to eat. There were ration cards, of course, but the food rations must have been adequate. I don't remember going hungry. I just remember adults reminiscing about the "good old times" when they could walk into the store and ask for half a pound of butter or sugar, rather than needing little paper coupons for everything. I do not remember when we started getting ration cards. I can only remember that they were always there and were a part of life. It seemed to be completely normal that, when my shoes got too small, we had to go to several places (government agencies) to request permit slips which we then took to the shoe store. The grown–ups were complaining about needing permit slips for everything as consumer goods began to disappear from the market. We did not own cars, so gasoline and tires were no matters of concern for us.

Berlin

"How could anyone ever come up with the idea of founding a city in the middle of all that sand?" wondered the French novelist Stendhal when he came to the Prussian capital in 1806. Berlin is located in the *Mark Brandenburg*, Germany's sandbox, where pine trees and potatoes thrive.

In the thirteenth century, two towns, Cölln and Berlin were located on the Spree River across from each other, and eventually they merged into one city—Berlin. As the city grew and spread, surrounding villages far beyond the downtown area were incorporated into the city limits. Keeping the original names of those villages as a part of the address was a good way of designating the location for the post office and for administration. Thus, Berlin is divided into twenty boroughs.

We lived in Berlin–Lichterfelde, which until 1920 was one of the outlying villages, and the rural flavor was still quite evident. Quaint, cobblestone streets lined with large trees were hiding expensive villas, interspersed with forest, rivers, and farmland. The stunning part of Berlin was the downtown area (*Berlin–Mitte*) with its grand avenues and monumental buildings, which included the castle and a magnificent cathedral called the "Dom."

The "Dom" was built in the nineteenth century and restored during the 1980's and 1990's.

Berlin covers an area of 883 square kilometers (330 square miles), as much as Munich, Frankfurt, and Stuttgart put together. Two major rivers, the Spree and the Havel, as well as numerous lakes and many miles of canals, comprise seven percent of Berlin's area, with a combined shoreline of more than 200 miles in West Berlin alone. There are 967 bridges spanning water—more than in Venice. Berlin can fairly claim to be the greenest metropolis in Europe with rural areas, parks, and the Grunewald forest totaling about a third of the whole city area.

Berlin is one of the youngest of Europe's great cities, its existence first documented in the year 1237. It experienced phenomenal growth. With two million inhabitants in 1900, Berlin became the fourth largest city in Europe. By the beginning of World War II, the city's population had grown to 4.3 million.

What really makes Berlin special, though, is the spirit and bounce of the city and its citizens. The Berliners have always distinguished themselves for their high–voltage energy, quick senses, and quick tongues, as well as a unique mentality. Berlin's dry wit expresses itself in a quick, sober, typically Berlin way of speaking and thinking. The notorious Berlin humor lies on the same wave length. It often sounds more biting than is intended and contains a large measure of irony. The Berliners have an undisputed talent for seeing the funny side of even the most unpleasant aspects of life. Their quick tongues, however, are by far outdone by their big hearts. *Schnauze mit Herz* (quick tongue with a lot of heart) is how those bold and daring types of humans, the Berliners, are labeled. They are tough and realistic, no nonsense types, and their quick wit and humor, especially during critical times, cannot easily be extinguished. They are survivors, although many of their fellow countrymen consider them a most rude species.

Berliners love their city with its numerous lakes, rivers, canals, parks and the *Grunewald* (Green Forest). In fine weather a Sunday is not complete without an excursion *ins Grüne* (into a green area), even if it is just an afternoon stroll in a city park. The fierce pride and love Berliners have for their 412,000 city trees is unparalleled.

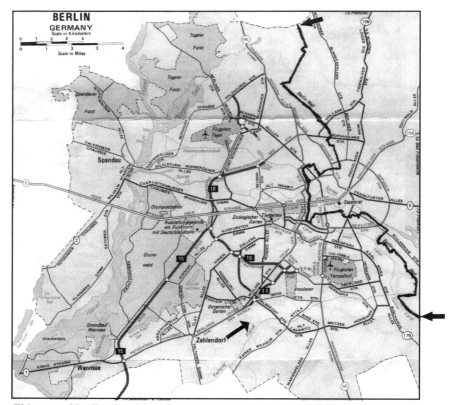

This map of Berlin also shows the infamous Berlin Wall, highlighted, running from the SE section up to the top middle of the map (see arrows). It was built in 1961 at the height of the Cold War. The bottom center arrow points to where we lived.

Where we Lived

We lived in a beautiful city. A ride through the *Grunewald* on the child's seat of Papa's bike was a real treat on a Sunday afternoon. In the summer we would stop at one of the lakes to swim, or visit Onkel Karl and Tante Martha at their garden. Onkel Karl's garden was a big wonder for me. Another innate desire of man is wanting to watch things grow. People who could afford it owned little garden plots in some not yet built up areas of Berlin. Grandma Stanneck's brother, Onkel Karl, was one of those lucky people, and we were lucky to know somebody who owned a garden! I got to pick and eat gooseberries, red and black currants, strawberries, apples, and

Papa and I in Onkel Karl's garden

pears. Tante Martha baked the best gooseberry tarts. There was a small cottage on their garden plot, but it was only big enough for the two of them to stay overnight.

I especially enjoyed visiting Tante Martha and Onkel Karl. Their apartment was in Berlin–Zehlendorf which, next to Berlin–Dahlem, was one of the nicest boroughs of Berlin located in the southwestern part of the city and bordering on the *Grunewald*. The subway stop there was special to me for a number of reasons. First, it was diagonally across the street from where they lived, and therefore not such a long walk. This was important to a little child. Second, it had a shopping

Tante Martha and Onkel Karl

We lived on the street level of this apartment building. The picture was taken in the early 1960's during a visit and before the building was torn down.

street along both sides of the underground station, and I always thought it was great to have all of the small grocery stores right next to each other rather than having to walk distances between the bakery, the butcher, the greengrocer, as we had to do where we lived. The subway in that area was not really underground but in an open depression, like a big ditch. The name of the station was, and still is, *Onkel Toms Hütte* (Uncle Tom's Cabin). After exiting the subway station there are pine trees everywhere, and one has the feeling of being in the forest already. *Grunewald* is the name of Berlin's beloved forest.

The apartment buildings were very contemporary, only three stories high, and painted in different pastel colors. That was really "far out" in the 1930's. I found it cheerful and very special. Tante Martha and Onkel Karl never had children, and they obviously enjoyed it when my parents brought me to visit them. I enjoyed being fussed over, I guess, after I got over the ordeal of being kissed.

Cows and Cobblestones

We lived in Berlin–Lichterfelde–West, and in the most wonderful place as far as I was concerned. During the Depression when Papa's job as a typesetter for a publishing house came to an end, he had been without a permanent job for five years. Just before my birth in 1934 he become a salesman for a tobacco company. He did not earn much and we could not afford to live in a fancy apartment building, so we lived in one of the plain ones located in a rural area of old villas. Until its incorporation into the city of Berlin in 1920, *Groß–Lichterfelde* (Greater Lichterfelde) was a popular suburb with the well–to–do.

In those days, milk did not come in cartons which were filled in factories, but rather from live cows. Even in the city there were stables in which cows were kept and milked every day. The milk was transported through the neighborhoods in large milk cans which were placed on horse drawn carts. Wherever the milk wagon stopped, the driver rang a bell and people came with their containers to buy milk, which was measured out in liters down to fractions of quarter liters.

Unlike the crowded inner city tenements, we were quite spacious in the suburbs. Our apartment building complex was a small one, consisting of two four–story buildings facing the street with about fifteen apartments each, and two buildings at right angles in the back, each housing two families upstairs and there were stables below. In the stables were the milk cows, of course, as well as draft horses and pigs. A few of the tenants kept chickens in a row of small stables farther in the back beyond the manure pit, which was next to the coal yard. The four houses were set in a horseshoe shape around a good sized square yard,

The courtyard behind our apartment. I am the small child looking over my left shoulder at Mom taking the picture. I was two years old. There was a coal dealer's stock yard at the rear of the yard beyond the flowering tree. The left side of the yard had cobblestones, but the right side was sand. Note the old vehicles.

Several mothers are sitting in the yard in front of the storage sheds enjoying the good weather. Mom is on the left and I am sitting on her lap.

half of which was paved with large cobblestones and the other half was packed sand. Fenced in at the far end of the yard was a coal dealer's stock area. This caused a spectacular fire after an air raid a couple of years later. A driveway went from the street to the coal yard through the center of this horseshoe.

Between our house in the back near the coal yard and the big house by the street was a row of sheds. One of them was a garage in which Herr Thieme, the taxi driver, kept his taxi. Another was the laundry room with large wooden tubs and a big kettle for boiling the laundry. The other sheds were mostly used for storing bikes and other outdoor items. This was on the sandy half of the yard. There were also large metal poles on which the clotheslines were strung. It was the sunny side of the yard and a popular place for the ladies to sit in the afternoons and knit, sew, and gossip while supervising young children at play.

The cobblestone paved half of the yard was to be kept off limits for us kids for safety reasons. It was where the wagon traffic moved. Besides, we were always skipping and running, then falling on these uneven cobbles and getting scraped and bruised. I remember Tante Else's wedding coming up in June of 1939 and Mom telling me that if I had skinned knees I would have to wear long stockings to the wedding to cover the unsightly scabs. Grandma Stanneck's knitted woolen stockings were hot and itchy, and it was almost summer so I enjoyed wearing anklets. I walked very gingerly during the week before the wedding and got only one little scrape on a knee. Mom's threat did not come true.

The cobblestone area was irresistible to us kids. There the wonderful wagons stood in their places in a row whenever they were not in use. Besides the milk wagons, there were hay and fodder wagons, animal transporters, and utility vehicles. We thought the wagons were the most wonderful places for play. I remember playing "wedding," decorating the "carriage" and ourselves with flowers retrieved from the nearby garbage containers. Another attraction was an occasional truckload of straw bales which was dumped at random when first delivered. This huge pile was by far our favorite place to climb on, hide in, and slide around on before the bales were neatly stacked in their storage area.

Our apartment was bright and sunny and had a large bedroom and kitchen. A little hall went off the kitchen to our living room, which was not quite as sunny in the summer because the branches of a pear tree shaded the windows. We used the living room only on Sundays, holidays, and birthdays when relatives and friends came to visit. Other-

Peter and I at a farm near Berlin. Those were happy days

wise we lived in the large kitchen which was always warm. The only praise Mom had for living in an apartment above cow stables was that we always had warm floors, and therefore warm feet. Otherwise she found it rather embarrassing to live there. For us kids it was sheer paradise. We had the benefit of a little bit of country life in a big city.

My Friends

One of my playmates was Alice Lochner. She lived in the house across the yard from us, above the horse stables. Her parents, whom I called Tante Frieda and Onkel Heinz, were good friends of my parents. They sometimes went to the movies together at night. We celebrated Christmas and birthdays together, and in the summer we went to the *Grunewaldsee* (Grunewald Lake) to swim. Alice and I kept in touch until her recent death, and we called each other "sandbox friends" because we played in the sandbox together.

Then there was Ursula Lusch. Her parents had a fruit and vegetable stand at different weekly produce markets.

Reinhard Engel had the most wonderful toys. Trains, cars, trucks,

In the yard with some of my playmates. I am in the center with the small wheelbarrow. Behind me are (from left) Hans Binternagel, Ursula Lusch, Eva Binternagel, Werner Henkel and Anneliese Huhn.

and soldiers. His father was a scientist with the government, and they were "rich" in our eyes. Reinhard was the boy who told me about air raids, airplanes and matchbox–size houses.

Anneliese Huhn was being raised by her grandmother. I caught the whooping cough from her. Eva and Hans Binternagel were twins. Their father was the coal dealer and their mother yelled a lot. Then there was Werner Henkel. I don't remember anything particular about him or his parents.

My Family

My brother Peter was born in 1938 and we have always been very close. We had no other siblings. As the older sister Mom counted on me to look out for and take care of Peter, particularly in later years when she had to work.

My father, Erich August Paul Stanneck, was born in Cottbus, about 70 miles southeast of Berlin. He was the third of five children, but all except he had died either in infancy or at very young ages. At some point the family moved to Berlin, most likely to find work. I never met Grandfather Stanneck, but I have a picture of him with a lawn mower and was told that he was a landscape gardener. He left Grandma when Papa was still a young boy. From what I heard, Grandma never got over it. This, plus losing four of her five children, most likely accounted for her unnatural attachment to her son Erich, who was all she had left The abnormally strong bond between mother and son was a wedge in my parents' marriage and eventually led to their separation and divorce.

My mother, Johanna Magdalene Elisabeth Hinniger, was born in Berlin–Lichtenberg, a suburb east of the city. She was the youngest of five children, having two brothers and two sisters, all of whom lived in Berlin with their families. Actually, seven children had been born, but infant mortality played a part in the Hinniger family as well.

Grandfather Hinniger was a butcher and owned a butcher shop in the working class area of *Berlin–Mitte* (city center), where the family lived. Grandmother Hinniger tended the store while Grandfather and an apprentice made all the sausages and cut the meats that were sold. The Great Depression, which also hit Europe, started when the Hinniger children grew up. The two boys found jobs at the city's

*From top left: August and Marie Stanneck (Papa's parents), Johanna and
    Erich Stanneck (my parents)*
*Middle row: Adolf and Martha Hinniger (Mom's parents), Charlotte Hinniger
    Tilch (Mom's middle sister),*
*Bottom row: Helmut Hinniger (Mom's younger brother), Hans Hinniger
    (Mom's oldest brother), Hildegard Hinniger Sawinski (Mom's oldest sister)*

Papa was an only surviving child. Mom was the youngest of five children.

slaughterhouse, and the two older girls were training in butcher shops, selling meats and sausage. Mom, as was characteristic of her during her entire lifetime, fell out of line. She sought an education and became a tailor.

Tante Hilda (Hildegard) was Mom's oldest sister. She and Onkel Rudolf lived in the same apartment complex as we did, in the house by the street, or the "front house," as we referred to it. They had no children, and I have very fond memories of them from my earlier years.

Tante Hilda's first husband, Onkel Hans, died before I was three. He was crazy about children. I have been told that in public Onkel Hans liked to pretend that I was his child. When we all went on outings together he would take me into a different car on the train or the streetcar, from where my parents and Tante Hilda were. He also bought most of my toys—the big toys, such as a doll carriage and a big doll, for my birthday. I remember him taking me into toy stores and letting me make selections.

Before the war, when candy was still available, I would go to Tante Hilda and beg a few pennies from her to buy gummi bears. Those were my favorite candies then, and still are.

There were also cousins. Mom's sister Charlotte (Tante Lotte) had two sons, Heinz and Klaus. She married Onkel Martin who was a butcher, and they owned their own butcher shop.

Mom's oldest brother, Hans, had a daughter, Erika. I liked visiting there. Erika is a year older than I am, and I got my middle name from her. She was an only child and did not have to share her toys or spend her play time watching a younger sibling. From experience I knew that a little brother can be a drag. On the other hand, I adored my little brother and was always proud of how cute he was.

Mom's youngest brother, Helmut, was engaged at that time.

Grandma Stanneck's niece, Tante Else, also lived in Berlin with her two little girls (her husband was away at war), and so did Grandma's brother, Onkel Karl and his wife, Tante Martha, whose garden plot we loved to visit.

Except for Tante Hilda, our family lived in different parts throughout the city, none close to each other. However, public transportation was excellent. Before the war and the bombings started, we would all visit with each other, especially on birthdays and special occasions. Later nobody ventured far from home, fearing to be caught in an air raid while separated from the rest of the family.

Happy Daytime Play and Frightening Nights

In the daytime we played happily in our farm paradise, but the nights became more and more frightening. During the fall months of 1940 when the days were still fairly long there were few air raids, and we kids nearly forgot about them. However, with early winter the nightly terror resumed, sometimes twice a night. Once the sirens went off signaling the start of an air raid, we usually did not have more than five minutes before the bombing and flak fire started. Mom had to dress herself as fast as she could, help me, and, running out of time she just wrapped Peter into a blanket and carried him. Since our building had only the stables downstairs, we had to run across the yard to reach the cellar of the front house. By that time the bombs were already falling and the flak was barking. We could often hear shrapnel falling all around us on our mad dash to the other building.

After too many of those scary dashes, and wondering how long our luck would hold before one of us got hit by shrapnel, Mom went to bed at night only partially undressed. Later, Onkel Rudolf who lived in the front house came over to help Mom with us and he carried Peter for her. One of the things we needed to do at the start of each air raid was to unlatch all windows so that they could blow open during the bomb blasts. This saved the glass from getting broken. Onkel Rudolf would take care of that while Mom helped me dress. I always froze with terror as soon as the dreaded sound of the sirens started up. My heart would pound, and I shook so violently that I could not manage to get into my clothes. Mom had to help me.

Eventually, when more often than not there were two air raids a night, Tante Hilda and Onkel Rudolf invited us to sleep in their apartment. Every evening after supper we "moved" to the front building. During the long nights of winter when darkness came before 4 p.m., the first air raid often came in the middle of supper. Mom and Tante Hilda consolidated the cooking and we "moved" before it got dark. Gypsy life had started for me.

Dinner conversation revolved mostly around speculations as to when the "Tommies" (British bombers) would show up for the first time that evening and how many hours they would stay. Would they come a second time tonight? And, most important to us, would we still be around to see the sun rise on another day? What cheerful subjects for a six–

year–old to listen to! I did not comprehend all of the things they talked about. Mom and Tante Hilda often whispered to each other, which was eerie, and I felt scared. I started to become afraid of nights because of the terror they brought.

Tante Hilda's apartment had only one bedroom. I slept on a chaise lounge in their room, Mom on the living room sofa, and Peter in a "basket" which consisted of two wicker chairs tied together. We were spending so much time in the cellar now that Mom fixed up a beach chair with blankets for me to sleep on, and moved the old baby carriage down there for Peter. I hardly ever slept. Bits of conversation picked up from the tenants' talk kept worrying me as much as the blasts of the bomb explosions outside. Somebody mentioned something about water and sewage pipes breaking and people drowning in the cellars. With each nearby explosion that shook the building, I anxiously looked at the many pipes on the ceiling.

When finally the "all clear" signal sounded, there would be sighs of relief. People were grateful that it hadn't been "our turn." However, everyone was sure that "our turn" would come—in time

2

1941
Our First Evacuation from Berlin
Age Six

The Eventful Year of 1941

The bombings went on throughout the rest of the winter and spring. Soon after we had started to spend most of our nights in the cellar, one of the handymen installed electric lights. The neighbors had long since stopped bringing their knitting and other crafts to the cellar at night. Everyone was too frozen with terror. The ominous thing was that the bombs whistled on their way down. If it sounded like a close one, we would hold our breath and pray that it hit right here rather than next door. Why? Nobody wanted to be buried alive or maimed— or drowned in sewage. A sure hit would get it over with fast, whereas a hit on the house next door or across the street would do only a partial job on us. Not all explosive bombs were large enough to do so much damage. We got pretty proficient at knowing by the whistling sound approximately how large a bomb was coming down. The magnitude of the explosion would confirm our guess.

Whenever a nearby bomb explosion rocked the building, dirt, plaster, and mortar fell off the ceiling and walls. The air pressure of the blasts was dreadful, and the noise deafening. Afterwards we would look around, surprised at still being alive, and anxiously make sure that our loved ones were all right, too.

Life was no longer fun, even for a six–year–old. During the day-time when we were playing we often found our fun would suddenly be disrupted by the shadow of fear of what might await us during the coming night.

I was nearly six–and–a–half years old and not yet in school. At that time in Germany, school started with first grade at age six. The beginning of the school year then was April 1, and my birthday is in September. The previous April, when I was not yet six, Mom thought I was too young and decided to wait another year. In the winter of 1941, however, the start of the school year was changed from April 1 to September 1. Consequently I was seven years old when I started school.

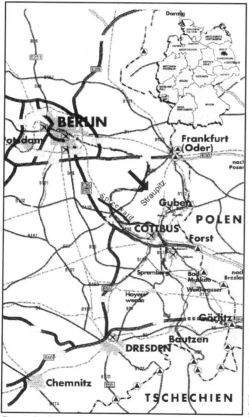

Our First Evacuation from Berlin

Berlin is quite far north, and in the summer the darkness of night is very short, perhaps only four hours. The planes needed this darkness to keep from being visible to the antiaircraft guns. As a result the summer days in Berlin went by with only an occasional air raid, and we could sleep in our own beds again. The novelty of moving to Tante Hilda's every evening had long since worn off. Mom dreaded a repeat of our moving routine once fall came with the longer nights and more air raids. So in August she decided to pack up Peter and me and move to a village about fifty

Straupitz is at the center of the map (arrow). Only fifty miles from Berlin, it took nearly all day by train. miles southeast of Berlin, to Straupitz in the Spreewald.

Narrow waterways wander throughout the Spreewald area. They are the "roads" in this part of the Spreewald.

"Spreewald" translates into "Forest of the Spree River." The area has always been quite a popular tourist and vacation destination, especially for Berliners. The Spree River makes a large curve, and inside that curve it splits into countless little rivulets. It is very picturesque. Some of the tiny villages which are located deep within the Spreewald have waterways instead of streets, and people get around only by boat. The children go to school by boat in the summer, and on ice skates in the winter.

Straupitz is one of the largest villages in the Spreewald, population then about six hundred. We knew about Straupitz because Tante Hilda had vacationed there and had friends in the area. She thought it would be a good town for us to move to.

The move was accomplished by train, taking only our clothes and essential household items—bed sheets, towels, pots and pans. It was somewhat like going on a camping trip, but by train. This meant that Mom had to carry everything, including three–year–old little brother. At age seven I could not be of much help to Mom in carrying things. Since it is said that necessity is the mother of invention, I can truthfully say that Mom invented the suitcase on wheels for that trip. Actually, we did not even own a suitcase. We did, however, own one of those wicker travel trunks which people used for ship voyages. It had been given to Mom by a friend, and it held everything we needed to take. But how could she move that trunk by herself? Well, we had a stroller for Peter, and Mom removed the chassis from the stroller and fastened it to the underside of the trunk. Then she propped Peter and the rest of the stroller on top of the trunk, and held me tightly by the hand while her other hand pushed the trunk.

First we had to go by electric elevated city train to get to the long–distance train station. I do not remember how she managed the stair-ways at the stations and interchange stations. I guess strangers were helpful to her. I do remember sitting in the waiting room at the long–distance train station and a man, staring in disbelief at Mom's travel-pyramid and exclaiming: "Oh, how marvelous—your travel trunk has wheels!" It surely was marvelous, for how could she have otherwise managed three train changes before we arrived at our destination?

I don't remember much about the village of Straupitz then. I do remember the family Wegener in whose house we had a room upstairs.

Tante Hilda (right) pictured here in the late 1930's wearing a Spreewald costume.

They were not farmers, but rather grew flowers in their garden and had a few little stables for domestic rabbits. I remember white rabbits with red eyes and some rabbits were gray; and there were many little baby rabbits.

Another memory is of the beautiful and colorful traditional costumes of the region which the women wore to church or on festive occasions. The same type of skirt with apron, blouse and scarf, but in black and gray colors, was worn daily to work around the house and farm. Work shoes were clogs which consisted of a wooden sole and a leather top front. The back was open.

"My first day of school" says the slate which Peter, age 3, is holding.

Starting School

September 1 was my big day. I started school—first grade. In Germany it is customary to get a *Schultüte*, a cone shaped colorful cardboard bag filled with candy. Mom had saved up sugar ration coupons to be able to buy some candy for me.

The school was diagonally across the street from where we lived. School children carried their books in leather bags strapped to their backs, with a wet sponge and dry rag hanging out on the side. We still used slates to write on, hence the sponge and rag which were attached to the slate with strings. I took school very seriously and enjoyed learning.

I had my seventh birthday two weeks later on September 13. We were working on an assignment near the end of the school day when the teacher happened to look out of the window. Excitedly he told me that my father had come home from the front. I argued, saying it could not be, because if Papa were coming home for my birthday he would

We are celebrating Papa's 36th birthday with the Wegener family. Papa had to return to the front the next morning. Peter is sitting on Frau Wegener's lap and I am standing between Papa and Mom.

have written and told us so. "Well," said Herr Maak, "I see your mother crossing the street with a soldier, and I am assuming that the soldier is your father. You come and look." Reluctantly I went to the window and Herr Maak lifted me up so that I could see. Sure enough, there were Mom and Papa, as well as my little brother, approaching the school. Herr Maak seemed almost more excited than I was. He urged me to leave right then and run to meet them, and he would pack up my school bag and bring it over later. I did run, but afterwards I brought Mom and Papa into the school to show them my classroom, and to meet my teacher and my friends. Papa was home on furlough for two weeks. It was to be a surprise for my birthday. Mom had known, of course. Papa's birthday was on September 25, so we could celebrate it together. He had to leave the day after his birthday to go back to war.

I continued to practice writing my numbers and letters on the slate. The written alphabet we learned then was the old Gothic script, which a year later was abolished by Hitler in favor of the universal Latin script. Thus, I had to learn how to read and write all over again when I was in second grade. My brother, being younger, never learned the old Gothic letters, and he could not read Mom's handwriting. It probably would not have mattered if we had stayed in Germany, but once Peter and I moved to the United States and received mail from our relatives, Peter always had to give their letters to me for "translation."

The schoolhouse in Straupitz had three classrooms. Two classrooms were in the main building. The first and second grades were together in one room, and grades three, four and five were in the other room. The two teachers, Herr Maak and Herr Schmitt and their families lived upstairs. Herr Maak circulated back and forth between the two classrooms located in the main school building. Grades six, seven and eight were in a loft above the carriage house across the school yard. Herr Schmitt was in charge there. During break we always went out beyond the fence to the edge of the surrounding wheat fields. The formal school yard was used only for the various physical education activities, mainly athletics, in place of a gymnasium.

Mom taught me how to knit and how to read the calendar. I had brought Rosemarie, my favorite small doll, with me from Berlin, and I knitted a white skirt for her. Mostly I enjoyed playing with Peter's little set of building blocks. I loved to build. When I put the blocks back into their little wagon, red, being my favorite color, always came first, blue second. Liking green and yellow equally well, these blocks took turns in third and fourth place.

3

1942
Back in Berlin
Age Seven

Berlin Again

Early in December 1941 we received word from Papa that he had been released from active duty until further notice because he was sick with dysentery. He was recuperating in Berlin, so we packed up and went home. I was happy to be back in Berlin for Christmas, but not about the air raids. However, Papa would be with us and that made the air raids seem less scary. It is interesting that a young child believes her father can prevent the bombs from falling on us.

School in Berlin was more exciting and impressive with the large school building, and the many classrooms and teachers. Each grade had its own room and teacher. There were about forty–five girls in a class, and usually at least two classrooms filled with the same grade, sometimes three, all girls. Boys and girls were segregated. There were separate school buildings for boys and girls. Both school buildings were down the block and around the corner from where we lived. The building of the Girls School had been destroyed by bombs, and dou-bling–up had to be implemented: 8 a.m. to 12:50 p.m. for boys—1 p.m to 6 p.m. for girls. The schedule was reversed each week.

Having a school less than two blocks away was a real relief for Mom. In the village of Straupitz she did not have to worry about my walking to school and being hit by a car, as she did in the city. However, Hitler in his wisdom had declared that each child should have at least a fifteen–minute walk to school, on the grounds that a walk in fresh air would clean out the lungs and the brain, and facilitate clear thinking. Accordingly, I was not permitted to attend the nearby school. Mom fought for the cause and won, and I did go to the school in the neighborhood for the duration of our stay in Berlin.

School

School in Berlin was very different indeed. In *Straupitz* we began and ended our school day with a folk song and a prayer. In Berlin we started and finished with a "hail to the army" type song, all the while holding up our arms in a *Heil Hitler* position. Twice a week in the six–day school week, we had *Appell*. The mere word installed terror in us first graders. It meant that we had to stand in the gymnasium with children of all grades and listen to speeches given by Nazi party members, holding up our right arms (for *Heil Hitler*) during the seemingly endless time. And we younger ones didn't even know what it was all about. Arms tiring, we tried to alternate between the left and the right arms, but if caught, we were severely reprimanded or physically punished. Girls from the older grades, if caught, were given speeches and slogans of Hitler's or other "top guys" to memorize and recite at the next *Appell* assembly.

More Air Raids

The air raids got worse, with longer duration and larger bombs. The men who were still at home because they were too old for active duty, or recovering from illness like Papa, were assigned to make checks during the air raids. If a fire bomb or embers from a nearby fire landed on any roof, they were to extinguish those or get help, if needed. This was not a casual threat. A fire on one of the roofs of the four houses or the sheds happened at least a couple of times a week. We were most concerned about the coal yard—it was like an ever present monster looming over us, threatening us with disaster. If the coal ever ignited we could never put it out. Yet we could not get rid of the dealer's supply. Everybody needed coal for heating and cooking. Wood was not

available, and oil was unknown to the home consumer.

Papa has always been a
handyman. He could repair almost anything, from little
things around the apartment to
painting and wallpapering. He
could also put new soles on our
shoes and make house slippers
for us on Mom's sewing machine. Houses had slate roofs.
Papa learned how to repair
these and was very much in
demand up and down the
street. He could put new glass
into blasted out windows, the
most common minor air raid
damage. In fact, one of the
musts when an air raid started,
was to unlatch all windows so
that they could blow open in a
bomb blast without breaking.

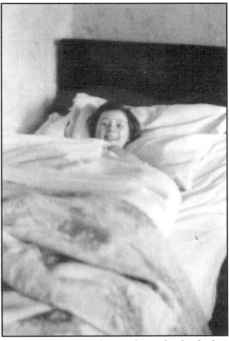

Keeping warm underneath my featherbed.

Windows in apartment buildings in Berlin open like double doors. We
also learned to always count steps on the dark stairways. Most people
did not own flashlights. Blackout laws were in effect throughout the
war. To this day, I count steps when I walk up or down anywhere, even
at the Lincoln Memorial in Washington DC. It has become a part of my
life from childhood days on. Counting steps simply is the way one
walks on stairways. I automatically count even though my safety no
longer depends on it.

Childhood Diseases

I loved school. The school year in Germany started on September
first and ended after the third week in July, so there were about five
weeks of summer vacation. We also had off the week between Christmas and New Year's and the rest of the week following Easter. The
only national holiday was May 1 (Labor Day). Easter and Whitsunday

had an extra holiday on the Monday following. Whitsunday is a religious holiday fifty days past Easter, which puts it somewhere into late May or early June, depending on when Easter is celebrated. Whitsunday is also a celebration of flowers and trees. Everything is in bloom and the trees have leafed out. It is the custom to decorate the house entrance or apartment door with birch tree branches for Whitsunday.

On Whitsunday in 1942, I coughed a lot while attending the engagement party of Mom's youngest brother, my Onkel Helmut. Relatives were concerned and advised Mom to take me to the doctor. She did. I had whooping cough. Not only that, but a few days later I came down with the chicken pox and pericarditis. The doctor wanted to hospitalize me because of the pericarditis, but Mom pleaded, assuring him that I would get much better care at home.

My case of whooping cough was severe. I nearly succumbed, coughing up mucus by the bath towel full. It was a nightmare for my parents. The neighbors in the house across the yard heard me cough during the night, and sent me candy, which they had been able to purchase for sugar ration coupons. They thought it was the last thing they could do for this dying kid. However, I was tough and survived, but I missed the rest of first grade, and I loved school. I especially loved to read. One of my aunts had given me a series of four little books which described how dolls were made. These books were my favorites, and I read them over and over. During my illness the doctor had prohibited reading, and Mom hid the books on me. I had seen her hide them on top of the wardrobe. In Germany we did not have built–in closets. Instead we had a huge piece of furniture called *Kleiderschrank* (wardrobe). One day after weeks of being very ill, I felt stronger and wanted to read my favorite books. I got out of bed, pushed a chair to the wardrobe, and tried to climb up to retrieve my books. Mom heard the crash as I fell to the floor. I had not been strong enough to climb up on a chair, but worst of all, I was caught in the act.

Luckily it was summer, so there were only a few minor air raids during the weeks of my illness. We stayed in our apartment.

During my ten years of school I was absent only one other time, the following spring, when I had the mumps. After that I was finished with my childhood diseases, and was from then on so healthy that I never missed another day of school.

This picture was taken in 1942. I am 8 and Peter is 4 years old.

The War Continues

Second grade started out like a dream. I had my eighth birthday, and Mom had made me a beautiful, wine red silk dress (pictured above) with a full pleated skirt, which I loved. Red was my favorite color. My Onkel Rudolf, another handyman, had built a bicycle for me from parts collected everywhere, including junk yards. I knew no eight–year–old who owned a bicycle, and I was on top of the world.

Germany seemed to think it was on top of the world, too. Things were apparently going well for Hitler, according to bits of adult conversation I picked up here and there. Papa was not for politics and tried to stay out of political things. After his return from the front he was sent to work in a factory. It was an electronics factory, Askania Werke, which was then manufacturing instruments for airplanes. I remember turn and bank indicators. Papa brought home a faulty one to show to us, and he explained how it works. The vision of the "houses looking like match boxes" and the airplanes that visited us every night returned to me, causing terror. I did not like turn and bank indicators. I pictured them in airplanes that dropped bombs on us. Many years later when I learned to fly an airplane myself, I still had a problem when looking at the turn and bank indicator.

Papa was against any political affiliation. He was not a member of the Party, but Nazi people caught him at work and made him join the Party. He was very distressed when he came home on that particular night, feeling that his freedom had been taken away by being forced into the Nazi Party.

Askania Werke gave a nice Christmas party for the children of employees. We attended a Christmas play, *The Nutcracker,* and afterwards a reception where every child received a toy.

Nazi Checks

We had a radio, a *Volksempfänger* (folk receiver). Like the Volkswagen car, it was a plain and simple radio designed to be affordable to the *Volk* (people). Hitler's voice sounded full of vigor during his speeches on Sundays, and one wouldn't want to be caught not listening! Even I noticed there was concern that someone might be checking, so the radio had to be going, and loud. I remember asking Papa who the man in the radio was, and why he was always yelling. Was he angry? As an answer, Papa put a finger to his lips and whispered "shsht." It was obvious that I should not have asked. There might be "informers" at work!

At different times, government people (Nazis, Gestapo, or whoever) came around on Sundays, the only day off from work, to check and make sure every household had a picture of Hitler "prominently" displayed and of adequate size. Papa was reprimanded for having only a postcard–size picture, and it happened to be behind the living room door—when open—which was hardly ever used. He told them we could not afford to buy a larger picture, but they made us move the one we had, and it looked ridiculous above the sofa.

Other times they came checking to see what people were cooking. Once a month was *Eintopfsonntag* (Stew Sunday), meaning we could not cook a roast—not that the ration cards provided enough meat to have a roast. It was quite disagreeable to have a stranger walk into our kitchen and look into the saucepan on the stove. The idea, I found out later, was to force people to cook an inexpensive meal instead of something more special on Sundays, and donate the money to the Nazi Party for the war effort.

We still had Christmas together. Mom knitted matching outfits for my five dolls—brown pants and white sweaters— from inexpensive and miraculously still available cotton yarn. Who would have thought then that in the cold fall of 1948, during the Berlin Blockade, I would unravel those doll outfits to salvage the yarn and knit socks and mittens for my brother?

4

1943
The Terror of the Bombings
and Return to Straupitz
Age Eight

Papa was ordered back to active duty early in the year, and sent to the Russian front. We resumed the nightly ordeals without him, sleeping fully dressed now so that we could just dive into our coats and run.

School was no longer fun. Whenever a girl was absent, it was assumed that something had happened to her during the previous night's air raid. Unfortunately, most of the time that was the case. Then the teacher would try to gently break the bad news to us. I remember thinking that the next day—or the day after—my name would be mentioned as one of the dead. I was sure of that. It was so hard for me to take the news of the deaths of little friends, and I became quite depressed. When I stopped eating, Mom kept me home from school.

Berlin was being heavily bombed, and for a child which could not yet comprehend why this was happening, it was a very hostile world to live in. There were people out there who hated us so much that they were doing all those terrible things. I often wondered what they might look like. Being from other countries "far away" and being so nasty and hateful, they were sure to look like monsters with two heads, or worse. Luckily we kids did not have movies such as *Planet of the Apes* or *Frankenstein* to further stimulate our imagination. I do not think I had ever been to a movie. Mom had taken me to several children's plays when I was quite young—I remember *Snow White and the Seven Dwarfs* as one of them.

Circus and Terror

Two air raids devastated our neighborhood. The aim apparently was to destroy two targets—a military academy less than a mile away, and temporary barracks built on a vacant lot behind our house, next to which the army stored 110 gasoline barrels in the ground. During a raid at the end of February, an extraordinary number of bombs were dropped on our neighborhood, but these two targets were not hit. Many buildings in our neighborhood were. We were worried.

In an effort to cheer me up, Grandma Stanneck took me to the circus on the afternoon of March first. I loved the circus, especially the animals. Mom was reluctant to let me go. Occasionally now there were air raids during the daytime.

I worried all day about the upcoming night and a repeat of another air raid like the big one we had a few days earlier. Even the fun of the circus could not block out my fear. The clowns' happy, smiling faces seemed ironic to me—as if they were saying "you laugh now, but wait until tonight!" I think I started to break right then. To me, the clowns' smiles suddenly turned into grimaces, and the audience's laughter into screeches of terror. I asked Grandma to take me home. I was feeling ill.

It was like the final straw—as if I had a premonition. That night, tons of incendiary bombs rained down on our neighborhood. Long before the end of the air raid, the men came into the cellar to report that they had extinguished a fire in the coal yard, but that the barracks behind us were burning, and the gasoline barrels in the ground could explode at any moment. There were 110 barrels. They told us we had better get out of our cellar and go somewhere else. If they exploded one at a time it would not be too serious, but if all of them exploded at once, it would take the apartment building down and bury us alive.

We started to run for our lives even though it was not yet the end of the air raid. We ran to put as much distance as possible between us and the fuel tanks. The whole world seemed to be on fire. The first barrel exploded. We ran faster. Nearly every other house on the street was burning, and there was no getting away from fire. Every so often we heard—and saw—the explosion of another fuel barrel. It is strange that we never gave a thought as to whether or not the house we lived in, and our belongings, would blow up. At the time we were completely detached from material possessions. They did not mean anything. Escaping with our lives was our main concern.

We ran endlessly through the inferno in the streets of our general neighborhood, wearing only our nightgowns, having shed our coats because of the intense heat from all the fires. We worried about where we would go if another air raid were to start. Most cellars were already overcrowded with people who were bombed–out earlier that night, and we might not be let in. Fortunately, there was no other air raid that night.

For a time, the explosions of the gasoline barrels became more numerous, often two or three together; and by dawn there was an eerie silence. There were burnt out houses everywhere. We returned to our street with much anticipation. The fire department had been there the whole time and had hosed down whatever they could, especially the coal yard and the house we lived in. The front building in which Tante Hilda lived had been saved as well. Wearily we went upstairs to our apartment and crawled into our beds. At least Peter and I did. Mom made plans. We were getting out of Berlin.

It was to be many years before I could even look at a fire in a fireplace without getting nearly hysterical. Today, sixty years later, I still can't look at a house on fire, or hear a siren, without my blood curdling.

Return to Straupitz

The air raids were terrifying enough to experience in the cellar of the house, but to be out in the streets and totally unprotected was a devastating experience. The fires had been terrifying. I could not wait to return to "peaceful" Straupitz. Mom promised me that we would get out of Berlin immediately, and on the very next day—March 3—we left.

I was so traumatized that I have no recollection at all of the trip to Straupitz. We obviously had to go by train. There was no other way. I was truly at a breaking point. The cumulative impact of the bombs falling all around us—night after night—and going to school only to find—day after day—that another one of my classmates had been killed, impacted me beyond what words can describe. I was only eight.

I also do not know how Mom made arrangements for a place to live in Straupitz. People had no telephones. However, we ended up living in the house of Herr Sasse and Frau Clärchen. I was very relieved not having to live in fear of air raids at night. We could see the sky over Berlin, only fifty miles in the distance, glowing red from the fires, and we could hear the sound of exploding bombs at night. Most nights I would wake up from the noise of the bombs falling on Berlin, and relive the terror. I cannot describe how relieved I felt being away from Berlin, even though we had only the most necessary items with us—no furniture, no toys, nothing familiar except for our clothes.

We had no relatives here. I realized that I missed everyone—Mom's brothers and sisters, Grandparents, as well as our cousins. I think I also missed Berlin very much. While it was wonderful not to have any air raids, I missed the tempo of the big city, its heartbeat. Despite the terror filled nights, there was something alive about the city in the daytime. Here in the village, everything was sort of "sleepy" in comparison.

In school, I was in second grade and doing well. It was still cold early in the spring, and I remember doing my homework in bed to keep warm. The next step after writing on a slate was to write on paper with a pencil, and then with ink. Writing with ink at that time meant dipping a pen into an inkpot. One time the inkpot tipped over and the ink spilled on the featherbed. I tried to wash it out before Mom came home from work, but it was permanent ink. She did not scold me. It was so cold in our room because we did not have any heat during the day when Mom was at work. She felt that Peter and I were too young to be left alone with a lit cast iron stove.

The school vacation schedule was different from the one we had in Berlin. Unlike in the city, here we had only four instead of five weeks of summer vacation, but then we had two more weeks in late fall at potato harvest time. Kids had to help with the harvest.

Farms in Germany are very different from those in the United States. First of all, they are tiny in comparison. A typical farmer in Germany owns a number of fields in which he grows crops for his own consumption and for levies. Most farmers then were peasants, working perhaps one or two hundred acres of land. They lived together in villages, and their fields and some forests surrounded the villages, either immediately or further out. Straupitz was such a village.

There were no trucks or farm machinery to help harvest the crops. The farmers walked to their farmland or rode on ox carts. All plowing, planting, hoeing, and harvesting was done by hand. The different grains were cut with scythes, gathered by hand, and each sheaf of grain was tied by hand and stood up with a number of others in a circle, to dry. After the harvest was in the farmers' barns and it became time for threshing, a threshing machine would make the rounds throughout each village in the area. It separated the straw from the grain which could finally be taken to the mill to be ground into flour. A long, hard labor intensive process. Backbreaking work!

My Friend Marga

For an outsider, especially one coming from the big city, it was difficult to "fit in." First of all, as is the case in most small communities, even people who have lived there for many years, often decades, were still referred to as "newcomers." One had to be born there to "belong" and to be accepted as "one of them." On the other hand, we were city dwellers and total greenhorns as far as farming was concerned, so in that respect we could not measure up to the local people. The Nazi Party's evacuation plan was just starting up, and the farmers were going to have to get used to the "foreigners" very shortly. In school I did not have quite the same problems that Mom had with the villagers. Children seem to be more accepting and accommodating.

My best friend at school was Marga Konzack. She lived across the street, and her family had the prettiest house and the nicest farmyard in the village. Marga's family did not live from farming alone. Her father was a carpenter, but he had been drafted into the army and his carpenter shop was closed. Everyone in the family, even the youngest, had to help in the fields and with the animals. That was where I got my little farm experience. Marga, being the oldest of three children, had to help. If I wanted to spend time with her, I could only do so by helping her with her chores. Together we raked hay, twisted the ties for bundling grain sheaves, helped pile them onto the wagons, and held the oxen or cows in check so they would not run off with the wagons. I loved this kind of work. We collected the eggs in the chicken house, and helped her grandma churn the butter when her arms got tired. Their kitchen was a separate building from the house. It had a brick floor with sawdust sprinkled on it and I thought it was wonderful. One would not get scolded for tracking in dirt.

I helped Marga pick the cherries off the trees in July, the apples, pears, and plums in the fall, and enjoyed eating some of them along the way. Cherries were my favorite fruit, and they still are. I liked them so much that I did not want to waste the pits. With great effort I planted them alongside a street which went out of town towards the flour mill, having visions of a whole street lined with cherry trees. To my disappointment, the street still had no trees when I revisited it 46 years later.

Late in the fall we would watch farmers harvest the potatoes. We hung around when the men dug "graves" for them, lined them with straw, and stored the potatoes in the pits for the winter, to keep them from freezing. Frozen potatoes taste sweet, which I did not like. At times we had to eat them when our rationed potatoes had frozen because we had not protected them well enough. Many years later in America, I would not eat sweet potatoes. They remind me of frozen regular potatoes, and I still do not like them.

Living in a village in the country was a child's paradise, as well as a learning experience for a city kid. There were so many things that were different from the big city. The streets were unpaved and the oxen dropped their manure wherever they went. Oxen and cows were the draft animals. Nobody owned horses anymore, except for the royal family who were allowed to keep a few for their personal use. All horses had to be given to the army for the war effort. Every Saturday we raked the street in front of the house to clean it for Sunday. I always volunteered for this job because I liked to rake, and I would rake nice patterns in the sand. Raking was a novelty for me, and Herr Sasse, being elderly, was happy not to have to do it.

There were a lot of things the dictatorial government did to us. Mom had taken us out of Berlin, to Straupitz, without waiting for an assigned destination in the government's evacuation plan. We were therefore "kicked around" all over Straupitz, and did not have a legal place to live. The government assigned apartments or living space to families, and Mom had dared to take it upon herself to fend for her children. We had come here because we had lived in Straupitz before and had friends here. As more evacuees arrived from Berlin, we were reduced from two rooms into only one, without the use of the kitchen. A family of four was assigned to move into our other, larger, room. The trouble was that we always had to walk through their room to get to and from ours. We thought this was the worst situation, however, more was in store for us.

School and Trains

Mom had started to work as a conductor on the railroad, the little narrow gauge train called *Spreewaldbahn*. It served the neighboring villages and connected with the nearby cities of Lübben and Cottbus, Schwieloch and Lieberose. Straupitz was the hub.

It became my job to take care of my little brother. He was then four years old and I was eight. Mom had to leave for work before five–thirty in the morning, so I cooked breakfast before I went to school. Every morning before 7 o'clock I walked to the dairy about half a mile away, bought the milk, and cooked a soup with noodles or tapioca for Peter and me. I left for school just before eight o'clock, and Peter stayed

Mom, on the left, with two of her colleagues. With most of the men in the army, women had to do this physically demanding job. The picture quality is poor but it is remarkable that it survived the war.

by himself in the safety of his crib until I returned at one o'clock in the afternoon.

Our three–classroom school was getting crowded as more Berlin evacuees arrived. The notable things about the Berlin kids was that they were much taller than the local children, and they were ahead in education. My friend Marga was an exception. She and I were at the head of the girls in our class academically. After us were mostly Berlin girls, and then the local kids.

We had a Duke living in Straupitz in a castle on the edge of town. The Duke's son, Hubertus von Houwald, called "Hubsie," became a good friend. His parents gave him permission to bring me to the castle to play. He was an only child and needed to have playmates. He had won-

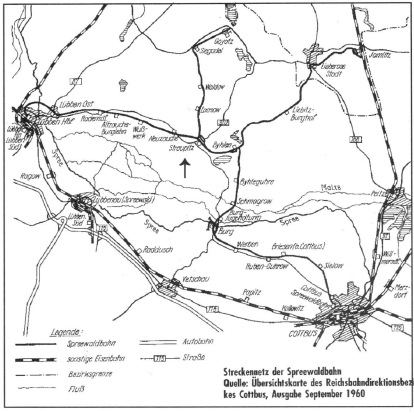

Straupitz (slightly above and left of center—see arrow) was the hub. From there the trains went to the surrounding cities and larger villages.

derful toys. However, I was an outdoor kid and preferred the grounds and the stream to the stuffy, spooky, though elegant castle. Mostly we carved little boats and floated them in the water. In the winter we skated.

When the Russians took over in 1945, the Duke and his family were ordered to "disappear." Mom, through her connections at the railroad, was able to help them reach a destination where relatives lived, and to cover up their whereabouts. Mom always stuck out her neck to help people, and several times she had one foot in the grave because of it. This was one of those times. The Soviets had no mercy.

Peter and I

My physical appearance was plain and awkward. Having lots of freckles across my nose, I was duly called "freckle face." Being extremely skinny, and very tall with long legs, the shorter, chubby local kids also called me "stork legs." The advantage of having long legs was that I could run fast and jump high, and I made my marks in sports, which won their admiration—but the freckles didn't earn me anything except teasing. I hated my freckles and skinny legs, and I thought I was the ugliest kid alive.

This was our two–room school. The two teachers and their families lived on the upper floors. We took this picture in 1991.

Unlike Peter, I was extremely shy and did not attract hordes of friends, but rather preferred one or two close ones. I have always enjoyed time alone, sewing clothes for my dolls or knitting, practicing embroidery stitches, or making things out of pretty paper, if available. I might have been more into crafts had there been materials available. Even at that stage of the war, a few short, colored pencils were much treasured relics from better times. I remember how much I liked colors. There was a noticeable lack of color in our lives at that time. Nearly everything we owned was dull, unless one liked black, brown, and gray.

Peter has always been an outgoing, charismatic boy who made friends easily. He was polite and friendly, loved the out of doors, had scores of friends, and was thriving in the village of Straupitz. Everybody loved him—his friends and their mothers alike.

Mom was very strict with us where it was necessary; on the other hand she was extremely understanding, and very fair. One thing she would absolutely not tolerate was dirty language. She was very insistent that Peter and I speak good German, impressing on us that how we speak tells people where we come from and what kind of an upbringing we have had. She also sought to make sure that the friends we chose did not influence our speech and behavior in a negative way. If on occasion a "bad" word did slip out, Mom reacted instantly and we felt her backhand right where the word had come from—as if she was shoving it back in. General good behavior, good manners, respect for and politeness towards others, and especially honesty, were of utmost importance to her. We did not get away with anything in those areas.

Peter and I loved the close community, our friends, and Mom's working on the railroad, where we could go riding along on the train with her anytime we wanted to. I loved the trains, especially the locomotives. Straupitz, being the hub of the *Spreewaldbahn*, had a switch yard and a repair facility. I enjoyed watching the repair work whenever they let me into the place. At the end of one of the tracks there was an old railroad car in which people lived. I envied them. This appealed to my gypsy nature because it was rustic and seemed like camping to me. Being so close to all the activity of the rail yard, I thought that those people were so lucky to live right in the middle of everything. Mom always had trouble prying me away from the rail yard.

My First Time away from Home

The Nazi Party's Socialist Welfare Department selected a number of needy children from the schools and sent them to the farmers in Saxony during the summer vacation to get fresh air and plenty of food. Being so skinny, I was the first one to be selected.

The town of Bautzen in Saxony is only about fifty miles south of the Spreewald, but by train, and having to change twice, it took most of the day to get there. It is beautiful country with rolling hills, forests, and tiny villages. Christa, also from my school, and I were met at the Bautzen train station by a member of my foster family who took us to the village of Blösa, four miles away. Christa was to live across the street with the post office people. Blösa was not even a village, but just about a dozen houses alongside a narrow country road. A window of the people's private home was all there was to the post office. I lived with real farmers who also owned an Inn, although at that time nobody traveled, and there were no overnight guests. The local men would come in on weekends or evenings and have a few beers.

I had a nice little room upstairs, and it was the first time that I ever had a room all to myself. The family was so happy to have me. The owners of the Inn, as well as their married daughter with her infant son, lived there. The young woman's husband was serving in the army, of course.

Even before I went downstairs for breakfast the next morning I was

on the verge of crying. It was my first time away from home and I missed Mom and Peter. I was beginning to be homesick, though I had hoped this would not happen.

Breakfast was a new experience for me. The kitchen was a typical huge farm kitchen. In one half of it there was a long

This 1999 photo shows the Farmhouse/Inn as it was when I lived there for five weeks. The window of my room is above the front door.

table with benches. On the other side of the kitchen was a large brick oven, two big work tables, and wooden troughs for mixing the bread dough. At mealtime the farmhands came in, about twelve or fourteen of them, and we all sat at that marvelous long table. I liked this. Although I did not know it at the time, this was probably the reason why I wanted a dozen children when I grew up. I always pictured a long table with a big bunch of kids sitting down for meals.

Then the food was put on the table. There were huge, rectangular cast iron frying pans filled with fried potatoes and bacon, different kinds of sausage, plus all the other things that go with a hearty farm breakfast. The odd thing was that there were no plates. The frying pans were lined up end to end in the center, and everybody just dug in with their forks. I watched this in disbelief. Here were adults eating right out of the cookware. At home this was considered very bad manners. Mom would never approve of it, but I thought it was great fun and wished that she could see it. I suddenly missed Mom so much and started to cry. My foster mother (I don't remember the name of the family) thought I was upset about the way they ate, and said she would get me a plate. She took a beautiful collectors plate off a high shelf on the wall, dusted it off, and put it in front of me. However, I ate only two bites. It was wonderful food, but I could not eat. I was homesick.

For the next three weeks, I was crying all of the time and unable to eat. The family became so concerned that they called for a nurse to come and examine me. Then I heard her tell my foster mother that if I lost another half pound, they would have to put me into the hospital. I started to force myself to eat, just so I would not have to go to the hospital. I also stopped crying and instead looked forward to being home in another week. About that time a social

56 years later—my flower meadow (vacant lot) next to the house across the street from where I lived still looks the same.

worker came around with the good news that they had been able to negotiate for us kids to stay an additional week. This seemed to be the end of the world for me, and I cried some more. I even missed my pesky little brother. But I survived.

The tiny village of Blösa was in a lovely setting. Behind the house was a brook where I liked to sit and watch the trout, endlessly. Sometimes I tried to catch one with my hands, however, they were too swift and slippery. There were woods on the other side of the brook, and directly behind the house was a large open area where the family grew all of their vegetables and berries. They found that if they let me help with little chores, I would be distracted and did not cry. I helped pick raspberries and red currants. The family was very good to me, and they wanted to spoil me rather than make me work. I convinced them that I really enjoyed helping with things more than just hanging around with Christa. She and I did play by the stream, as well as at her house or mine. There was a big meadow with lots of wildflowers next to the house in which Christa lived. I loved to pick flowers, and at the Inn they let me put them into vases, which I set on the tables in the guest dining room.

One Saturday there was a wedding, the reception being held at our Inn, and the whole village attended. Christa and I enjoyed seeing the beautiful bride. All of the food and cakes were prepared by my foster family, and I had fun watching, and helping. I loved being around my foster mother. She was wonderful to me, and was sad that I was homesick. She baked all of the bread in the big brick oven in the kitchen. Interesting to me was that the baking sheets were round, about twenty inches in diameter, and used for both the sheet cakes and the bread. This solved the puzzle as to why we always had such huge slices of bread at meals.

One afternoon about a week before it was time for me to return home, the young woman took me to the town of Bautzen, four miles away, on the back of her bicycle. There we went to a jeweler and she bought a silver ring for me. In exchange for the silver, she gave one of her silver teaspoons to the jeweler. It was my first ring, a silver band with horseshoes and four–leaf clovers on it. I loved this ring and wish the family knew how often I thought of them. Even after the ring no longer fit me, it was worn by my brother until the soft silver wore so thin that the ring broke.

The thoughtful gesture of giving me this little ring as a remembrance did much to etch the experience into my memory. Fifty–six years later, in 1999, I went back to find Blösa. All I had to go by was the name of the village and the memory of what the house and its surroundings looked like. I found it.

Almost nothing had changed from the way I remembered it. Having been a part of East Germany after the war, time had stood still as far as progress was concerned. Even the vacant lot next to the house with the post office across the street still had wildflowers growing on it. That house was in a terrible state of disrepair. The former Inn, where I had lived, had been kept up beautifully. While I walked up and down the street taking pictures from all angles, a woman came out with her bicycle, ready to go somewhere. I told her my story. She was interested, told me that the then young woman's name was Frau Nimschke, and that she had died just a few years ago. Her son—the little boy she had when I was there—lived some distance away, and he sold the house five years ago. Frau Nimschke's husband did return home after the war, which I was happy to hear, since the family had been so good to me when I lived with them.

The house is no longer an Inn, but little of the exterior has changed. They had done some remodeling of the interior, I was told. I asked about the little room at the top of the stairs which had been mine, and the woman told me that it is now a bathroom. They had also found the former brick oven in the kitchen when a wall was removed during the most recent remodeling.

It was quite an emotional experience for me to have seen the place at which I spent five weeks during my childhood. Despite my homesickness, I have very fond memories of that time.

Our Own Furniture and no Place to Live

Papa came to visit us in Straupitz whenever he was on furlough. In October of 1943 our apartment in Berlin was bombed. Luckily Papa was in Berlin at the time spending part of his furlough visiting his mother. He and neighbors saved most of our furniture from the burning building. It was the menacing coal yard which this time was hit by enough fire bombs to be beyond salvage. The fire burned for two weeks and the coals glowed for another three weeks, which prompted the pear tree near our house to flower in October.

Grandma Stanneck stored some of our furniture in her one–room plus kitchen apartment. The rest, including my doll carriage, was shipped to Straupitz. It was quite a special day when our very own familiar pieces of furniture arrived. It is difficult for me to describe how I felt. I guess I felt like we were put together again. We belonged somewhere because our furniture was where we were. I was not totally a gypsy—yet.

5

1944
Being Kicked Around Within Straupitz
Age Nine

Gypsy Life

We were being kicked around by the government. Farmers had to share their living space and take in evacuees from Berlin. We were not evacuees under government law because Mom had left Berlin on her own; therefore we apparently had no right to a place to live. The impossible situation of living in one room next to a family of four in another one room was solved by the local *Ortsgruppenleiter,* (town official) Herr Hesse, in the summer of 1944. He assigned us temporarily to one of the three rooms occupied by a government agency, the "National Socialist Agency—Help for Mother and Child Department." We were to live there until further arrangements could be made for us. Unfortunately we could enjoy the lovely, large, bright room for only a few weeks.

In September we were given the right to move to a charming two–room summer cottage in a large garden at the edge of the village. It would have been ideal except that it was fall and temperatures were dropping. The cottage was built of wood and we could see outside through the cracks. I thought this was neat. I loved peeking through the cracks and seeing the garden outside. Mom was afraid to light the wood burning stove, the only source of heat, before she went to work early every morning, for fear that her kids might go up in flames before waking up.

Peter and I had the best time in that cottage. My doll carriage became a train which carried our friends on wild rides throughout the vast yard. One of the stops was at the pump—water pump, of course. Most houses in the village had no running water and people got their water from a pump in the yard. There was no indoor plumbing either, and outhouses were no fun during the cold winters.

Building Toys

Papa had built a doll house for me when I was two years old. It was still in Berlin, and I missed it. Now during the long hours after school I built a doll house and furniture from cardboards. On a recent visit to the office at the Straupitz train station I had noticed discarded file folders in the trash can and asked if I could have them to play with. Instead of playing "office," I found a better use for them now. They became the doll house walls and floors. I stitched the file folders around the edges and sewed them together like a postcard house. The doll house furniture was made of the little cardboard railroad tickets which Mom sometimes brought home for us to play with. Peter helped me. We glued the railroad tickets together with paste made of flour and water to make the furniture. It had not been easy to talk Mom out of some of our precious flour. Flour was food—and food was scarce. Our Mom was always sympathetic, knowing from her own childhood during World War I how deprived we children were of a normal childhood.

Third class "beige" ticket.

The railroad tickets were our favorite building materials. Being about one and a half by two and a half inches in size, they were made of heavy cardboard and came in different colors. My favorites were white tickets with a diagonal red stripe, which were issued for express trains connecting Berlin with other large cities. They were also the rarest. The second class tickets were green, and third class tickets beige, which were by far the most common and the least coveted. Not until years later in America did it occur to me why we had so much fun with those little pieces of cardboard and got so excited about the colors. We lived in a country depleted of everything, and nothing was packaged colorfully if packaged at all. We were starved for color. Everything we owned was drab, practical, and hopefully durable.

Railroad station in Straupitz

Everyday Life

Mom wore her railroad uniforms and did not need most of her dresses. Being a tailor, she had no trouble making dresses for me out of hers. Her sewing machine was in Berlin and she had to do the stitching by hand. Mom was very good at designing, and I always had by far the nicest dresses in school, which I hated. Kids do not want to be different. I dreaded going to school whenever I had to wear a new dress because it would catch everybody's attention and admiration which embarrassed me. I would much rather have worn old clothes like everybody else did. Other mothers needed their own dresses, and not every mother knew how to sew. This was also a time when I was growing extremely fast and outgrew my clothes continuously.

Shoes were a big problem. We found that by cutting holes into the toes of my outgrown shoes I could wear them longer. Next I wore Mom's galoshes which were too big, and the spaces for the heels had to be stuffed with paper. Being made of soft rubber, they were quite uncomfortable. Eventually we ran out of "raw materials." I then had to wear rags and homemade sandals. A homemade sandal is a piece of wood which we cut to a shape somewhat similar to a foot, with straps or string nailed on it. It could be considered a forerunner of Dr. Scholl's. Peter was always the lucky one to inherit my outgrown clothes which had been remodeled for him by Mom. I don't know when she found the time for all this. She worked a heavy schedule at the railroad. It was actually a man's job, but with most of the men fighting in the war, women had to do their part.

Occasionally Mom ran into people on the train who were coming from one of the nearby cities and were peddling goods. They hoped to trade those goods for food from the farmers. We had nothing to trade since we were living on only our ration cards. One day Mom came home with a pair of wooden shoes for each of us. She had talked the man into letting her buy them with money. Peter and I were elated to have wooden shoes like those worn in Holland, which we had seen in pictures. We did not know whether they were an imitation made in Germany or the real ones from Holland, but we found them terribly uncomfortable. The problem most likely was that our feet were not used to being enclosed in something so rigid. We were getting blisters by the scores, and could hardly wear those wonderful wooden clogs.

It has always been my responsibility to handle everything related to ration cards and food shopping. I certainly knew how important it was not to lose a coupon, and I could be trusted. Rarely would I let Mom go to the store because she inevitably lost something. Later on as food became less available, shopping became nearly a full time job. I would spend countless hours in food lines. But for the time being we were not starving. Peter and I got a good sandwich now and then while hanging around with our farm friends.

Visiting Berlin

We traveled to Berlin on several occasions to visit the grandparents and relatives, but each time we fled back to Straupitz sooner than planned after being caught in an air raid.

The trains from Lübben to Berlin were always extremely crowded. Mom would get us into the conductors' compartment by taking advantage of her railroad uniform, hoping that her slightly different railroad insignia would not be noticed. This would have given away the fact that she worked at only a secondary railroad. The advantage was that we not only were sure to get on the train, but we could get seats in the compartment reserved for conductors. Even so, it was not easy for Mom—she had to pretend being asleep to avoid questions from interested colleagues as to which route she worked on.

The conductors' compartment was marked "For Railroad Officials Only" on the outside. However, on one of the trips a lady yanked the door open and tried to get on just as the train started to move. Peter, not yet five years old, was leaning against that door straining to be able to see out of the window. When the door opened, Peter fell out of the slowly moving train. Mom grabbed him instantly by the suspenders of his little outfit and pulled him back in. He got away with a scraped face, and bumps and bruises from being dragged along the station platform for a moment. We were thankful that he was not seriously hurt.

The Big Disappointment

In the fall of 1944, Onkel Rudolf was drafted into the army. Tante Hilda wrote to say that she would come and visit us in Straupitz. We were always close to Tante Hilda having lived in the same apartment house, and later across the yard from her, and I was excited about her upcoming visit. She had written only an approximate date of arrival. Wearing my prettiest dress I met every daily train from Lübben for nearly a week. Sometimes I even rode my bicycle to the previous stop, Neu Zauche, hoping to see her that much sooner, but she never arrived. Then came her letter. Tante Hilda had found out that she was pregnant, but complications were expected and she needed to stay in Berlin. The prospect of a new little cousin somewhat made up for the disappointment. Unfortunately, during one of the last air raids on Berlin in early May 1945, Tante Hilda delivered a stillborn little boy while down in the air raid shelter.

Papa's Visits

Papa came to visit us whenever he was on furlough. On one of those visits he took Peter and me to Forst where his Onkel Wilhelm lived with his family. Forst is located on the Neisse River which in 1945 became the border between East Germany and Poland. The Neisse is a swiftly flowing river. Peter and I were impressed when Papa swam across, arriving at the opposite shore quite a ways downstream. On another day we walked across the bridge of the Neisse River and on to the village of Hohjeser four miles away. Hohjeser was the birthplace of Grandmother Stanneck. This village is now in Poland and I am glad to have been there and seen it. Onkel Wilhelm was the youngest of Grandma Stanneck's seven brothers. He and Tante Jenny owned their own home in Forst. Peter and I enjoyed their big yard where they kept chickens, geese, and rabbits. Their grown daughter, Herta, spent a lot of time with Peter and me. She was married, but her husband was serving in the army. We must have behaved well for we were invited back.

Air Raids Again

We were not so lucky the next time we tried to visit Forst. From Straupitz we had to travel on Mom's train to the city of Cottbus, twenty miles southeast, then on another train from there to Forst. About three miles before Cottbus as we passed by the airport, we suddenly saw bombers starting to drop their bombs. The engineer stopped the train immediately and we all ran into the forest, threw ourselves down, and buried our faces in the ground. We prayed that the train would not be hit by bombs. Mom was on duty and had to stay with the train. It was awful for us to watch those bomb bay doors open and discharge their deadly cargoes. The bombs were glistening in the sunlight and whistling ominously on their way down. While the Cottbus Airport was hit hard, nothing happened to our train. Peter and I were shaken up and begged Papa to take us back to Straupitz, not wanting to leave Mom there with the train and be separated from her. We still had to go on to Cottbus and wait until it was time for the train to return. Of course we worried about another air raid on Cottbus, but we were lucky, and at least the four of us were together.

With the nearby small cities being bombed now, we no longer felt quite as safe in Straupitz. But then our daily life offered distractions.

Gypsy Life Continues

With upcoming winter and Christmas, Mom insisted that the "authorities" assign appropriate living quarters to us. She did this by showing up at Herr Hesse's office every day after work. We could not spend a cold German winter in a wooden summer shack—or could we? Herr Hesse finally either had mercy for us or he wanted to get rid of Mom. He knew of another family which was living in Straupitz "illegally," a war widow from Berlin—Frau Wischnewski. Like ourselves, she had arrived in the village on her own with three children. The two boys were hers and the girl, Ingrid, was her orphaned niece. Ingrid had lost her father in the war and her mother in an air raid. Frau Wischnewski was told by Herr Hesse that we had been in Straupitz longer than she had, and that we therefore had a right to her apartment. She was to evacuate the two small rooms and tiny kitchen for us, but she was not told where to go instead. Naturally she refused to move.

A few days later while Frau Wischnewski was at work and the children at school, Herr Hesse sent several men to her apartment. They removed her furniture from the bedroom and piled it into the small living room. Then they moved us into the tiny bedroom, and I mean it was tiny! The men piled our few pieces of furniture up to the ceiling as they had done with the Wischnewski's in the other room. In our room there was space for only one of the single beds and Peter's crib. The table was jammed in between the two so we had to sit on the bed. No room for chairs. It was like camping, and I liked it.

The Berliners are well known for their talent to see the funny side of even the most unpleasant situations. Our Mom was a typical Berliner. Her incredible cheerfulness and good spirits combined with a large measure of humor were to help us unbelievably during the difficult years that were still ahead.

Mom's working hours were dependent on the train schedule. The runs to the different destinations were assigned to the conductors in rotation. Thus, depending on how early Mom had to leave in the morning she could be at home as early as three in the afternoon. That day Mom was home when Frau Wischnewski returned from work and found us all moved into part of her apartment. Frau Wischnewski was speechless but she did not have a chance to get angry. Mom stood in the doorway and said: "Well, you were expecting us, and here we are. I know you don't want us, and we don't want to be here. This was an 'Act of God' and there is no point in the two of us becoming enemies. We might as well be friends and make the best of the situation, which is both comical and sad."

Mom's approach worked. Being true Berliners, both women broke into laughter about the piles of unrelated furniture, and suddenly everything was funny. We all became friends and had a great time during the few weeks we lived together.

Straupitz Day Care Center. Peter is sitting at the far left. I am the tall girl in the back row on the far right.

We could not invite any of the Wischnewski family into our room. There was physically no space. When we opened the door we were in bed. After landing on the bed we had to slide across the table or crawl under it to get to some standing room in front of a piece of furniture, on top of which was our hot plate. As before, we continued to do all of our cooking on that hot plate to spare Frau Wischnewski the annoyance of having another party in the tiny kitchen.

During the long winter evenings, Peter and I joined the Wischnewski children in their room where we could sit on top of different pieces of furniture and play games. At bedtime we helped "build" beds for them. This meant clearing the sofa and some floor space of furniture pieces by piling those onto the table for the night to make room for a cot for Ingrid. The two boys camped on the sofa. Frau Wischnewski slept on a makeshift bed in the kitchen which had to be removed every morning to allow access to the stove and sink, as well as to the only door leading outside.

Mom insisted that Peter and I be dressed and ready for school in the mornings so that both of us walked through the Wischnewski's room together only once. We were not to run back and forth. We stopped in the kitchen to wash up—this house had running water—and then left. Mom, of course, had sneaked through their room much earlier to start her day of work on the train. She had to climb across Frau Wischnewski in the kitchen, then squeeze through the door to the outside which was mostly blocked by her bed. It was a good thing that Mom was very athletic. In her youth she had been a member of an acrobatics club for six years.

When school was out, Peter and I spent a few hours at the day care center until Mom stopped by to get us after work. We were not under any circumstances to go back to the house and inconvenience the other family in any way.

Moving Once Again

Christmas was approaching and there was no way we could have even one Christmas tree between our two families. Mom and Frau Wischnewski discussed their dilemma. Both of our families were not wanted in Straupitz on account of not having been evacuated on the government's evacuation schedule. In fairness, Mom admitted that Frau Wischnewski had the right to the apartment since the owners of the house were friends of hers, and the arrangement for the apartment had been a private matter. We should not be there in the first place and would move out as soon as we could. The question was: Move to where? Berlin was being bombed day and night, all year round now, and more evacuees were arriving constantly. There were no more rooms available in Straupitz or in any of the neighboring villages.

Mom had an idea. She knew where there were three empty rooms. We had lived in the largest of those rooms for a few weeks before being sent to the summer cottage. They belonged to the National Socialist Agency's "Help for Mother and Child" Department. Straupitz had no medical facility. Approximately once a month, a traveling doctor together with our village nurse would come and see mothers and children. Mom's reasoning was that during this critical housing shortage three rooms should not be left vacant for a single monthly visit— that two rooms would be ample. Mom decided to appropriate the same room which we had once occupied. She had a locksmith make a key, and one night after midnight about two weeks before Christmas we moved in. I was not only training to be a good camper but also a pretty good apprentice furniture mover. This was our fourth move in less than five months.

I shall never forget the next morning. Peter and I sat in bed to keep warm—no heat yet. Most houses had wood or coal stoves. This room didn't and Mom had to see what she could do about it. (She later traded Peter's crib for a wood burning stove.) On that morning she had come home between train runs expecting an official visit from Herr Hesse, the town's Nazi Party representative and keeper of the "official order." In a small village nothing remains a secret, not even a middle–of–the–

night move. Herr Hesse was a small, thin man, but it seemed that he could blow himself up when he exercised his political importance. He lectured me for twenty minutes once after I had greeted him with "good day" instead of the required "Heil Hitler."

That morning he looked about twice his size. His face was red and he was so angry that he even forgot to "heil" his Hitler.

What are you doing here?" he shouted at Mom. Mom calmly answered: "I live here."

"Don't you know that this is an official NSV place?" he asked. "Yes," said Mom, "I know this well. In fact, the metal plaque by the door says 'National Socialist Agency—Help for Mother and Child.' I am a mother with two children and I need help; therefore I feel that I am in the right place. You have obviously not been able to provide alternate acceptable living quarters for us, and I shall stay here with my children until you find us a place to live. I have been living in this village before most other evacuees arrived and have been kicked around the whole time. Now I am staying right here."

Herr Hesse's face got even redder from anger when he shouted: "I shall have you blown up." Then he stomped out of the room. I was most upset about the man's last comment. Having experienced the bombings in Berlin, I really believed that he could arrange for a bomb to be dropped on the house to blow us up. Mom assured me that Herr Hesse could not do this and I wanted to believe her, but still I was frightened.

This was a huge, bright and sunny room, especially in comparison to our previous cramped living conditions where the piled up furniture had taken away whatever little daylight came through the window during the winter. We ended up living in this wonderful

Recent picture of the "NSV" house in which we lived until we left the Spreewald. The front door was between the columns and our window was to the right of it.

Kurland, December 29, 1944

My dear Daughter!

Thank you for your letter of December 19, 1944 in which you send me greetings and best wishes from Straupitz. You made me very happy with the beautiful folded star which you made for me. For this, my dear child, I thank you with all my heart. I am glad to hear that.....

room throughout all the turmoil of the collapse of Germany and until our return to Berlin in December of 1946.

We had a wonderful Christmas and letters from Papa which turned out to be his last from the Russian front. In one letter he mentioned being encircled by the enemy.

My Christmas present from Mom was her own sewing box. She had owned it since the time she went to school to learn tailoring. Now she was happy to see how delighted I was with it. Ever since I can remember I had watched Mom sew, and I had learned how to sew with her guidance. As a young child I would endlessly watch Mom and be fascinated by her sewing with a machine. Later I would sit alongside her and make doll clothes from scraps that she could spare. Now there were but few colors of thread left. Replacements had not been available for years. But I was enchanted not only with having received Mom's own sewing box which she obviously treasured, but it also contained cloths showing all of the stitching and embroidery samples which she had to make for her final examination to become certified for the tailor trade.

6

1945
War Reaches Straupitz
and Arrival of the Russians
Age Ten

Our Swing

The National Socialist Agency house in which we now lived belonged to Herr Ruben who was a cabinetmaker. His workshop was a separate building in the back yard, but he lived somewhere else. He was an older man who had not been drafted by the army. Materials were not readily available so that he was seldom in his workshop. Whenever he was working I would go and watch him. He seemed to like it when I came around, and would patiently answer my many questions about his work.

A barn was located opposite Herr Ruben's workshop where he stored what little lumber he still had, and there were also some small

Herr Ruben's workshop was the brick building in the back on the right. The barn with our swing was the building opposite. Photo taken in 1991.

stables which were empty at this time. The outhouse was behind the stables, all the way in the back.

One day I asked Herr Ruben if he could spare a board to make a seat for a swing. I had noticed two hooks above the barn entrance which no longer had doors, and I figured out that a swing may have been attached there at one time. Herr Ruben cut and finished a board for the seat, found some rope, and then he helped me put the swing up. I thought he looked sad as he helped me, as if he remembered his children or grandchildren swinging there. He was a quiet man and never talked about himself when Mom paid the rent, nor did he ever mention his family, if he had one.

Peter and I, as well as our friends, had much fun with the swing, and Herr Ruben always smiled when he was in his workshop and saw us swinging.

Mom's Carbide Lamp

Mom had a carbide lamp for her work on the railroad. She needed it for giving signals to the train's engineer. The lamp had an upright rectangular shape. The back panel was the reflector, the front had clear glass, and the side panels were covered by doors. Upon opening the door on one side the lamp would give a red light, and on the other side the light was green. With this lamp Mom could signal to the engineer whether or not everybody was on board the train.

Peter and I thought that Mom's lamp was wonderful. We would have loved to have borrowed it to play with, but Mom would never let us tinker with it. She was of quite a different opinion about the lamp being so wonderful. After watching the "show" many times early in the morning I sympathized with her.

The way the lamp worked was as follows: Inside the lamp there was a container for a smelly, gray, grainy chemical called carbide and a reservoir for water which, when properly mixed and lighted, would give a flame. To be able to light the lamp the speed of the water droplets hitting the carbide had to be just right, otherwise the lamp would either flood or refuse to light up. If it flooded, the carbide had to be cleaned out totally and the lamp refilled. This was a time consuming process, especially when one was running late to start with. Trains do not wait.

Now, here is the scenario: Mom had to light the lamp before she left for the train station in the early hours of the morning. She was usually arriving there at the last minute and needed her lamp immediately. Alarm clocks, at that time, were the wind–up kind which did not keep accurate time. That, combined with Mom's innate lack of punctuality, meant that she was always running late and did not have time for a prolonged lamp lighting ceremony. Mom's frantic efforts to get the lamp lit every morning turned into a daily comic show for me as I would wake up and watch. The more I laughed at her futile attempts to get it going, the angrier Mom would get at the stubborn lamp. I can still see her gritting her teeth and muttering "curses, curses." Having inherited punctuality from Papa, I failed to see why Mom could not get up earlier to allow extra time for her lamp which obviously required patience.

Feeling sorry for Mom, I offered to take over the nightly job of preparing the lamp for her. I had noticed that most of the time Mom did not get around to cleaning it out the night before, and piling fresh carbide on top of the old sludge just would not work. She had confessed to me that her lamp would often be out before she arrived at the station, and that then she had to borrow somebody else's. Mom was quite relieved when I offered to clean out her lamp every night and refill it with fresh carbide. After learning how to adjust the water drip I would light it for her in the morning since I had more patience with the drip adjustment, which was crucial. Mom was happy about my taking over the nasty job of keeping the carbide lamp in working order, but she felt badly that I had to get up earlier than I needed to. I told her that I usually woke up from the commotion and her cursing the lamp, and we laughed about it. I had also felt guilty about "enjoying the show" rather than helping Mom out. Our solution to the problem turned out to be a good one, and together we got the lamp lit every morning.

School

I was in fourth grade and enjoying it. Schoolteachers at that time were men who were too old to be sent to war. Our teacher was an evacuee from Berlin, and he drilled us mercilessly in math. I can't recall his name, but I do remember how much we learned, and I wish he knew how many times later in life I thought about those drills and thanked him for his teaching. He always complimented me for the essays I wrote, and I felt embarrassed when he read them to the whole class. He recommended to Mom that I be sent to high school, if we could afford it. High school in Germany had to be paid for, and it was for rich kids. We had not been born into that class, although at that particular time everybody was more or less in the same boat. Money was nearly worthless. As a conductor on the railroad Mom earned much more money than we needed to buy our rationed foods. There was nothing else available for purchase. The village did not even have a movie theater. Twice, a small circus came to town and we went to see every show, plus helped them set up and take down. I envied the circus people because they could live in wagons and move from place to place. This appealed to my gypsy nature.

Mom did give serious consideration to the teacher's recommendation to send me to high school. On her salary she could more than afford it. However high school in Germany started after the fourth grade and went on for eight years. If I went, I would be starting in the coming fall and have to travel daily by train to the city of Lübben, fifteen miles away. It was 1945 and Lübben had air raids. The decision, however, did not have to be made until summer. At the moment there were new problems to be faced almost daily.

Teacher Schmitt

Herr Schmitt was one of the original two teachers. He and his family lived on the upper floor of the school building. Herr Maak—who was my first teacher when I started school in 1941—had also lived upstairs, but he was gone when we returned to Straupitz in 1943. The nice teacher from Berlin must have moved away, and Herr Schmitt now became our teacher. He specialized in hitting kids. Those were still the days when school children were spanked for everything they did or did not do: being late for school, not having done homework, making mistakes in reading, or not writing good or long enough essays. Girls were slapped in the face or hit on the hands with a stick which often caused welts. Boys got their backsides whacked, and all boys wished they lived in Bavaria and owned leather pants. Sometimes when Herr Schmitt spanked a boy too hard his stick would break. His hobby was gardening and he grew a bush in his garden which supplied him with his sticks. He even told us about this special bush, and we were sure he grew it for that purpose only.

One local boy, Günter Royk, was late for school almost every day and he seldom did his homework. He got so many spankings that everybody felt sorry for him and wanted to help. The suggestion of a notebook in the pants for cushioning did not work. It was discovered immediately. So was the pillow which cushioned his seat another time.

I did not agree with the teacher and thought that Günter was basically a good kid. One time he gave me two kittens which he had rescued from being drowned. This told me that Günter had a kind heart. The problem was that those kittens were too young to be away from the mother cat, and no matter where we hid them or locked them up at our place, they always disappeared during the night. The next morning Günter would be back in school with the two kittens in his pockets. The kitten business went on for nearly two weeks. Then one morning Günter came to school without the kittens. They were gone.

Günter was an orphan and was being raised by elderly grandparents. He had to help a lot with the farm work and did not have much time for homework. Günter had to milk the cows before coming to school. However, this was not an excuse for tardiness as far as the teacher was concerned. Luckily Herr Schmitt's "reign" was short–lived.

Nearing The Long Awaited End

Somebody Gave His Life for Mom

The work week in Germany was six days, of course, but I do not remember Mom ever having a day off except for a "wash day" to do the laundry once a month. While the trains were running on reduced schedules on Sundays, they still had to run seven days a week. The conductors took turns working the Sunday runs. There were also other railroad related jobs to be done such as digging fire lanes in the forest alongside the railroad tracks. With pit coal no longer available for the railroads, pressed brown coal (lignite) had to be used. This soft coal created a great volume of sparks that were carried by the smoke, and could easily start forest fires. I remember Mom having to go and help dig fire ditches on Sundays as a "service to the country."

As the war was winding to an end and the German army retreated, there were countless wounded soldiers to be relocated. On some Sundays, a freight train consisting only of boxcars lined with straw, transported those men. Lack of medication, especially pain killers, made for much suffering for the soldiers but also for those who had to watch their misery, unable to help. Mom would come home all upset after witnessing the suffering and dying of so many brave men.

On one particular Sunday it was Mom's duty once again to accompany such a train. The resort town of Schwieloch had converted a hotel into a military hospital, and a trainload of wounded soldiers was to be transported there from the city of Cottbus. One of Mom's colleagues, Herr Winkelmann, who was also the grandfather of one of my classmates, told her to stay at home. "You spend this Sunday with your children," he told Mom. "It is an easy run." There was only the milk to be picked up along the way, and since the train carried no regular passengers, no tickets needed to be sold. This kind man insisted that Mom stay home with us, and that he take her place.

The train carrying the wounded soldiers was bombed as it left the city. Everybody—including the conductor—was killed. Mom would have been on that train!

Last Days of School

We owned a radio but it was in Berlin. Herr Hesse was probably the only person in Straupitz who owned one. We knew this because he always had it turned up very loud and we could hear it down in the street. I suppose he wanted everyone to hear Hitler's speeches telling the *Volk* about the *Vaterland's* many victories.

For a couple of weeks we kids picked up pieces of conversation from adults about the war not going well, and that the German army was retreating in several areas. We discussed this with each other in school, but being only ten years old nobody seemed to really comprehend what was going on. We were seeing quite a few refugees wander through town lately, begging for food. Grocery deliveries had begun to be somewhat erratic and we could not always get everything for which we had food coupons. The farmers were the only lucky source for the begging refugees, but soon there were so many of them that even the farmers could no longer give to everyone.

One morning near the end of January 1945, school had started when Günter Royk came in late again. He went straight to the teacher's desk and bent down for his usual whacking. We all laughed when Herr Schmitt reached for his stick and found it broken. Gleefully he left the classroom to go out to his special bush and cut himself a new weapon. We began to wonder when he had not returned after ten or fifteen minutes. Something was wrong. Suddenly he came rushing into the classroom, empty handed, and said: "Pack up your things, stand up, and go home." No explanation. No song. No prayer. When somebody asked if we were to be back the next day, he said "no—you will be notified." We were confused, and even Günter looked questioningly at Herr Schmitt, wondering what had happened for him to forego the spanking. Herr Schmitt waved to Günter and told him to get going. This was to be the best thing that happened to us for a long time to come: Günter got away this time, and the nasty Herr Schmitt was upset about something.

The Refugees' Tragedy

The next day we found out why we had been sent home from school, and also that there would be no school in the foreseeable future. The school building was being turned into a refugee camp. It was only a drop in a bucket, but quite an important drop for the few dozen lucky people who could be accommodated.

The refugees were coming from East Prussia, Pomerania, and Silesia, the most eastern parts of Germany which were later given to, or reoccupied by, Russia, Poland, and Czechoslovakia. As the German army retreated and the country was invaded by the Russians, most of the people who lived in those areas fled west to escape the Soviets.

By the middle of February there was a continuous column of refugees moving through our village. It was the most pitiful sight, and as I am writing this almost sixty years later I feel nearly sick to my stomach, remembering. Exhausted from their long trek, those people were just barely moving along, pulling behind them hand carts loaded with a few necessities, as well as with sick or old people, small children, and babies. Older children were walking along with the women and older men. As the farmers were no longer able to give food to the countless begging people, they gave up even trying. People were sick and dying, starving, falling by the wayside; children were separated from their mothers and lost, or orphaned when the mother collapsed and died. Items were discarded along the way when they could no longer be carried, and the people trekked on and on with no destination. It was torture for us to watch them, seeing the despair in their eyes and not being able to help.

Riding the Spreewaldbahn

In early March Mom stuffed a few clothes for each of us into a pillowcase—we did not own a suitcase—and took Peter and me with her on the trains. She was afraid something might happen that would separate her from us. The cities to which the trains traveled were being bombed regularly, and railroad bridges could be destroyed which would cut us off from Mom and the train. The trains were especially crowded now, carrying refugees who rode back and forth aimlessly with nowhere to go. Peter and I could sit in the special compartment which was reserved for the conductors. For the next few weeks we were railroad bums, continuously riding back and forth on Mom's routes.

One morning at the railroad station of Lübben we saw something odd and extremely disturbing. The station and tracks of our narrow gauge railroad were parallel to the station and tracks of the long–distance trains, and the two stations were separated by a fence. The station platform on the other side was crowded with people who looked ragged and starved. Many had little camp stoves and were cooking on the station's platform. It looked like they were camping there, too. We had seen countless refugees lately, but there was something different and even more pitiful about those people. They looked haunted, and scared. I asked Mom why they were cooking there, and why they were staring at our train with such big, sad eyes. She had wondered about them, too, and asked another conductor if he knew who they were. He did not know, but he guessed the people might be Jews who were being transported. However, he thought there was something odd about their being there. Some of the unbelievable facts were starting to leak to the population. Years later upon learning the horrible truth, we figured out that those people had been Jews who were being relocated from a concentration camp in territory which was already invaded by the Russians. Their skeleton–like appearance and unspeakably sad and pained faces have haunted me all of my life.

By early April, one of the Spree River bridges was destroyed and the trains stopped at Lübben–Ost, the eastern part of the city. From there people had to walk three or four kilometers to get to the long distance railroad. Not long after that all trains of the Spreewaldbahn stopped running. People were no longer traveling. Mom could now stay home with us.

To Leave or Not To Leave

One day some of the retreating German army came to Straupitz. There were soldiers in army trucks and others with horses. The army was retreating, along with the still steady trek of refugees. Mom tried to make arrangements for us to get a ride in a truck back to Berlin or to wherever they were going, but the officer told her they could not take civilians. I was fascinated with the trucks and disappointed not to get a ride in one. I don't think I had ever been in a car or a truck. The soldiers who had horses let us ride them, with their guidance. They stayed in our village for two days.

When they moved on, Mom considered joining the refugees in their retreat. Three different times within two days she strapped that pillow case with our clothes to her bicycle and we started walking. Each time we walked a relatively short distance, then turned around and returned. Mom felt unsure of our venture. On the third try we walked a ways into the forest before we stopped. Mom then asked me if I thought we should continue. I think I wanted to go but Mom had second thoughts. "I don't feel good about this," she said. "Some inner voice seems to tell me to stay." Once again I teased Mom about her "inner voices," but we turned around and went home. A few days later we heard that the forest near the city of Halbe where we would have been by then was full of refugees at the time dive bombers attacked it. Thousands were killed. Mom's intuition, and our Guardian Angel, saved us once again.

Fifty–nine years later I drove on the autobahn by the city of Halbe and suddenly there was an exit labeled: *Forest Cemetery and War Memorial—Battle of Halbe—Mass Graves*. I shuddered, picturing that we would have been there but for Mom's intuition. There were few survivors.

Dive Bombers

My best friend, Marga Konzack, and I were together in the Konzack's farmyard one day in mid–April, when the first dive bombers hit Straupitz. Marga's grandmother was in the hen house gathering eggs into her apron, and we were helping her. We were horrified when without warning airplanes swooped down firing machine guns. We ran into the stable and sought solace with the cows. As we sat huddled on the floor in the straw, Grandma was so shaken up she must have squeezed the precious eggs in her apron too hard. Most of them were broken when it was all over. I was the only one who had experienced air attacks before, yet I was as stunned as everyone else. The village of Straupitz—I had believed—was safe.

We emerged from the stable a long time after the attack, thinking it was over. No sooner were we outside when the bombers returned. This continued all afternoon. Somewhere between attacks I managed to run to our house, three doors away, where Mom had been very worried about me. She had not wanted to leave Peter alone and go looking for me, or expose him to danger by taking him with her.

The Last Days of World War II

Except for short intervals, we were being dive bombed steadily, day and night. For the next ten days we hardly left the cellar. No store was open during that time, and I don't remember that we even ate anything in between the attacks, or for days afterwards. We must have, Mom would have seen to it, but I sure don't remember it at all.

Unlike the four or six–story apartment buildings in Berlin, the cellars of the mostly single family houses in Straupitz were just barely below ground with windows above the ground. This was a dangerous situation while we were being dive bombed. We tried to stand against the wall between windows, but at the same time tried not to be opposite any on the far wall. With heartbeats felt in our throats, we watched as shrapnel and fragments of exploding bombs flew in through the windows from all sides.

The first thing people did in between dive bomber attacks was to fill bags, buckets, and containers with sand, and place them in front of the windows. There were no burlap sacks we could fill, so any container we could find had to do. The safest barrier was my brother's equivalent of a "little red wagon." Peter had a wooden wagon which was made out of a box and mounted to the wheels of his old stroller. This "vehicle" had served us well throughout our many moves within the village. In it we also hauled home our potato and coal rations. Now the box was taken off the wheels, filled with sand, and placed in front of the window in the smaller section of the cellar. This area became the safest place in our cellar, but it also became crowded as refugees came in and took shelter with us.

The house in which we lived had three apartments. We occupied one room of one apartment. The other room and kitchen of that apartment belonged to the "sacred" National Socialist People's Party and stood empty. Fräulein Konrad, a lady in her 60's who gave piano lessons and was also the church organist, lived in the other apartment on the ground level. Frau Karsten, a young woman with a four–year–old daughter, lived upstairs. She had taken shelter underneath a bridge near the castle during the first dive bomber attack, and a piece of shrapnel had hit her shoulder. There was a nurse in town who had bandaged her right after it happened. Sadly, I remember all the days and nights we spent in the cellar, and the poor woman moaning with pain. Her blood soaked and crusted bandage was never changed.

The endless trek of refugees had almost stopped with the numerous air attacks, and people took shelter wherever they could. On the second day of the attacks several families had taken cover in the barn without a door, where our swing was. A woman in the barn was hit by the dive bombers' machine guns and killed. When the war was over, seeing the bloodstained boards of Herr Ruben's precious lumber kept reminding us children of the poor woman, and took away some of the enjoyment whenever we used our swing.

On this second day we also received visitors. Onkel Wilhelm, my Grandmother Stanneck's youngest brother, arrived with Tante Jenny, and Herta, their grown daughter. They were among the refugees having trekked from Forst on the Neisse River, about fifty miles southeast. We had visited them with Papa just the previous summer. Now they came to stay with us until "the end," whatever the end would be, death or peace.

We thought Onkel Wilhelm was so funny. At a time like this when nobody cared about material possessions, he was bemoaning the fact that his good felt hat had gotten muddy when they were taking cover in ditches along the way. At first we thought he was just trying to cheer us up with the way he carried on about his hat, but we soon realized he was serious. We remembered from Berlin how people would run back into a burning building and risk their lives to save some unnecessary item—a book or a record, for instance—instead of something essential such as warm clothes, or the indispensable featherbed.

What we did not know then was that people were starting to crack up. They had long since given up on Hitler—given up belief in his victories and his promises of a better life. People threw their money out into the street and nobody bothered to pick it up. For as long as I could remember, money did not buy anything other than food provided in our ration cards. There was nothing available to purchase. The country was depleted. Totally.

The End

We were spending all of our days and nights in the cellar now, huddled together on piles of potatoes and coal. Somebody had set up a bed for Frau Karsten, the injured woman. The foot end of the bed was opposite the wooden cellar door, and subject to being hit by whatever came flying through this door which was riddled with machine gun holes after a few days. There was no room to put the bed elsewhere. Frau Karsten's little four–year–old girl was in bed with her mother, whimpering softly.

Crouched on the coal, we relived the Berlin bombings. More and more people tried to get into the cellar for shelter. Eventually there was standing room only and we had to lock the doors, feeling awful about turning away people who were seeking shelter. Days and nights blended together, accompanied by the machine gun fire and explosions of bombs—and the moaning of Frau Karsten who was in much pain. There were horror stories going around about the Russians who were approaching, and about the inhuman things they would do to us. I did not understand about rape or what it was, but I heard something about earrings being torn out of ears because they wanted the gold. I asked Mom to remove my little earrings which I had worn since I was less than a year old.

Everybody was at the breaking point, and some people told funny stories trying to cheer everyone up. I think I was only semi conscious because all the memories are blurred. People were talking about wanting to get it over with. Did they mean the Russians coming, or ending life? I was puzzled but it did not really matter. We had no choice over what was coming.

The Russians are Here

Finally one night—it was towards morning of one of the last days in April—it happened. There had been an ominous silence for hours after the air attacks stopped. With mounting anxiety we waited for something unknown to happen—then the first Russian soldiers walked into our crowded cellar. They were looking for German soldiers, guns, and women. My first impression was surprise. The feared Russians looked like human beings, people like we were. Unlike the enemy monsters I had pictured in my childish imagination, they did not have two heads, or looked like any of the bad characters in fairy tales. They looked every bit as human as we did. The only difference was that they spoke another language. A number of them seemed to know some German, especially the two words which installed terror into every woman: *"Frau komm"* (woman, come).

After all the horror stories that had circulated about the Russians, I was relieved to find that they seemed to be polite people. They had not walked in slashing and killing, as I had imagined. However, being a child it escaped my notice that they were looking the women over. Most of the refugees in our cellar, including our Miss Konrad, happened to be older people. Frau Karsten the wounded woman, Cousin Herta, and Mom were exceptions.

Mom's incredible sense for self–preservation and the protection of her young had her come up with unbelievable ideas. Here she was, a woman of only thirty–six and fairly attractive, she was a prime target to fall prey to the young Russian soldiers. I am still amazed at Mom's incredible coping ability and resourcefulness. To look as unattractive as possible, she smeared her face, neck, and hair with dirt from potatoes and the nearby pile of coal. Then she twisted her hair into a bun on the back of her head as most old people did. To top it off, she stuffed Peter's little pillow under her dress in the back so that she looked as if she were a hunchback. Mom would have won the grand prize for looking repulsive. She escaped degradation. Mom also looked out to protect me. Being only ten years old, but tall for my age, she was afraid that I would be judged older, and raped. I wore my hair in pigtails, and Mom made sure that the pigtails were showing to make me look younger. She also smeared my face with dirt and insisted that I bend my knees when I walked so that I wouldn't look so tall. At the time I did not understand why she was so concerned about me, and Mom did not explain.

Onkel Wilhelm

My Grandmother Stanneck was the third of ten children. Onkel Wilhelm was the youngest of Grandma's seven brothers. Kaiser Wilhelm, the Kaiser of Germany at the time Onkel Wilhelm was born, also had seven sons. He let it be known that he would be godfather to the seventh boy of any family which had seven sons in a row. Well, my Grandmother got in between the seven boys "in a row" and messed it up, but from what she told me, Kaiser Wilhelm still sent a present and a letter of congratulations to the family. Onkel Wilhelm, of course, was named for the Kaiser.

Onkel Wilhelm did not think the dive bomber attacks were as bad as what he and his family had experienced during their trek to Straupitz, and he had elected to stay upstairs in our room the whole time. He came down into the cellar soon after he heard the first Russians arrive. There was a group of several soldiers and an officer. What Onkel Wilhelm did next was unbelievable and nearly sent everyone into shock. He shook hands with the officer and said: "Welcome!" Then he raised his right arm and saluted with "Heil Hitler." There was a collective gasp to be heard from all of us. Had anyone had a gun we would have shot Onkel Wilhelm. We were actually waiting for one of the Russians to do so, and then to shoot all of us as well. Instead the officer said in broken German: "Hitler dead," and to our great relief Onkel Wilhelm agreed: "Oh, yes, yes, Hitler is dead, thank heaven." We were surprised and relieved when the officer accepted this and nothing happened. However, everybody in the cellar was ready to hog–tie and gag Onkel Wilhelm for fear of what kind of trouble he would get us into next. He might have made a mark with Kaiser Wilhelm by being born the seventh son of a family, but it sure did not look like he was going to make any marks with the Russians.

Looting

All Russians asked for watches. *"Uhri, Uhri"* was the magic word, and one could almost save one's life with a watch. We never even owned a watch, and nobody else in the cellar had one except for Onkel Wilhelm. He was promptly relieved of it. Now he was really becoming a menace. Upon arrival Onkel Wilhelm had been upset that his precious felt hat was muddy, and now he lost his watch. He scared us to death by carrying on like a crazy old man, telling every Russian who came into the house that he wanted his watch back. By the time it was morning, many more Russians had marched through our cellar and we could see their "loot." Some of them had watches strung all the way up both arms.

For the next several days, four or five times a day, all of us were ordered to go upstairs into our room and to wait there while the cellar was searched for weapons, German soldiers, and possible hidden treasures. In the turmoil, more refugees drifted into our house. Back in the cellar we hid in the darkest corners. There was continuous screaming upstairs from women who were being raped by the Russians. For lack of enough young women, older ones had to do. I was aware of something terrible and unspeakable going on because the adults were whispering to each other, terror stricken, but Mom did not explain anything to me.

Next coming through the area were the Mongolian Russians. Those were feared the most and said to behave like animals. Actually they were people who lived in primitive circumstances in Mongolia and Siberia. Our modest living facilities seemed fantastic to them. They had never seen "water come out of the wall," and they were playing like little kids with some of the simplest gadgets around the house. Clocks fascinated them endlessly because they were ticking. They seemed to be alive. Weeks later I saw a Russian tinker around with an appropriated alarm clock. When it started to ring and he could not stop it, he shot it with his gun. That shut up the clock but it also broke it. Then he cried because his *"Uhri"* was dead, and he cradled it in his arms.

Days drifted on as in a nightmare. Eventually after the initial commotion had quieted down a bit we staggered upstairs to our room, weak from hunger and fright. The place had been ransacked. There was blood on the floors and our few belongings had been scattered. Nobody cared. The only thing people cared about at that time was to have gotten away alive—but then we asked ourselves "what for?" There must be a will to survive installed in every living thing to fight for survival right now even if it means falling prey to the next predator.

I don't even remember what we did next except that Mom cooked some soup and tried to get Peter and me to eat it. We had not had anything warm in our stomachs for more than ten days.

We spent the days in our room with a steady stream of Russian soldiers walking in at any time and looking for things to take. The pillow case stuffed with our clothes was spared. It did not look attractive enough to be hauled off as loot. Fräulein Konrad's two neatly packed little suitcases were long since gone. Having the Russians look through our things became an everyday affair. Had their parents or the Bible not taught them that it is a sin to steal other people's belongings? "Of course" answered Mom to my question, "but this is a part of war." — War, always war, I thought. Though war had been a part of my life ever since I could remember, I still did not understand it. It seemed that everything could be done in the name of war.

It scared us when some Russians tried to get into our house during the night. Mom did not feel comfortable about our door just being locked, and very evening I had to help her push a china cabinet in front of the door. My furniture moving experience came in handy.

Mom's new bicycle had been stolen. Being resourceful, Mom removed the front wheel from my old bike to "disable" it. It was the one Onkel Rudolf had built for my eighth birthday. I was happy that nobody had stolen it, and it still served Mom well for another year and a half.

Eventually Peter and I ventured outside to see what was going on. The street was littered with discarded items. Besides money, there were clothes and household items. Nobody bothered to pick anything up. Nobody cared. Nothing mattered. Life seemed to be destroyed.

PART II

THE ATERMATH YEARS

7

1945
Post War Under the Russians
Age Ten

May 8, 1945 marked the official end of World War II. This end had been long awaited by the war weary German people. Now we have Peace! Everything will improve from now on. So we thought.

Peace

An era in the history of Germany had come to an end—a chapter of our lives closed. The air attacks had stopped, the Russians had invaded us, and the war was over. Life would be normal again from now on, I thought. Yet I did not know what a normal life really was. To me it meant no more air raids and no ration cards. I think I expected food to appear on the scene instantly, to be purchased for money and without needing those nasty little ration stickers. I heard people speak of peace, but I did not know what that meant. I was sure that it meant no air raids and no Russians and no ration cards.

I was anxiously looking forward to peace, although I remembered something somebody said during an air raid in Berlin: "Enjoy the war—peace will be frightful." This was to become true in the following years. Hitler's famous promise of a better life: "Nobody shall be hungry—nobody shall freeze" was quoted often and with mockery when we were trying to survive miserably cold winters, and when we felt lucky if we had one piece of bread every day and a featherbed to keep us from freezing to death.

Still worrying that we might be separated from Mom in some way, Peter and I did not go out of sight of the house. Mom needed our protection, too. The Russian soldiers were not finished raping women. Each time a group of them approached the house, Mom would pick up Peter, swing his legs behind her to hide the fact that he was older, and pretend he was a baby. She was hoping the soldiers would have mercy on a woman with a baby. Mom always fixed me up to look as ugly as possible for fear that they would think I was older than my ten years, and take me. I did not know what it was all about and Mom did not explain, so I resented her efforts to make me look ugly.

Peter and I thought the Russians were really nice. To be fair, they were wonderful to us children. After all, they were human beings and had suffered from this war as much as we had, or even worse. Seeing us children probably reminded them of their own children back home in Russia.

Some Russians still kept coming to loot despite military orders to stop. Others came just to look around and visit. Those were nice to people, and all were good to children. Frau Karsten, the young woman who had the injured shoulder, was suffering terribly. We had a nurse in town who came by occasionally and changed the dressings, but the wound seemed to be festering and not healing at all. One afternoon Frau Karsten was sitting outside in the sunshine moaning with pain, with her little daughter staying close to her. I sat near her on the steps with the door behind me open. This way I could keep an ear tuned to make sure that Mom was all right. Several Russians came wandering into the back yard. They looked friendly. The officer who was with them spoke some German, and took an interest in Frau Karsten's injury. She told him what had happened and he seemed to want to help. He told her they had a doctor, and that he would send him. We did not believe it, but the doctor did arrive soon afterwards. He examined the wound thoroughly and found that the piece of shrapnel was still inside her shoulder. He told Frau Karsten with sign language and a tiny bit of German, that he would make arrangements for her to be taken to the hospital in the nearby city of Lübben. Later in the day, a Russian vehicle came and picked her up. Her little girl went with her.

Always Hungry

Grocery deliveries were very erratic and we did not receive all of the meager food rations which were printed on our ration cards. The Russian army had set up a field kitchen around the corner from where we lived. Peter and I would go there with containers and beg for some of their stew. Quite often we were lucky. The Russians were kind to children. Six–year–old Peter was little, and adorable, with huge brown eyes and a sweet smile. They usually gave some food to him, even if it was just a slice of bread. The Russian army was not well fed, but we did not know this until years later, and then we appreciated their kindness even more. No wonder they seemed to always cook cabbage soup or cabbage stew.

On two occasions when army supply trucks moved through town, Peter and I, as well as a bunch of other kids, ran after them and begged for bread. By that time we knew the Russian word for "bread." The Russian soldiers who sat in the backs of the trucks smiled as they threw loaves of bread down to us and saw how happy they made us.

A New Beginning

The Month of May brought sunshine and flowers. The trees began to leaf out. Mother Nature was creating new life. In the turmoil of the time we needed this constancy. It helped restore our energy.

Our lives began to get somewhat back to normal. Peter and I went out to visit with our friends, however, I tried to keep an eye on the house and on Mom. The trains were still not running, so she was at home. Russians, as well as Poles who had come across the not so distant border, still came to loot, even though it had long since been prohibited. Recently they came with long sticks and metal rods, having found out that many people had buried treasured belongings in the ground. They would poke the ground wherever it looked recently disturbed or soft, and find the buried "treasures."

During one night just before the end of the war, Mom dug a large hole about the size of a grave in the ground behind the house. With my help she placed our small china cabinet into the hole, then filled it with our nice china and glassware, as well as other cherished items which we did not want to have stolen or broken. As was her way, Mom thought ahead. Her common sense told her to cover the obviously recently dug up ground with our firewood. Ours was not discovered, although nearly everybody else's buried treasures were.

One day I was sitting on the back steps of the house and talking to Frau Karsten who was finally recuperating and wearing a smile on her face. Two Russians had come and were messing around in Herr Ruben's carpenter shop hoping to find things to take. Most Russians drank everything that was in bottles. After a time the two Russians came back out of the workshop drinking from a container. One of them proceeded to light a cigarette and in horror we watched him spitting fire. He died before help arrived. They had been drinking denatured alcohol. Another horrible experience to add to our war scars.

The Russian Military Headquarters for the area had been set up in our village and we had Russians walking around town all of the time. Once I got home just as a very handsome young Russian officer was about to leave. Mom introduced me and the man said some complimentary things to me. He spoke fairly understandable German. After shaking hands with both of us, he left. Mom told me that he had tried to make a date with her for that night. Not wanting to be rude to him because he treated her with respect, Mom had the intuition to tell him that she was sick with tuberculosis. She suggested she was contagious and that he might not want to meet with her. It worked. The officer thanked her and was shaking hands with Mom and wishing her well as I entered our room. At least Mom could produce one of her children she had been telling him about. When he first asked her to meet with him, she used us as an excuse, but he had offered to send somebody to watch us.

"Nobody Shall be Hungry—Nobody Shall Freeze"

That, apparently, was a "promise" Hitler was making to the German *Volk* in his speeches. Could he have heard how often his slogan was mockingly quoted, he would have spun like a top in his grave. We had ration cards, but they lied. Anything can be printed on paper. It did not mean we received what it said we should get. From now on much of my time was spent checking the grocery store, the bakery, the butcher, and the greengrocer to see if they were open. If one of those stores was open, it meant that they had received supplies, and I needed to get into line immediately before those limited supplies ran out. Sometimes there would be a note on the door telling people when the store would open and which food items would be distributed—if they knew ahead of time what they would be receiving. In that case, people would line up hours ahead of the opening time to ensure that they got their rations before supplies ran out, which happened all too often.

By summer our little railroad line was running again on a reduced schedule, and Mom was back at work. However, the trains had to stop east of the destroyed bridges near the city of Lübben until temporary bridges could be built. The whole transportation system did not yet function. We were at the mercy of the Russians who were hauling off to Russia everything they could, including railroad tracks and food. Once the railroads were back in operation, they had to run on single tracks with very few sidetracks on which to wait for oncoming trains. This, combined with the many destroyed bridges, caused monstrous delays in the transportation system, which at that time was almost exclusively dependent on the railroads.

One of the worst times was when there was no salt. We were used to not having any sugar, but a flour and water soup without a dash of salt tasted awful. At that time our bodies must have been critically depleted of salt. I don't remember feeling ill—we were so hungry and weak all the time that not feeling well was normal for us. I remember when word spread that some railroad cars carrying salt for the cattle had arrived at the Straupitz station. There was a regular migration to the railroad station. We just climbed up into the open box cars and started licking the unrefined salt, which was a salmon color and came in huge chunks. We took some small chunks home with us to last until distribution of table salt resumed.

Typhus and Other Diseases

There was something wrong with the cattle. The cows had hoof and mouth disease, and we had to boil the milk before using it. Later that summer every infant and child up to the age of two died of dysentery in Straupitz and in all the neighboring villages. Knowing everyone in the village, it was quite distressing to us kids when the church bells rang and another tiny white box was carried to the cemetery. We usually followed the procession for a distance, silently saying our own good byes to the small brother or sister of a friend.

Everyone had to go and get typhus vaccinations. Those were a series of three shots which were jammed into people's chests with dull needles. The loathsome needles were pre World War II equipment. After each of those shots we could not get undressed for more than a week because we could not lift our arms. The typhus shots were so awful and so dreaded that people had to be forced to get them. This was done by requiring the vaccination certificates in order to receive our ration cards.

Many people had typhus. When Peter got very ill with it, we thought we were losing him. Somehow from somewhere through connections, Mom was able to get a big bag of oats. She cooked oatmeal without sugar or salt, strained it, and fed the slime to Peter to coat his stomach. We swear that it saved his life. Mom made me eat it, too, just in case. Without at least a dash of salt the oatmeal slime tasted so horrible that for decades I avoided eating oatmeal.

Survival in the Russian Zone of Occupation in 1945

Most of the time there were no grocery distributions until near the end of the month, and then we did not get our full allotment. Not owning any land on which we could plant a garden, Mom had to take measures to keep us alive during the rest of the month. She was seeing too many homeless people (unsettled refugees) riding the trains, aimlessly, until they were dead from starvation. Since they had no permanent place to stay, they were not registered anywhere and therefore received no ration cards.

Because of her work on the railroad, Mom had certain opportunities which she took advantage of, though often at tremendous risks. For a while she was able to get into the milk supplies which were being transported to the Russian headquarters in Straupitz, by skimming the cream off the top of each of three or four milk cans. She also went to "harvest" some of the potatoes outside of town. All potatoes were earmarked for the alcohol still in the castle, where the Russians made their vodka. To be caught would probably have meant death, or worse. One night Mom was picking string beans, when the Russian guard walked past the field. Quick thinking saved her. She crouched down, pretending she "had to go," so the guard discretely looked the other way. When he was out of sight, Mom continued the harvest and we had a rare meal of string beans.

Our fare was always stew. Turnips, cabbage, carrots, potato soup. Sometimes we could flavor it with a little meat or a bone. The very meager meat rations had to be stretched for flavoring. Never did we have enough food to be reasonably full. While the vegetable stews were a very healthy fare, the body needs fat, too. I was nearly eleven years old now, and growing. So was little brother. Seven–year–old Peter with his hunger pangs confronted Mom and me one evening, accusing us of not giving him all the food he was entitled to, and then demanding that we give him his portion so that he could manage his own rations. Mom gave it to him just as bread and jam were available. Peter ate his whole ten day ration, which was less than one loaf of bread and about three ounces of jam, within a day and a half—then remorsefully came to us begging for food. He admitted that there wasn't enough food allocation at any time if we ate until we were no longer hungry. He had learned his lesson, but Mom was hurting. To watch her children being hungry, and Peter would often cry when he was hungry, must be one of the worst things in the world for a mother.

Mom did what she could to get us through the rough times. She often came home from work with a sandwich, a few potatoes, or whatever she had been able to get in return for a favor she had done for somebody. Most of the time, the favor consisted of getting some overweight farmer a seat on the crowded train. There were no seat assignments and a crowded train in Germany was, and still is, one where people who are sitting down are nearly piled on top of each other. The alternative was standing up. At that time nobody was fat, and to clear a space for a heavy person meant having to talk two people into giving up their seats. Only Mom could do this kind of thing. She had the personality for it. She also had a Guardian Angel protecting her during some of the risks she took.

One time Mom came home with about five pounds of sugar beets which she had dug up somewhere. She thought they could be cooked like carrots, but they stayed hard no matter how long she cooked them. Being hungry we tried to eat them hard as they were but the taste was awful. She then decided that perhaps we could get some molasses by cooking the beets long enough. However, all we got was very dark brown water which tasted bitter. Mom gave up and threw the brew away. Peter and I were disappointed because the word sugar beets implied that somehow Mom ought to be able to coax sugar out of them.

Now that people no longer had to "volunteer" to work for the *Vaterland* on Sundays, Mom had to take her turn on the train only once a month. On Sundays the trains were running on a reduced schedule, mostly just to pick up the milk.

On several Sundays in the fall, Mom went on excursions into the nearby forest to gather mushrooms with people who knew which ones were edible. Being so hungry, she often ate a few mushrooms after she picked them. One time she ate a poisonous one by mistake and was awfully sick for a couple of days afterwards. Peter and I were terrified and afraid that we would lose our Mom. What would we do if something happened to her? We did not even know whether or not we still had family left in Berlin, not having heard a word from anyone. Mail service was nonexistent at that time, at least in our village, although we were only fifty miles away from Berlin. Fortunately, Mom recovered.

Boils, Lice, and Soup Dispensed by the School

When we were back in school we received *Schulspeisung,* consisting of one half liter of hot soup every day. This was better than a precious gift! We were "thriving" on this extra special allotment of watery bread soup, cabbage soup, and best of all, pumpkin soup. Nevertheless, due to malnutrition our arms and legs started to break out with boils which were very painful. We did not know the cause at the time, but many years later in the United States I had a friend, Tove, from Norway. We compared notes about the years following the war, and she told me that they also had those boils. Tove was a number of years older than I and confirmed that malnutrition had caused them.

Lice became a general problem. There were two kinds—hair and clothes lice. Mom made me wear my braids wrapped around my head so I wouldn't pick up lice in school, or especially in the food lines where there was closer body contact. I liked my long braids, but Mom insisted that they were perfect "louse ladders." We never picked up hair lice, though many of our friends had them. However, one day Mom noticed that Peter kept scratching his neck and shoulders. Upon inspecting his clothes she found clothes lice on him. She was nearly hysterical, and searched all of our clothes day and night for a couple of weeks until she was sure we were rid of them.

Poetry

Throughout all of our school years we had to memorize a lot of poems. The old German poets seem to have specialized in long ones. If a poem had only twenty stanzas, we considered it a short one. Many of them went on for forty or fifty stanzas. I must have had a good memory because I had no trouble memorizing them, but I certainly had no practical use for poems. To me they seemed a lot of flowery language to say something that could have been said in a sentence or two.

One contemporary poem, a post war one, hit me hard. I cried when the teacher read it to the class, and it was very embarrassing to be crying in front of my peers. Then the teacher asked me what it meant to me, and when I told him, some other kids cried also. It was the story of a soldier returning home after the war. He found the city destroyed and went looking for his mother. Eventually he went to see his minister who took him to the cemetery. There the soldier stands at the grave with his head bowed and says: "You are wrong, the dead one does not rest here. How could a space so small ever enclose all the love of a mother!"

At the time we had not yet had any word from Papa or from anyone in Berlin. In my mind I pictured him, in ragged POW clothes, returning to Berlin and looking for his mother. Perhaps her apartment building had fallen prey to bombs. We could not even be sure Grandma was alive. The poem pictured the scene so vividly for me that I thought it was cruel. It did not help that my peers were teasing me about crying in school.

News of Berlin

Very late in the summer of 1945, Grandmother Stanneck arrived in Straupitz. With the transportation system still chaotic and mostly non-existent, she had walked a good part of the fifty miles from Berlin to get to us. She came to see if we were all right. Then she told us all the bad news from Berlin. The city was reduced to rubble—seventy–five million tons of it covered what was left of our Berlin, a city praised in songs and by poets as the "Athens on the River Spree."

Some of our relatives were dead, including Grandma Hinniger, Mom's mother. Tante Else, first cousin of my Papa and very close to

Cousins Hannelore (3½) and Rosemarie (5) were killed on the last day of the war when a shell hit their basement shelter.

Grandma Stanneck in that she had been raised by her, had met with a terrible fate. On the very last day of the war, with the city already surrounded by the Russians, Tante Else's mother, father, husband, and two little girls all died. Shellfire had hit their shallow basement shelter. People went flying through a wall from the blast and were killed. Tante Else's parents had come as refugees from a town southeast of Berlin. Her husband had lost both legs in the war and he had been released from the army and sent home. He perished.

Tante Else was dug out of the rubble and patched back together. She was the only one left. Grandma said that when she saw her in the hospital, her hair had turned white. I could never get over the death of my two favorite, adorable little cousins, Rosemarie and Hannelore, ages five and three. Fifteen years later when visiting Tante Else in Berlin, she suggested we look at pictures, and I had to tell her that I couldn't. She certainly had more courage than I will ever have.

Grandma had no word from our Papa. We did not know where he was and what may have happened to him.

I do not remember how long Grandma stayed with us, most likely only overnight. Nobody could feed extra people on non existing rations. Even if regular rations were available, it was not possible to share food with other people for any length of time. Everyone knew this and accepted it. Mom took Grandma on her train to Lübben–Ost, then walked with her across an emergency pedestrian bridge, and four kilometers to the long–distance railroad station. There she put her on a train headed towards Berlin. Since bridges were out everywhere, most trains ran only as far as they could. Then people had to walk.

School and New Teachers

In September I had my eleventh birthday and entered fifth grade. We were now the "big" kids. Our ranks were swollen with all the refugees the village had absorbed, and our three–room school house was getting too small. We started attending in shifts. This, as well as Grandma's visit, reminded me of my year in Berlin and I felt homesick. Now that there were no longer any air raids, couldn't we just move back to Berlin? This was only a dream, and I knew it. Our apartment building was gone and so were

I am third from the right. My best friend, Marga, is second from the left. This photo was taken in the fall of 1944 by the father of one of these girls.

many, many others. The once beautiful city of Berlin was a heap of rubble and had a critical housing shortage. Nobody received permission to move back. There was nothing left to move to.

In Straupitz we made do with the existing quarters at the school house. The fifth and sixth grades were together in the smaller of the two classrooms. Grades one to four were in the large room. The seventh and eighth grades moved into the attic room above the carriage house. This was a small and somewhat dark room with small windows, and quite a contrast to the large, bright rooms of the school house.

Going to school in shifts—8 a.m. to 1 p.m. and 1 p.m. to 6 p.m.— did not work out. The farm children hardly ever showed up for the afternoon shifts. Once they were involved with helping in the fields, it was difficult for them to get away during planting and harvest times. Late in the spring of 1946, several rooms in the castle were made available for use as additional classroom space. Grades seven and eight moved to the castle, and grades five and six moved into the attic room of the carriage house. Despite being small and on the dark side, I found it charming and cozy. Now we could drop the afternoon classes which had been quite inconvenient for the farm children.

Our teachers were qualified men, having either returned from the military or been found among the refugees. I do not remember their names, but a couple of those teachers stand out in my memory for different positive reasons.

Fun

Despite the hunger which sapped our energy, Peter and I also had fun. Remembering her own bleak childhood during World War I, Mom let us do many things which most mothers would never permit. At times when she was not too tired and lacking in energy after work, Mom would even be a part of it. Peter and I built a tent with the only blanket we owned. A blanket was something special—it was a luxury item. I'm surprised we even owned one. Our covers at night, summer or winter, were our featherbeds—huge pillows filled with feathers. Mattresses of German beds came in four sections. Mom would let us take those off the bed and "camp" on the floor with them, using the blanket as our tent. I would be the instigator on camping and moving around the room, with the "campsite" being in a different area of the room every night. I don't think camping was known in Germany at that time, so my different place to sleep each night was more like "gypsy-ing" around.

With Peter's crib having been traded for a stove, the three of us slept in the two single beds which were put next to each other as they would be for a married couple. Together they were then the size of an American king–size bed. This was quite an adequate sleeping arrangement by the standards of that time.

The most marvelous thing to me was that we had a sheet of masonite. It was our table top, and I discovered one day that it could be lifted out of the table's frame. Delighted with a new building material, I found different uses for it when we did not need the table. For a while, Peter and I put it up in the center of the two beds every night. It held up the blanket for our tent above the beds like a center post, with the effect that Peter and I had our separate little tents.

A fringe benefit was that one side of the masonite was smooth, so I could write on it with chalk and erase it. In school I had just learned how to solve what I thought were the most complicated math problems. I loved them and spent at least an hour every night giving myself problems and solving them on the board on my side of the bed tent, while Peter slept. Mom never complained about not having a table whenever we used the masonite top. When it was time for Mom to come to bed after she was finished with the household chores, she squeezed in next to whichever one of us was not too sprawled out in our sleep.

In the daytime when we were not in school or with friends, Peter and I often played cards together, such as *Schwarzer Peter*, the equivalent of Old Maid. We also liked building things. The trouble was that there were no building materials and nothing was available for purchase. I had already made cars out of some of Peter's building blocks, having sawed empty spools of Mom's sewing threads into slices to make wheels which I attached with nails begged off of Herr Ruben. However, nails were precious and Mom's threads were nearly gone.

Chores

Besides being the keeper of our valuable and irreplaceable ration cards and standing in food lines, my chores included washing the floor of our room every Saturday after school, as well as raking the street and sweeping the sidewalk, both of which were unpaved. Peter had to dust and help me as best as he could with the raking and sweeping of the street. Mom worked on Saturdays, as all people did, and she did not get home from her last train run until late in the afternoon or early evening. By helping her with the cleaning we could enjoy time together on Sundays without Mom having to do all of the chores.

Mom usually cooked our next day's stew during the night. This took a couple of hours. Not wanting to stay awake, she would set the alarm clock for the time at which she thought the stew would be done. Then she attached a string to the electric cord of our hot plate and tied the end of the string to the headboard of the bed. When the alarm went off, she'd pull the plug out with the string. That way she did not have to get out of bed during the icy winter.

Actually (she did not tell us this then) she had pleurisy that winter, but dragged herself along without ever seeing a doctor. There was no doctor in our village or in any of the neighboring ones. In the nearby city they would have put her into the hospital, and she was not going to abandon her children.

This train was so slow it was said that you could jump off, pick flowers, and still catch up with the train and get back on.

Wheels and Yarn

I liked wheels. Even at age six I had taken all the wheels off my doll carriage and used them to make other things. Much to my parents' anger, I had also taken apart every car of my brother's train set which had once belonged to Onkel Rudolf, mostly to get the wheels for which I found other uses. So much for my mechanical streak.

Peter specialized in clocks. We had to literally hide our only alarm clock after Peter had taken it apart several times The problem was that he did not know how to put it back together, and Mom and I had to do so. Mom had to catch her train quite early every morning, and that was a problem for her even with an alarm clock. Punctuality was definitely not one of Mom's strong points. I cannot count the number of times she raced after the train with her bicycle, to catch it at the next station. Luckily, the *Spreewaldbahn* was renowned for its slowness. How else can it take more than two hours to reach Cottbus, only twenty miles away. There were rumors of posted signs saying: "It is prohibited to get off and pick flowers while the train is in motion." This was the typical milk train which stopped not only at the stations, but also at designated farmers' fields along the way to pick up the milk, or a passenger.

By the end of the summer I started to knit a lot. Both Onkel Wilhelm and Tante Jenny had worked in a weaving mill. When they left us to return home after the end of the war, they left with us an assortment of cotton yarn suitable for knitting. By then I could knit well enough to make sweaters for myself and Peter. Growing despite the lack of food, we needed clothes for the upcoming winter.

Mom had time to knit whenever the train was at its destination. There were usually two or three hours layover before the return trip. The schedule had to accommodate the connections with the long–distance trains. One time Mom had spent countless hours knitting a jacket and short pants for Peter. He was to wear this darling little suit on an excursion to the city of Cottbus where Mom had planned to take us on a Sunday afternoon. Mom had Peter dressed in this new outfit a little early. My dear brother was a hopeless case as far as staying clean, and sure enough he got the front of his jacket dirty when Mom was not looking. She then had to wash that part of the jacket. We had a wood burning stove to heat the room and she hung the jacket close to it to dry. She must have hung it a little too close—the next thing we saw was the front of the cotton jacket catching on fire. Mom nearly cried as we watched Peter's new jacket, worn less than five minutes, burn.

Sitting in Caskets

One day in the fall, I noticed that Herr Ruben was quite busy in his carpenter workshop, building something. This was most unusual at that time. Since I loved watching people build things I went to look, and I saw that he was building boxes—specifically caskets. He had been ordered by the Russians to build thirty–two caskets in three days. Our village square was going to become a Russian cemetery. The remains of deceased prisoners of war were to be dug up and buried in caskets in the middle of our village. Herr Ruben was frantically working to get some crude boxes made by the deadline. Poor quality lumber and a meager supply of nails which the Russians had allotted for this did not permit a halfway decent job. Speed was of the essence. The orders needed to be obeyed—punishment usually was severe.

For the first time Herr Ruben asked me to help. I handed the valuable nails to him without dropping even one. Because of being short on lumber, the boxes were mummy shaped, meaning wider at the head end than at the bottom, with slanted sides. As Herr Ruben tried to nail the first box together, it kept slipping because of the slant. He asked me to sit in the box to hold the edge down. I was petrified. Sitting in a casket when I was still alive was about the worst thing I could think of, and most likely bad luck, too. I could just hear my superstitious Grandma Stanneck! However, seeing that Herr Ruben really needed my help, this was my turn to help him out. He had helped me build the swing the year before. After a while it stopped bothering me to sit in the caskets as I forced myself to concentrate on getting the job done fast. We were a pretty good team and made the deadline. Then a Russian army truck came and picked up the boxes. I felt proud that I had assisted with building them and that I had been able to be of help to my grandfatherly friend.

A couple of weeks later, our village square was a cemetery with a red fence around it. On top of each fence post was a red Soviet star. What a gloomy sight. I hated passing the square but, being right in the middle of town, there was not much choice.

Recovering and Surviving

Near the end of 1945 the spirits of the people slowly began to recover. The Russians no longer bothered us, and life had fallen into a routine. Peter and I were back in school and Mom was working on the railroad. We were always anxiously awaiting Mom's return, hoping she would bring home some food. Mom would risk anything for the survival of her children. The Russians claimed everything and there were quotas to be filled. The farmers had difficult and scary times. If, for instance, their land was assessed to raise a given number of tons of wheat, they had to come up with those tons, even if they themselves were not eating. Nature had a way of controlling the yield, but the Soviet administration did not care about that.

Another area in which the Russians collected heavily was livestock, especially pigs. Some farmers smuggled a couple of pigs to relatives or friends in other villages whose stock had already been counted, and in that way having a lower count when the officials came around. Later on they would retrieve their two hidden pigs for themselves. Mom helped several times in that she assigned a railroad car in the back of the train to a farmer alone with his squealing pigs, and then left one car empty as a cushion so that the passengers would not hear the pigs. She would stand outside on the stations' platform and announce for everybody to get into one of the front cars of the train, and that the back was all filled. In return she would receive a few huge slices of bread, a jar of homemade liverwurst, and other sausages from the grateful farmer. Nothing came from nothing—Mom stuck out her neck a number of times, and if caught she would have been dead. She saw to it that we "kept our heads above water" and survived. Had she later been asked where she got the ideas and found the energy to execute them, she would not have known the answer. She did believe in "Someone" watching over us and giving her intuition and strength to fight for our survival.

Christmas came and went, and the very eventful year of 1945 came to an end. Though the struggle for survival continued, we clung to but a glimmer of hope for a better future.

It had been a year since we had heard from our Papa. Where was he—was he still alive?

It is difficult to understand a war, unless one is in it. War never takes us to a better place—looking at history, everyone loses in the end. Even though we felt we would have lost everything if we lost our Papa, we still dared to hope.

8

1946
Escape from the Russian Zone
Age Eleven

Red Stars

Our village square where we had experienced happy times whenever the circus came to Straupitz, had been turned into a Russian cemetery.

One morning a dreadful thing was discovered. The fence around the Russian cemetery had been vandalized. Besides damage to the fence, the Soviet stars on top of the fence posts were bent and quite a few were missing. The Commandant of the Soviet Military Headquarters gave the village two days to repair the fence and to put up new stars—otherwise all children under twelve would be killed. It was assumed that children had done the damage.

Mom was frantic, and so were all mothers who had young children. The problem was not that it was impossible to repair the fence in the two days given, though the damage was extensive and paint unavailable—it was the question of where to get sheet metal to replace the missing stars. There were no materials available. Cans might have been usable, but there were no canned goods. The baker wanted to donate some of his baking sheets, but this did not work because the shiny aluminum would not hold the paint and the stars had to be red. Our blacksmith said he could make stars if he had metal. Seeing that suggestion as the lifesaver, people eagerly donated whatever small metal items they had around the house and which the blacksmith found suitable. He melted everything together and fashioned the stars. I don't know where they found the paint, but the fence was repaired and Red Stars were back on the posts by the deadline.

We had once again survived two horrible days, and we children were allowed to go on living thanks to the combined efforts of the whole village. From then on, nobody ever even went near that dreadful cemetery again.

Disappearing People

My friend Marga was standing outside our window talking to me one day when our former and not very favorite teacher, Herr Schmitt, came by. He stopped to talk to us. To our surprise he had become quite humble and seemed almost nice because he no longer had any authority to exhibit. As it turned out, it was the last time we ever saw him. About a week later we heard that he, as well as Herr Hesse and other Nazis, had disappeared without a trace. We knew by then that when the Russians "cleaned up," the people who disappeared were either shot or sent to labor camps in Siberia.

Learning Russian

As was required in the Russian occupation zone, we started to learn the Russian language in school. It was my first foreign language and I liked it. I especially enjoyed learning how to write the cyrillic alphabet. The Soviet Military Headquarter was located in our village, and whenever we had a chance we would try a few words with some of the Russian soldiers who were walking around town.

On one particular Sunday it was the birthday of a German woman who had joined the Communists. She was now an official as well as the interpreter at the headquarters. The teacher selected me to memorize a Russian poem and recite it for her birthday the next day. I struggled all evening and the next morning, but not knowing what the words meant, it was difficult to memorize the Russian words. It was quite a long poem, too, and I realized that there was no way I could recite it from memory by that afternoon. Reluctantly, I had to go to the teacher's house and tell him I couldn't do it. He then asked me to write the poem nicely on a sheet of paper and present it to the woman. In addition he taught me how to say "congratulations on your birthday" in Russian. Despite my stage fright, it all went well. The Russians who were present during my presentation smiled and complimented me for my effort (said the interpreter).

Our Lives Change

Easter 1946—The Happiest Easter

A week before Easter we received a very special letter which would change our future. It was a letter from our Papa. I could not believe my eyes when I saw his beautiful penmanship, which I so admired. The letter was dated and postmarked a week before Christmas and had taken all that time to get

I always admired Papa's penmanship. The number "2" in the circle is the ZIP code, which Germany had initiated during the war.

from Berlin to Straupitz, only fifty miles away. Papa wrote that he had returned from Russia, and that if he were well enough to travel he would visit us at Easter. Since he did not say on which day he was planning to arrive, Peter and I went to the station and met the train from Lübben every day after school during the week before Easter. If Mom was on duty on the Lübben run when our Papa arrived, she would have the good fortune of seeing him a few hours earlier. I was so looking forward to seeing our Papa again that I could hardly concentrate in school that week.

It seemed like the longest week of my life, but Good Friday was really good to us. As usual, Peter and I met the train from Lübben, and on that day it brought our Papa back to us. He looked the worst for the wear—nearly unrecognizable, old, and he was quite weak as well. Mom had to help him out of the train—but he was alive and with us. After hugging Peter and me, his first words were: "I wrote you a letter, why did you not write back? I was very sad about that." I had written back immediately, of course, but he had not yet received my reply. It was hard for him to believe that we received his letter from December only a week ago.

What a happy Easter! For Peter and me, anyway. Our parents continued with their marital problems. These problems had become obvious to me during some of Papa's visits to Straupitz on furloughs. Among the many victims which this war had claimed were relationships. Due to the continuous sacrifices that a war requires, many couples found they had changed so much that they could no longer live together. Mom has always been a free spirit, and she came to like her independence. She also loved her job on the railroad which kept her outdoors most of the time.

Mom and Papa talked things over and decided to try for a "new beginning." This meant we would move back to Berlin, if we could get permission to do so. Papa stayed with us only throughout Easter. He was going to start working after the holiday. Tabak Erbach, where he had worked until the beginning of the war, was giving him back his old job as a tobacco goods salesman. What tobacco goods? Naturally there were inventive minds at work in all fields, and they came up with unique ideas to improvise.

The Heart–Wrenching but True Story
of a POW's Return Home from Russia

The following is the story of Papa's arrival in Berlin as Grandma Stanneck told it to us. First a few words about the setting.

The apartment house in which Grandma Stanneck lived in Berlin–Steglitz (American occupied sector) had remained intact at the end of the war, except for blown–out windows, crumbling stucco, and roof damage. It was a small building with about sixteen apartments, each consisting of one good sized room and a kitchen. The building dated back to the nineteenth century and initially had no indoor plumbing. At one time it had been modernized in that toilets were added in the corners of the landings between floors. The apartments still had gas lighting. The kitchen stove was fired with coal for cooking, but it also had two gas burners.

Grandma had been living in this apartment for nearly forty years and Papa had grown up there. Just before the war he installed electric lighting into the room, but the kitchen still had gas light. Grandma's apartment was on the second floor (the third floor by American way of counting, where the ground floor is counted as the first floor). This detail is important in the story to come.

It was early December of 1945. Grandma was looking out of her kitchen window and noticed in the street below a *Heimkehrer* (home comer), as the returning POWs were called. Those ragged men, just barely able

Resting to gather strength to make it home. A typical POW returning from Russia—in rags, barely able to walk and almost starved—This is how Papa appeared on Grandma Stanneck's doorstep one day in December 1945.

to stay on their feet and dragging along from lack of energy, were a familiar and pitiful sight. From the sorry sight of them, everyone could tell that the poor men were returning from Russia. No other country sent their POWs home in such deplorable condition.

Returning POWs were seen everywhere at that time, often searching for their families whom they had left such a long time ago. Would they still be living in the same place or was the house gone? If it was, where could they find them? More importantly, would their loved ones still be alive?

Our Papa was such a *Heimkehrer*. The war had been over for more than seven months and we had not heard from him in over a year. At that time he was near Stalingrad. Statistics say that of the armies who were fighting in Stalingrad, 90,000 were taken captive, of which only 6,000 survived. Chances were slim that Papa would be one of the survivors.

While we had hope, the odds that he was still alive were not good. At the time of his arrival we were living in Straupitz—which was in the Russian occupied zone—but he could not have known that we were still there. In any case, after getting out of Russia, he would not have wanted to go anywhere in the Russian zone. He therefore returned to his mother in Berlin, to Grandma Stanneck's second floor (third floor in America) apartment in the district of Steglitz.

Here is the heart–wrenching story of Papa's arrival, in Grandma's words:

When I looked out of the window and saw the POW so very slowly round the corner and approach the house, I said to myself "another poor *Heimkehrer*—I wonder who are the lucky ones whose son or husband is returning." I kept watching from the open window as he moved along the sidewalk. It took him forever to cover the distance alongside the building. When he was halfway along and opposite my window, it seemed like he lifted his head ever so slightly, though not far enough that I could see his face. Then I noticed that he bent his elbow up to waist level and moved his hand, as if to wave. He was not able to lift his arm any higher. Poor man, I thought, he seems to be awfully weak. But it did look like he was trying to wave to someone.

As he got to the end of the building, he turned in. I thought, oh my, he is coming into this house. I wonder where he is going. Which is the lucky family to get him? I went to the kitchen door, opened it and listened, hoping to find out where he might be going. Nothing happened for a long, long time. After more than 15 minutes of listening, I heard someone approach so very, very slowly. Then I saw him round the stairway at the landing below me and drag himself up, very slowly, one step at a time. It took minutes until he was on my level. I stood as if paralyzed, watching him, and all the while wondering where he is headed. Then, ever so slowly he approached me and said in the lowest voice: "Mother, I am home."

I looked at him and could not see any resemblance to my Erich. So much crime happened these days out of desperation, and I thought this man must be someone who had nowhere else to go, and he is trying to find a place to stay. I tried to get rid of him and close the door, but he kept insisting that he is my son Erich and to let him in. Finally I did. But I still did not recognize him. He looked like an eighty–year–old man, and my son would be just barely forty. This stranger could not be my son, but from what he said, it seemed like he was determined to convince me.

I thought, well, the poor devil seems to be awfully weak and cold. At least I could give him something warm to eat and let him stay long enough to warm up in my kitchen before I send him on his way.

It wasn't until he had eaten that he felt strong enough to talk some. Then from the things he said about the past, and about his wife and children, he convinced me that he was my son.

I could not believe the condition he was in, wearing nothing but rags, even on his feet. He told me he had walked most of the way from Russia, having occasionally stowed away on a freight train to get farther along the way.

After he had eaten, I helped him clean up and get into bed. He needed to sleep. He seemed to be very sick, though mostly weak. It was a week before he was strong enough to write that letter to you.

Every time I reread Grandma's words I can vividly remember the sight of the returning POWs—and tears stream down my face.

* * * * *

Seventh Grade

As I described in the last chapter, the fifth and sixth grades had been combined in one classroom. The teacher knew that I always participated in the work for both grades. He felt that I had absorbed and could handle the material he taught to the sixth grade, so that at the end of the school year I was told to skip the sixth and move right into seventh grade. What a treat! Not because I could skip the sixth grade, but because I could now go to school in that spooky castle.

A Different World

The castle was a paradise in which to go on exploration trips, inside and outside, though what a sad difference since I had been there playing with Hubertus only two summers ago. The interior had been stripped of every piece of furniture and decor. Only a couple hundred pairs of antlers on the walls above the grand staircase were a hint of the former luxury of the place. In awe we walked up and down that stairway to and from classes every day.

We wondered why those marvelous antlers had not been hauled off. Everything else was gone, including all door handles. Here our classrooms had very large, ornate double doors, but no handles to open those doors. There were just holes where the handles would normally be. Being so in awe of the castle, we thought that perhaps there was a special way in which the doors would open—some magic or "spooky–ghost" way that we were not familiar with. "Open Sesame" did not work. We had tried it. Our teacher had a simple explanation. Door handles, especially in a castle, are made of solid brass—and the Russians took them. Meanwhile, the doors kept locking on us and only the teacher could open them with his pointing stick.

One morning during class, one of the boys was sent to stand outside the classroom for disturbing the lesson, one of the mildest forms of punishment. He went exploring instead, and found a "magic" door opener. He used the point of a small antler horn to unlock the classroom door after he had found this horn in an out–of–the–way room which contained a large pile of antlers. During break, some of us hurried to that room to select small single horns so that we could have our own door openers and did not have to wait for the teacher each time we locked ourselves out during breaks. In addition, with that horn we had access to every locked room in the castle. There were many, and we were curious. Our teacher, however, forbade any roaming and exploring. Locked doors were to be left locked.

This teacher was very young, and after returning from the military service and not being able to get permission to move back to Berlin, he landed this job in our village. He had secured one of the horns for himself before he chased us out of the "treasure room." He found it much more convenient to carry his "door opener" in his pocket rather than having to walk around with the long pointing stick all day. He explained to us that the antlers can be sliced and buttons made out of the slices, and that the best buttons were always made from horns.

Not long after the day of our important discovery, a large Russian truck parked in the circular drive at the main entrance of the castle and men came in, tore all the antlers off the walls and threw them into the truck. They did not forget to take the big pile from the locked room. We thought that Russia surely must be desperate for buttons!

While watching those magnificent racks of antlers being thrown onto the Russian truck, our teacher remarked that we should have taken more of the little horn pieces for ourselves. For once, at least, he seemed to be human. Otherwise we thought that he was unreasonable to the point of being nasty. To be sure, he was not exactly happy about being stuck as a village schoolteacher. That much he had admitted to us. He did go to Berlin to visit his girlfriend whenever possible, but he could not get permission to move back. After each of those visits he would be noticeably upset and unkind to us.

He loved giving us stupid assignments. For speaking when not asked to speak, he had the pupil write "I shall not disturb the class" fifty, seventy–five or a hundred times, depending on the mood he was in. If homework had not been done with the excuse "I forgot," the assignment might be to write two hundred fifty times "I shall not forget to do my homework." One boy whom he did not like, and who had disturbed the class a couple of times that day by talking to his neighbor, was assigned to write about it, an unreasonable seven hundred fifty times. There was no way he could do this by the next day, and we each wrote as many pages as we could, to help him. Some of us were still writing when the teacher walked into the classroom the next morning. The boy handed the stack of papers to the teacher. He was surprised at the many pages and counted. There were eight hundred seventy–two sentences saying "I shall speak in class only when I am asked to," written in many different handwritings. The teacher was impressed with our teamwork, and he even laughed, which was rare.

Can We Return to Berlin?

Upon inquiry, Mom found out that we could get permission to move back to Berlin because we met all three criteria: 1. Our father had returned from being a prisoner of war in Russia. 2. We did not demand a place to live because Grandma offered to share her tiny apartment (one room and a kitchen) with us. 3. Mom did not need a job.

Consequently, Berlin would let us back in—*if* the *Kommandatura* of the Russian occupation zone gave approval to let us out. That was the big question mark! Luckily, things were not so strict at that time. Mom found out that there were three scheduled time periods for which permits to move out of East Germany were issued. All moves were to be completed before the end of 1946.

Mom was undecided. She loved her job at the railroad and life in the country. What was waiting for her in Berlin? A bleak, destroyed city, moving in with her mother–in–law who saw in Mom a rival for her son's love, and a marriage that was no longer quite intact.

Mom had often turned to me for confirmation of a decision she had made, or to get my point of view before making one. While I was much more serious and responsible than a child of my age would normally be, at eleven I was still too young to help make weighty decisions which would affect our lives. However, Mom valued my second opinion, and she somehow seemed to find it helpful to either have her own thoughts confirmed or to consider another course of action.

At this time Mom asked me whether I thought we should move back to Berlin, and gave me her reasons for wanting to stay. I wanted very much to move back. Despite enjoying the magic of living in the country, I still missed the big city with its hustle and bustle as I remembered it. Little could I imagine that the hustle and bustle had been bombed out of that city! My objective now was that I wanted the four of us to be together again and be a family. I had fond memories of celebrating holidays, especially Christmas, as a family with Papa present, and I dared hope that it would be that way again.

The Decision and the Paperwork

Mom really would have liked to have stayed in Straupitz. I, being half a gypsy by now, wanted to move back to Berlin. While I had loved living in the country, we had been there long enough as far as I was concerned, and I wanted to go home.

My reasoning against Mom's was that we may not like all of the circumstances—I was quite aware of the conflicts between Mom and Grandma Stanneck—but at least we would be in the West (West Berlin). What we had seen of the Communist system so far was enough to turn us against it. Mom's intuition told her that this fact alone by far outweighed all the others, and that it would be wise to get out of the Russian occupied zone while we still could. Years later, when East–West relations deteriorated, Mom told me how her intuition had connected with my words "at least we would be in the West," and how she knew instantly that the move would be the right thing to do.

We started to make plans. I was happy. However, I could not share my happiness with my friends because Mom told me not to say anything to anyone. There were always envious people, and our permit to leave for the West might be in jeopardy. It could even be revoked after having been granted. We had already learned that nothing was for certain. Under the present administration, rules and regulations were changed arbitrarily at the Soviets' whim. Mom thought it necessary to be so cautious that we did not even tell Peter about moving back to Berlin, feeling that he was too young to be trusted with keeping it from his friends.

Mom had to travel to Berlin to collect the necessary papers for permission to move into the American sector of Berlin, where Grandma Stanneck lived. Those papers had to be presented to the Soviet Military Headquarters in our village before an exit permit was issued. We were then assigned to the third and last exit block with a departure date of November 30, the last day on which our permit was valid.

For fear of anything going wrong at the last minute, Mom did not want anyone to know about our leaving. She did not quit her job, but just stayed away from work. Peter and I did not show up at school on the day we planned to "disappear" from Straupitz. Once again I have to marvel at Mom's intuition, about her feeling that we needed to be super cautious and not trust others in matters which concerned our fate so profoundly. During the year and a half under Soviet administration we had learned a lot. We knew better than to trust a "final" regulation, or a piece of paper with the word "Permit" on it.

The Arrangements

We were lucky to find that another Berlin family living in Straupitz was moving back to Berlin on the same day. Friends of theirs in Berlin owned a truck, and they were able to make arrangements with them to come to Straupitz and move their furniture as well as ours, and all of us to Berlin. On the "magic day" we waited anxiously and with anticipation—all day long. It was not easy to contain Peter who kept wanting to go out and see his friends. Finally, at nearly 6 p.m., the truck came. It had had mechanical problems. Our belongings were loaded first, and then those of the other family who lived on the way out of town. Neither of us had much, and by 9 p.m. we were on our way.

The truck was a medium sized, open bed one. There was not enough room in the cab for all of us. The other family and the driver knew each other and had arranged for this transportation, so it was their place to sit up front with him. Mom, Peter and I sat in the open truckbed. It was cold, but we did not mind. It was a rare treat to be riding in a car rather than on a train, and it certainly beat walking!

The Adventure

Hurrah! We were on our way to Berlin and would be there in a couple of hours. So we thought.

However, fate had other plans for us. It was a miracle that there was a truck available at all which agreed to move us to Berlin. That we had a flat tire twenty minutes into the trip was not surprising, although we had not considered the possibility. No equipment maintenance was available, and good tires would have been more than a miracle. There was a spare but it was in poor condition as well, and the driver had to do some of his own repair on the road. Much delay.

We had no watches and did not know how long we sat there, freezing, but it seemed like an eternity. Mom managed to get to one of our featherbeds, and we huddled together beneath it.

Once we were on our way again, it was not long before we had another flat tire. Knowing how long it would take to repair it, we were starting to worry about the time. The problem was that our permit to leave the Russian zone of occupation expired at midnight, November 30, and we figured it was probably past that time already. There was nothing we could do about it, but wait and sweat. We were no longer cold!

It was not our last flat tire, either. There was one more as the night crept on and we crept (literally) closer to Berlin. Actually, we were not traveling the shortest distance from Straupitz to Berlin. Because of destroyed bridges across rivers, and having to use the only then existing controlled border checkpoint from East Germany into West Berlin, the fifty–mile–trip turned into at least one hundred and fifty miles. Not only did this mean more wear and tear on our very fragile tires, but we were in for an experience which we hoped would never repeat itself in our lifetime.

The Petrifying Experience

Most bridges across rivers were destroyed at the end of the war. The Autobahn to Berlin crosses one of Germany's major rivers, the Elbe, twice near the city of Magdeburg. By the end of 1946, wooden emergency bridges had been built on this major artery to Berlin.

It was a dark night and drizzling rain. Our truck entered the first wooden bridge and it started to sway, gently at first, then more as we got farther along. There were no guardrails and the bridge was narrow. In the glow of the headlights, water was all we saw on both sides of us. The water looked black and cold in the darkness. We seemed to be skimming along on water, and swaying horribly on this seemingly endless bridge. Hands clenched and holding our breaths, we wondered whether we were still on the bridge or about to be in the water, while the seconds dragged on. Finally the terror ended, and with sighs of relief we welcomed good old terra firma (the more firmer, the less terror)!

Not being able to talk to the driver, we did not know that this had been the shorter one of the two bridges we had to cross. A few minutes later we entered the next bridge. Our hands got bloody from hanging on so tightly. I remember thinking "if this is it, so be it. Then it is not meant to be that I shall see my beloved Berlin again." The second bridge was much longer and it swayed violently. When it was over with, we could not believe that we had survived this. Fate, obviously, had decided that we should live.

The Arrival—Our Exit Permit had Expired!

It was nearly five o'clock in the morning, and we had been on the road for eight hours, when we reached the Soviet Border Checkpoint Dreilinden at the city limits of Berlin. It was December 1, 1946, and

We came home to Berlin—a city that was destroyed beyond recognition.

our exit permit to leave the Soviet zone of occupation had expired at midnight, five hours earlier!

We were cold, wet, hungry, weary from our ordeal, and nearly beyond caring, although ready to put up a fight, if necessary. The fifteen or twenty minutes it took for the Soviet border guard to check our papers thoroughly seemed like an eternity—all the while we were praying that we would not be turned back. This was the very last chance to get out of the Soviet zone with permission.

Then a miracle happened. We were surprised that without any debate whatsoever we were cleared into the American occupied sector of Berlin! Suddenly we no longer felt cold or hungry—we felt only the relief of breathing freedom. Three weary warriors had returned home!

Berlin and Freedom

Was this Berlin? The city looked different—destroyed beyond recognition. In the dim light of pre–dawn and the few remaining street lamps it looked eerie, like excavated ruins of antiquity. Exhausted, but happy, we reached Grandma Stanneck's apartment just before six o'clock. Grandma had some hot tea and bread for us. White bread—a taste of America! It was the whitest bread we had ever seen, and it tasted like cake. This American style bread was not very filling, but it didn't get stuck in our throats either, like the bread made from rye that was not threshed, which we had received in the Russian zone. We had to consciously remind ourselves now that we were in American occupied territory. The thought was incredibly reassuring!

The best part of arriving was to be home with Papa. He had just gotten up and would leave for work soon, but said he would try to get home early that day, and he did.

Daylight came slowly and the city awoke. There wasn't much traffic, but, not having seen any cars and buses for more than two years, we watched each one with interest and curiosity. It was so much fun watching from the window of the second–floor apartment that Peter

These signs became a familiar sight everywhere in Berlin

and I did not want to go to bed. We were afraid of missing out on something. City life seemed absolutely wonderful!

Exploring Our New Surroundings

The next few days were packed with new impressions. Grandma lived in an apartment building at the corner of a secondary street and a lesser cross street, about four blocks from one of Berlin's main arteries. Mom, Peter and I took a walk to explore what was left of Grandma's neighborhood. All of the stores were closed. They had nothing to sell.

Grocery stores were open for two days out of ten after supplies for our rations arrived for distribution. Our monthly ration cards were divided into three decades, or ten–day periods. Unlike in the Soviet occupation zone, here we actually received what was printed on our cards.

Peter and I were most interested in vehicle traffic. After years of living in a village where everything was moved by ox cart, this was a unique experience for us. All traffic, of course, was related to the American occupation. There were big, shiny limousines—Cadillacs, and other big American passenger cars. We had never before seen such large

Trümmerfrauen (rubble women) performed the backbreaking work of clearing the city of rubble.

cars. Then there were U.S. Army trucks of different sizes, and even an occasional tank clattered down the street.

There were army buses which transported the families of the military personnel around the city, and bright yellow buses with the words "School Bus" on the front, which transported children. We were totally unfamiliar with school buses and were fascinated by them, wondering why those children could not walk, or ride the streetcar or subway. We envied them for being able to ride on a bus. What a treat, as far as we were concerned. It never occurred to us that the Allies were effectively living in enemy territory and provided their own transportation. To us they were the liberators. We did not think of them as enemies.

The most wonderful vehicle we encountered often, and which was by far my favorite, was the Jeep. It said "Military Police" on it, and if the weather was nice, the top was open and the occupants would wave to us. I thought the Jeep was the greatest vehicle in the world. There was no luxury car I admired as much as the Jeep, and more so once I learned that a Jeep can be driven over any terrain, even when there are no roads. I practically fantasized about this miracle of a vehicle. Many years later during my four–wheeling expeditions in our desert southwest, I often thought of my love affair with the Jeep, and I have not gotten over it. One day before I die, I still hope to own a Jeep.

"Trümmerfrauen"
Rubble Women

On sidewalks, and often blocking parts of the streets, were mountains of rubble which needed to be cleared away. The rubble as well as the countless ruins were grim reminders of the city's recent past. However, there was activity everywhere. The major job available for women was a newly created one: *Trümmerfrau* (rubble woman). Women by the thousands were hired for the job of clearing rubble, which consisted of picking up every brick and checking it for reusability. Each whole and partial brick that was still intact enough and could be cleaned of old mortar so that it could be reused, was carefully worked over and stacked. The other, physically more demanding job of the rubble women was to load the leftover rubble into lorries and push those to a collection point, where a *Trümmerbahnlokomotive* (rubble train engine) would pick them up.

An illegal business grew alongside the clearing activity. It was the salvage of usable metals—brass door handles, steel girders, copper pipes, etc—which were stolen out of the ruins and rubble piles and brought handsome prices from scrap dealers.

Sad News

On the day after we arrived in Berlin, I thought I would surprise Tante Hilda, Mom's oldest sister, by dropping her a postcard and telling her that we were back in Berlin. She had planned to visit us in Straupitz when the war was still in progress, but circumstances did not permit it. Having always been close to Tante Hilda, I was quite anxious to see her and anticipated her visit as a result of my postcard. She did indeed arrive the very next day, but with bad news. We had returned just in time for Grandpa Hinniger's funeral. Mom's father had died of starvation. He had been living with his oldest son, Mom's brother Hans and his family, in the Russian occupied sector of Berlin.

As long as we were living in Straupitz, we had not been in contact with every part of the aftermath of this horrible war. In the country there was always a chance to "come by" some carrots or potatoes, beg a sandwich, or appropriate something edible, somewhere. The big city was a different story. It was a tragedy. Being surrounded by Russian occupied territory, it was like living on an island—an island of stone and ruins. The outskirts of Berlin were not accessible to us without red tape and the risk of getting stuck in communist domain. There was no way to supplement our meager rations until the black market came into being, although that was a solution for only very few since one needed either a lot of cash or "hard currency items" to trade with.

At this time, everyone was dragging from lack of energy. Some people's legs looked grotesquely fat. It was water. Some people were "fat" all over. Those had edema and were near death. That is what had happened to Grandfather Hinniger.

School in Berlin

Having recently skipped the sixth grade and been promoted to seventh in Straupitz, I continued in seventh grade in Berlin. The teacher told Mom that if I could handle the curriculum, I could stay in seventh grade. Here in Berlin the curriculum was more advanced and I needed to do some catching up, but it did not take me long to get back to the top part of the class.

As far as my classmates, there was a difference in atmosphere from what I had known in the village of Straupitz. It was a heavy atmosphere, laden with something I cannot easily describe. We twelve–year–olds were not as carefree as children that age ought to be. We all had experiences from which we needed to recover, some more horrible and indescribable than others.

We were quiet, disciplined, and turned inward. We were pleasant students, thankful to have a school building, teachers, and lessons. We were thankful that we had clothes to wear, and even shoes, and that we had paper and pencil, a soup bowl and a spoon for the half liter of hot soup we received every day at school. We had been through some gruesome experiences in our short lives and had learned to be thankful for everything.

We had freedom—a freedom which the generations after us no longer have—a freedom to go wherever our abilities would lead us. There were no set expectations, no peer pressure, and no pressures from parents with expectations for us which would feed their own egos.

We saw how our parents struggled just to get us through the misery and hard times until we could be on our own. We did not have to be asked about our homework, or what we did in school. Of course, we used the golden opportunity to learn what we could. Quietly, without complaints. With many of us having lost most or all worldly possessions, we had come to know that knowledge is a tangible asset which cannot be taken away from us. We had also learned to do what we were asked to do. We were serious and mindful children. Nobody thought that youth was a particularly happy time, or expected that a child always had to be cheerful.

We were a mixture of backgrounds and ages. Some children had not been to school for a year or two because of disruption of the system, forced relocation, or months of trekking to no particular destination. We were anywhere from eleven to fourteen years old—we were native Berliners, refugees, orphans, children of divorced or widowed parents, country children and bombed–out city children. We had many different pasts and the firm resolution to forget the horrors of those pasts. There was an unspoken agreement never to talk about it and never to ask. We were polite, considerate, and helpful to each other without getting to know one another. Our world had been so shaken and proved to be so brittle that we wanted no trouble and no problems. We criticized nothing and asked no questions for fear of inviting another catastrophe.

The classmates which we did get to know had not been selected by us, but rather were determined by specific circumstances: geographic proximity, book availability, timing. If there was one book for five or six students, the teacher organized it: who can study with whom until, say, 4 o'clock, and who was responsible for taking the book to the next study team. After censure, no books existed for some subjects, or perhaps only the teacher had one copy of a new edition. In that case it was read to us and we took notes.

The highlight of every school day was the half liter of soup we received. For most, this was their only hot meal.

9

1947
Readjustment, Shortages, and Hunger
Age Twelve

Surviving the Coldest Winter

The winter of 1946 and 1947 will remain in our memory forever. Not only was it the coldest winter so far this century, but it was so much worse because of circumstances. Most people's apartments had a number of broken windows. Glass was not available. We had repaired our windows with cardboard, wood, or rags to keep the wind, rain and some of the cold out. With none of the materials available we had to make do with whatever we had among our belongings. Wood panels could be taken out of certain pieces of furniture, such as a back wall out of a china cabinet or a wardrobe. While none of the substitutes insulated as well as glass, we were grateful for the protection we did have.

During that winter the temperatures went down to minus twenty degrees Fahrenheit, and most people did not have enough warm clothes to wear. Whatever coal had been rationed to us was needed for cooking. Our kitchen was almost warm because of what little cooking we could do, and the unusual fact that most of the glass had remained in the kitchen window. By wearing our winter coats we could be reasonably comfortable in the kitchen. In the bedroom it was nearly as cold as it was outside. Our coats were taken off only when we went to bed at night. We were fortunate in that we had not lost our featherbeds during the war. Not all people were so lucky to still own this lifesaver.

Featherbeds were priceless possessions which, especially during Germany's countless decades of war and oppression, were items that had been handed down from generation to generation.

Schools were open, but not for classes. There was not enough coal for central heating systems. It was a definite plus to live in the old apartment building in which Grandma lived. These apartments still had the old style ceramic tiled stoves which reached nearly up to the ceiling and were fired with coal. Each room had its own source of heat, and as far back as I can remember only one room in each apartment would be heated because of limited coal supplies. Usually it was the kitchen because of cooking. Once coal became rationed, tenants of the newer buildings which had central heating systems, either from within the building or from a distant power station, had to find a way to heat a room independently, such as an iron stove.

I was one of the very few children who owned a warm winter coat. It had been a little fur coat when I was six years old. My great–grand-mother, then in her mid–nineties, had given Mom her foal jacket and told her to make a coat for me out of it. Mom did this at the time, but as I grew and the coat got too small, she combined the original fur part of the coat with plush velour. Over the years she kept enlarging it with miscellaneous real or fake scraps of fur. This winter saw the coat's third major remodeling, when some other artificial fur–type material was added. Her creations were unique and attracted attention, which I did not like. However, I had the warmest coat in school and even a matching hat, as well as a muff to keep my hands warm. The muff was the envy of all, adults and children alike. Women stopped me on the street to admire it.

Winter Activities

We did go to school every day, not for classes, but to receive our vital half liter of soup. We would sit at our desks dressed in coats, hats, and mittens and eat our soup before it got cold. Then we children went home to our bleak existence and spent a lot of time in bed to keep warm. Our featherbeds were our lifesaving possessions.

I enjoyed walking and being outdoors a lot. After years of living in a village where ox carts were the only traffic, the very limited traffic activity of the city was exciting to me. Germans did not own cars at that time except for a few businesses who ran trucks of various sizes. Otherwise all vehicle traffic was military. Most of the supplies for the city came in by rail and ship. Berlin has two major rivers and a network of canals.

Within the city the Berliners traveled by streetcar, electric elevated and underground trains. For lack of gasoline, the bus lines were not yet operating, except for some electric buses wherever it had been possible to repair the overhead electric lines.

The streetcars were a sorry sight. Dented and pockmarked by shrapnel, they looked as though they were survivors of combat, which they were. With most of their windows blown out and glass unavailable, they had been repaired with cardboard and plywood. Inside they were dark, stuffy, and always overcrowded.

Money was practically worthless. The black market did not yet exist, and our meager rations did not use up our very small earnings. I had a lot of fun exploring the city by walking and by riding the streetcars back and forth. However, my lack of knowledge about traffic nearly landed me under a car one day. I was the first to jump off the streetcar after it had just barely stopped, and darted across the street without looking. A big American car brushed my coat as it zipped past me. My legs turned to rubber from the shock, and I had to sit down on the steps outside the closed department store which was right there at the corner. I was shaking for quite a while and could not get up to walk. People who had seen the incident gathered around. Some were sympathetic and others lectured me like a little child about "looking before crossing the street." I was awfully embarrassed, but too shy to tell them that I had just arrived from spending more than three years in the country, and that I was not used to looking out for traffic. I learned my lesson exceedingly fast. This had been too close a call. I realized once again that I was not yet meant to die.

Since people earned money and there was nothing to spend it on, one type of the little enterprises which sprung up here and there were booths of the kind one sees at amusement parks. They sold chances and people could win prizes. There were also skill games such as ring toss, and at another booth one could try to throw balls into containers, which usually bounced back out. The prizes were worthless junk, but so was the money. I enjoyed those games for a short period of time, then got bored with them.

The rest of the long, dreadful winter passed with treatment for an itchy skin rash which most people broke out with. I remember going to a clinic twice a week for three or four weeks, where we had to strip and a nurse would smear some kind of white salve all over our bodies. It was no fun, but preferable to continuously itching and scratching.

Sometimes Papa let me help him with his tobacco goods job. There was not much tobacco to be sold, though adult ration cards included a small tobacco ration. The rest of the time Papa's firm sold tobacco related items such as lighters, flints, lighter fluid, cigarette papers, and little gadgets in which to roll cigarettes for people who wanted to roll their own. This was usually done by mixing the meager tobacco supply with tea leaves or other dried weeds to "stretch" the tobacco. Papa also distributed other, unrelated goods for his company as those became available, one of which was saccharin. He appreciated having my help with assembling the orders for delivery to his retail customers. I also helped him insert the flints into the lighters before he filled them with lighter fluid. It made me truly happy to be able to help Papa. This turned out to be one of the very few times in my life when I had the opportunity to do so, and to spend time with him.

During one of those special times together, I once again asked Papa to tell me about his POW time in Russia. As he did before when I had asked, his face turned gravely sad and, obviously holding back tears, he just shook his head.

Grandma's Mysterious Abilities

At some point during the winter I had such a painful sore throat that it was getting nearly impossible for me to swallow. Grandma had a supply of salt brine from some herring of long ago, and she insisted I swallow three spoonfuls, which I reluctantly did. She assured me that my throat would get better, and it did almost immediately. The salt must have burned the infection right out of my throat! In the years to come I gained a lot of respect for those good old German home remedies, as horrible and unappetizing as some of them seem.

Grandma was an extremely superstitious person and we used to tease her about it. There were many things which, according to her, were bad luck. Hanging up laundry to dry during the week between Christmas and New Year's meant that someone was going to die. Other actions brought good luck. On New Year's Eve it was the tradition to "pour lead." The lead would form many different shapes and Grandma interpreted the fragments and told us what it meant for our future. For those not familiar with this tradition, the lead is heated on a stove until it is melted. It then gets poured into cold water, and as it solidifies it forms different shapes and fragments. At that particular time we wanted to believe in the lead fragments as we were hoping for a better life to start soon.

Sometimes women came to have their fortunes told by Grandma. They would mix a deck of cards and Grandma put the cards on the table in some particular pattern and then tell people things. I liked to listen to what Grandma was saying. Since we were all living in the kitchen, there was always the opportunity to do so. I found it amusing because often I heard similar fortunes, only in a different order. The women would be paying Grandma with small amounts of food or with something tangible, such as a household item.

Grandma's abilities, especially when it came to healing, were somewhat mysterious to us. All throughout the winter I had a boil on the shin of my left leg. It had been oozing for months and made no attempt to heal. Mom was worried about it, but one went to see a doctor only with major problems. Such a doctor's visit would have to be paid for with goods, preferably food, which we did not have to spare. One night Grandma decided to heal my leg. Mom did not like the idea of Grandma doing her "witchcraft," as she was sure that the devil was being promised my soul. However, Grandma persuaded Mom to let her try it. The conditions were right that night, she said. There was a full moon. I had to sit in the dark room by the open window with the moon shining in. Grandma positioned me so that the moon shone on my festering boil. Then she said some abracadabra, whispering all kinds of unintelligible stuff, while her hand went over and over the sore part of my leg. I was petrified. Having heard Mom voice some of her fears about the devil, I was sure he was going to appear at any moment and get me. After perhaps ten minutes it was over with. I vaguely remember some instructions about do's and don'ts.

The amazing thing was that my leg started to heal immediately and the wound never opened again. A deep hole down to my shinbone remained. I could stick my finger into it, and it took many years before the scar became less deep.

Spring 1947

Eventually the seemingly endless winter came to an end and spring arrived. It was as if awakening from hibernation. I don't remember Easter and Whitsunday, or even Christmas—we might as well have been hibernating. Some sunshine, and days which were getting longer brought life back into us. Energy. We were thawing out. It was as if we had been paralyzed and could now begin to slightly move again. Whatever trees had survived the war, began to leaf out. With that, hope returned. Optimism, and even some enthusiasm for life. A new beginning.

The eternal gray sky of the typical North German winter was gloomy enough. The ruins of the destroyed city compounded the bleakness. Unfortunately, our beloved *Grunewald* emerged from the winter with additional heavy damage. Bombs from the war had done a great deal of devastation, but now people desperate for firewood had further crippled the forest. Anything that was burnable had been used to supplement the inadequate coal rations. There was no wooden seat left on a single park bench in the city.

It was not until we pulled out of this winter that we realized we had survived it.

Flower pots—a sign of spring. The window shows typical emergency repair—cardboard and small panes for which the glass was gleaned from framed pictures or cut from broken panes.

After a ruined building had been cleared of rubble, the land was used to grow potatoes and vegetables.

Life Goes On

The resourceful Berliners did not give up their fight for survival. We needed more food and could even grow some ourselves if we had land. That would be the answer. We needed land—a little patch of soil on which to grow some vegetables. Every empty cage in the zoo was already utilized for growing potatoes, carrots and cabbage. All empty lots and patches of soil within ruins were used to grow food. Lucky were the ones who had access to those places. Others planted vegetables in the flower boxes on window sills and balconies. Those who did not have flower boxes and could come by some kind of building material, built some. To "come by materials" did not mean purchasing them for money. Money could not buy anything. Instead, something had to be given in exchange for the item wanted.

The schools reopened, but on a reduced schedule. We could not sit in an unheated building for too many hours at a time. Early May is still cold in northern Germany.

Having been mostly shut in during the cold winter, we were happy to get out of the apartment and move around. We played hopscotch on the sidewalk, as well as other children's games. There was only a tiny yard between the apartment building in which we lived, and the next one. This yard was paved and just big enough for the apartments' trash cans and to hang up laundry to dry during the time of good weather. Throughout the winter the laundry was hung up in the attic of the building, where it always froze. Then we had to find space for it somewhere in the heated kitchen to thaw it out and let it dry.

Whenever the laundry was hanging outside, it was usually my job to sit there and watch it until it was dry. People could easily come off the street and steal our only bed sheets and the few clothes we owned. This type of thing happened all of the time if one was not watching. Peter and I took turns, but he was less reliable because he would go off and play if one of his friends stopped by. I did not mind sitting there by the trash cans and using one of them as a table to do my homework. I loved being outdoors. Even sitting next to a trash can was preferable to sitting indoors.

Food and Survival

My main responsibility was to stand endlessly in line for food rations. I was the logical one to be given this ongoing job since Grandma was elderly and weak, Mom was occupied with the household, and Peter was too young to be trusted with the family's irreplaceable ration coupons. Unfortunately I had troubles with fainting spells while standing in line for hours because of the lack of enough nourishment—and I was always hungry. This was extremely embarrassing to me, though people were kind and understanding, and sometimes they let me go to the head of the line, especially if they knew me. At times Mom or Grandma would come and relieve me if I had been gone for too many hours.

In a German book which someone lent me recently, I found a list of the rations we received in Berlin during the years before the Blockade. This is helpful since I do not remember the exact quantities. I just know that it was barely adequate and that we were always hungry. While it may not seem so bad to the reader, it has to be remembered that we had been living on those amounts, or on less, for quite a few years by then. Being undernourished was a normal condition at the time, especially for children.

The following quantities are for the ration card category IV—Children—ages 9 to 14, which included both Peter and me at the time.

Daily Rations:
>   Bread – 10.5 oz.
>   Meat   –   ½ oz.
>   Potatoes – 14 oz.
>   Noodles, or flour, or beans, or oats, or other starches – 1 oz.
>   Fat (butter or margarine) – ½ oz.
>   Sugar – ½ oz.

Monthly Rations:
>   Salt – 14 oz.
>   Tea – ½ oz.
>   Coffee (not from coffee beans but made from roasted grains, called *Ersatz* (substitute) – 3½ oz.

Peter still received some milk rations, whereas I did not. Cheese was seldom available, and if there was any, it would be exchanged for coupons of butter. Now I have osteoporosis, as do many of my contemporaries.

Adults received slightly more bread, starches, and meat, but less fat, and the same amount of potatoes for all categories. Adult rations depended on the type of work people were doing.

The most effective way of taking care of immediate needs, other than food, was through exchange. Everywhere throughout the city, fences, plain house walls, even trees and lampposts, became bulletin boards for exchange notices, such as: "Have: Woolen Sweater—Want: Pair of Shoes, size 38." Everything imaginable was being exchanged by one person for something another person might have and not be able to use.

Food was a separate problem. Nobody in the city was in a position to do any exchanging with foods. Our calories were counted out and barely enough for survival. However, for as long as Berlin's outlying farm areas—though in Russian occupied territory—were still somewhat accessible to West Berliners, there was trading done with the farmers. The farmers took advantage of this and their trading bordered on highway robbery. The hungry and desperate Berliners would take the last of their precious possessions that had survived the bombings—china, crystal, oriental rugs, jewelry—even their wedding rings as a last resort—and trade them for food. Piece by piece their remaining

A typical "bulletin board" with exchange notices—as described in the text.

valuables were taken by the farmers who at some point were saturated and began to specify what they wanted. The joke was going around that their cows were wearing diamond earrings and the stables were lined with oriental rugs.

Eventually as some measure of trust was established, the Allied occupation generated quite a few jobs and contributed to the survival of many families in a curious way. German men and women who were lucky enough to secure jobs at a military base had access to the Americans' garbage cans. The wasting of food that is done by Americans became legendary, and many German families survived by scraping cans and food wrappers which they took out of the garbage, as well as by collecting food leftovers that had been thrown away.

Later on when American households were allowed to hire German help, those employees often received gifts of food and other desirable goods such as used clothing or household items, from the families for whom they worked.

These examples may seem abstract today to those who have never been hungry for more than a few hours. We were hungry continuously for years!

CARE Packages

One day in the spring of 1947, Grandma received a notice in the mail telling her to go to a certain place on a specific date and pick up a CARE package from America. We did not even know what a CARE package was, but upon mentioning it to friends, we quickly found out. We also had several offers from friends wanting to be present when we had the package in our possession and opened it, or to come along and help us pick it up. This was not because people expected to get a share of it. Everyone accepted that sharing food during that particular time was not customary, and certainly not expected. These offers were out of curiosity—for having the chance to see that food exists, somewhere—and what that food from another country might look like.

I accompanied Papa to a warehouse somewhere in Berlin and we picked up this huge, heavy (about twenty–five pounds) package. Knowing that it contained precious food, we guarded it with our lives on the train and streetcar trip home.

The CARE package had been sent to Grandma Stanneck who was one of the oldest of ten children, by the youngest, her sister Martha, who lived in the United States. Aunt Martha had emigrated to America as a young girl in 1929 and eventually settled in New Jersey. While Grandma and her sister had not been able to keep in contact with each other during the war years, Aunt Martha now remembered her siblings and the privations they would be suffering.

After getting the package home, all five of us gathered around it while Papa set out to open it. This turned out to be quite a job despite the many tools he owned. The first CARE packages then were military rations for soldiers who were encircled by the enemy, and the boxes were made to withstand being dropped from aircraft. First there were

I accompanied Papa to a CARE distribution center like this one to pick up Aunt Martha's gift of "hope." She could not have imagined what it meant to us.

metal bands to break. The tightly sealed and waxed heavy cardboard box proved to be quite an obstacle. When we thought we had "made it," we found that the large box contained four smaller ones which were equally as tough and as difficult to pry open. It seemed like hours later when finally all the goodies surfaced. There were foods such as raisins, which the adults had forgotten even existed. Peter and I did not know what they were. Then there were other dried fruits, small cans of meats, cheeses, crackers and breads, as well as dessert bars, and other strange foods which we did not know at all. One of those was peanut butter, another was chewing gum. All cans and packages were individual servings and each of the four boxes contained two or three full meals.

Some of our friends stopped by just to take a look at the strange foods which had come from so far away—and in our minds and hearts we worshiped the mysterious angel in a faraway land who had been so kind to send us this priceless gift. While we desperately needed every bit of food we could get to help us along—and even for five very hungry people this was an important drop in the bucket—this thoughtful gift was so much more than food. It was a bright light of hope in a nearly hopeless existence. Somebody was out there in this woeful world of ours who personally cared about our survival.

We later received another CARE package as well as a personal package from Aunt Martha. She sent us clothes and shoes which she had collected from people with whom she worked. Some of the dresses fit either Mom or me after minor alterations—we were extremely thin then. Others provided materials for Mom to make clothes, either for us or for trading to get food and various items that we needed. The shoes Aunt Martha sent were much too small for either of us, but the solution to that was the Shoe Exchange.

Shoes and Shoe Repair

There was an extremely effective self–help business starting at that time, called the Shoe Exchange. One of Berlin's chain of shoe stores had the idea to open up and take in shoes for exchange. For a modest fee one could exchange shoes for other sizes, as well as exchange a pair of women's shoes for a pair of men's shoes. Nobody cared about style or color, all we needed was protection and warmth for our feet.

The Shoe Exchange had a large selection of used shoes. We were able to trade the small, high heeled shoes which Aunt Martha had sent for some more practical ones that fit us. Peter needed a pair of shoes most urgently, which we were able to get for him.

Shoes were always a problem, especially for children whose feet grew. By the time Peter received my outgrown shoes which initially had been Mom's, they were quite well worn. Peter would finish them off.

One day in the summer there was a notice on the door of one of the big shoe stores on the main street. It said that they would receive materials to resole fifteen pairs of shoes. The store would be open on a certain date at 10 a.m. and the first fifteen customers could each drop off one pair of shoes. Papa's shoes were in dire need of repair. Grandma, among others, got in line early in the afternoon of the day before. I relieved her after school and she returned after supper, so as not to lose our space among the first fifteen customers. We were number eleven. During the night, Mom and Grandma took turns sitting in line. Grandma had one of those little folding chairs. Not everyone was so lucky.

I well remember the delight I felt when I accompanied Mom to pick up Papa's shoes two weeks later, and how appreciative he was of the trouble we had gone through to get new soles for his shoes.

Occasionally now some other goods became available in a unique way. There were all kinds of little enterprises sprouting up, and at some point there came a solution for worn–out shoe soles. Worn and no longer usable truck and auto tires had been cut into shoe soles of different sizes and were offered for sale. What a salvation! What a brilliant idea! Papa had the tools and the knowledge to repair shoes. The tire soles were permanently curved, thick pieces of rubber and extremely hard to work with. Papa had to struggle, and soon he was repairing shoes not only for us, but for our relatives, friends, and neighbors as well.

The Black Market

I don't know when the black market came into existence, or where the food available on the black market was coming from. I read that food and other desirable items could be obtained at the black market in exchange for cigarettes, coffee, and chocolate and even money, although at very high prices. Suddenly our money was no longer worthless, and this triggered inflation. The black market was illegal, but if one knew where to go and had enough money, one could get a pound of bacon for three hundred marks, a pound of butter for five hundred marks, and a loaf of bread for sixty marks. Those were horrendous prices when compared with the earnings at the time. Our currency then was still the old *Reichsmark*.

Papa did not earn enough money in a month to buy a pound of butter at the black market. Once he saved up for a long time to buy bacon for three hundred marks. He sent me to pick it up at somebody's house. I understood that this was a risky business and one should not be caught at it. While I was not told about the details, from the grown–ups' puzzling comments I sensed that it was something forbidden, or illegal. Papa did not feel good about it. I heard him say to Mom afterwards that we would not do this again. I was glad because I did not like being sent.

There was also criminal activity connected with the black market. Horrible stories were told about dog and horse meat being sold. The most terrifying for me, being still a child, was that children were slaughtered and sold for meat. This was said to be true and I remember being told that during one particular police investigation parents were able to identify a body part of their missing daughter by a distinctive birthmark.

Additional Help

A number of times when Mom was desperate, she sent me to visit her sister Lotte who owned a butcher shop. Onkel Martin had returned after being an American prisoner of war, and now they had reopened their butcher shop for distribution of rations. In the food business it was always possible to weigh a little short. Every grocer did this to gain some extra food for his own family. On several occasions I was sent to Tante Lotte, and she gave me some sausage to take home to the family. Mom did not like to beg from her sister, but there were a couple of times when our very survival depended on it.

Summer 1947

Sometime during the summer Mom took on a temporary job. Sitting in a one–room plus kitchen apartment with her mother–in–law who did not really want Mom in her son's life, had been going on her nerves. Mom looked for a job and found one that she thought would be enjoyable. It turned out to be just what she wanted.

A little amusement park had started up on a large lot cleared of rubble, at the corner of the main avenue and a side street, not far from where we lived. It consisted of an antiquated, squeaky merry–go–round, some swings shaped like boats which could go so high that they turned over at the top, and a booth with funny mirrors. There was also the usual ring–toss stand where one could win, but never did, a primitive homemade teddy bear—or was it a dog? Had they let anyone win the mystery animal they would have lost their one and only grand prize, for I am sure that it was the only one in existence.

Chances were being sold at another stand. That's where Mom worked, and she was good at it! She had this charming salesperson personality, and in her humorous way she could talk people into buying almost anything. I forgot what the winner of the chance was promised. It could not have been much. However, Mom sure had fun advertising it. Peter and I enjoyed going there just to watch her "in action."

The Hungry Berliners' Arduous Trips to Werder

Werder is a peninsula surrounded by lakes which the Havel River created. It is located southwest of Potsdam outside the southwestern edge of the city of Berlin, in Russian occupied territory. Werder has always been known for its fruit orchards. In my earlier childhood I thought of it as being a magical place. Some of my playmates whose parents could afford it would go to Werder on Sunday excursions in the springtime, to see the fruit trees in bloom. During normal times, Berlin's surrounding farm country supplied the city with produce. Werder has always been especially well known because of the fruit orchards. There were cherries, plums, apples, pears, and even some peaches.

At this time of privation, Werder and the surrounding fruit farm area came back into the memory of the hungry Berliners. Whenever some of the fruits and vegetables were ripe for harvest, a mass migration started from Berlin to the outlying farm areas, especially to Werder. The difference between the orchard owners in Werder and dealing with the regular farmers for all other food items, was that permission could be received from the orchard owners to pick the ripe fruit and pay for it with money, rather than having to trade for it with precious possessions.

The first time I went to Werder with Grandma, I saw, and was part of, the following scenario and unforgettable, shocking experience:

The station southwest of Berlin from which the train to Werder started was in the Russian occupation zone. It was already packed with people when we arrived by *S–Bahn* at seven o'clock in the morning, approximately three hours ahead of the *estimated* departure time. People were standing and sitting on both platforms which ran alongside the track on which the Werder train was to come in. I wondered why about half of the people were on the wrong side for boarding, but found out when the train moved into the station that it was necessary to "assault" it from both sides. Grandma and I found a place as close to the tracks as we could, and after standing for awhile we sat down and waited. In typical Soviet administration fashion, nobody knew when the train was scheduled to come in or depart.

The cars of the German trains in those days were not sleek like they are now, but rather primitive in comparison, and people could not pass from one car to another on the inside. There were running boards along the outside of each car, and the cars were connected to each other with chains and connectors where the two bumpers of one car met the ones of the next.

The Train Trip

As the two station platforms filled with thousands of people, I started wondering how long the train would have to be for everyone to get on. It suddenly occurred to me that getting on at all would be the big challenge. No train could be long enough to carry away all these people. I began to worry.

Finally the train rolled, ever so slowly, into the station. Before it stopped completely, people who stood in the front lines jumped on and everyone from the rear started pushing. Grandma and I frantically tried to avoid being pushed under the wheels. The train stopped, and like a flow of lava the masses of people started coating the train on all sides. Doors were not enough. Being summer, all windows were open and people assaulted the train from both sides by climbing into windows and onto the roofs of the cars, while others had secured themselves a

The train's cars were packed like sardine cans, people clung to the outside and even sat on the locomotive. Many did not get on at all, as the picture shows.

space outside on a running board. People sat on the bumpers between the cars and even on parts of the locomotive. Eventually the train was packed tighter than sardine cans and completely coated with humans clinging to it.

My own reaction just before the train stopped had been to not try for a door. Unless one happened to be immediately in front of me, there would be no chance of getting to one. If a window happened to be in front of me, I would climb into it. That was exactly what Grandma decided to do, except that the window which stopped in front of us was a small one from the restroom. I was amazed at Grandma. Agile like a cat, she climbed up and squeezed through the tiny window, then pulled me in while people behind me pushed from the outside. Needless to say, the restroom was already filled with people by then, but we still crowded in. It was hot and we were so tightly packed that we could hardly breathe. I was quite worried about Grandma because she was old, and I kept hoping she would not faint, or even die. I would not know what to do then.

It was only about twelve or fifteen miles to Werder. The train being heavily loaded, and that's an understatement, proceeded at snail's pace without stopping until we got there, about an hour later. The crowds got off the train and dispersed in different directions. Some went to the orchards, others to barter with the farmers for assorted foods or to gather whatever vegetables were available. There were trains returning to Berlin at different times during the day, and though crowded, it would be nothing in comparison to the first train that had left Berlin in the morning.

This was July, cherry season. After picking the amount of cherries we were allowed to pick, Grandma and I walked back to the Werder station in mid afternoon, carrying our precious allotment. Upon entering the station platform, everyone had to go through a control since we were in the Soviet occupation zone of Germany. East German border guards checked us out. We had heard rumors that the guards were often taking away whatever food items people had been able to bargain for. It was said that it depended pretty much on the whim of the individual guard whether he took away everything, part of it, or nothing.

We came up to one of the guards and were asked a few questions. Bins filled with confiscated fruit were lined up near the wall behind him. He then proceeded to empty out half of the cherries from each of our bags. I did not want to believe this after what we had gone through to get on the train in the morning. When we were past the guards and standing on the station platform, I was shaking and crying. Others told us that they had not been so lucky. Some had lost everything and were going home empty–handed. Soviet harassment had begun.

Exhausted, but happy to bring something home for the family, we arrived with our precious harvest and had the luxury of eating delicious cherries for a few days. Cherries have always been, and still are, my favorite fruit.

More Trips to Werder

After another trip with Grandma where she and I stood on a running board on the *outside* of the train during the trip to Werder, Mom would not let me go again. She was angry with Grandma for permitting this. Instead, Mom went by herself. Peter and I remember one horrible night when she did not return. We were sick with worry. Our worst fear was: What had the Russians done to her? Mom returned in the early evening of the next day. It turned out that the guards had taken everything away from her and, determined to come home with some food for the family, she and some other women decided to stay overnight and try again the next day. Nobody had telephones in those days and we were devastated just thinking about all the things that might have happened. Mom and the other women had spent the night outdoors in a ditch by the street, freezing, then continued their search for food the next day. I don't remember what she brought home, and it did not matter. Peter and I thought we had lost our Mom, and all that mattered to us was to have her back. I did not want to let her go again after that, and she was not eager to go back. She said it was the longest night of her life. They had no food or water, and nearly froze to death. North German summer nights are usually quite chilly. The memory of this last trip must have been awful for her because she did not go again, until winter came.

Berlin

Slowly the city was digging out of the rubble in an effort to recover. There was more traffic now. Some German businesses had gotten back on their feet, mostly in the areas of service and reconstruction. I still found it entertaining to walk a lot, or to ride the streetcars in order to see what was going on elsewhere. I was undeniably fascinated by living in a big city and realized that I must have missed it more than I thought.

Not too far from where we lived was a building which formerly housed one of the best known concert halls in Berlin, the *Titania Palast*. It had been turned into a club house for American military personnel. At the height of about the fourth floor there was a balcony which ran the length of the building facing the main avenue. This particular balcony was just a narrow, decorative one with a wrought iron rail. There we could see the American soldiers sitting on chairs with their feet up and sticking through the balcony rails. We had never seen people sit with their feet up on anything. In Germany, manners dictate that feet belong on the floor, and not only we kids but also the adults found this custom of "feet up" strange and quite hilarious. When riding the streetcar past that building, there was never a time at which people did not point and comment about the strange custom. In fact, it turned into an attraction—a highlight of the streetcar trip and a reason to laugh during our difficult times.

How did we feel about the American occupation? Good! America was to us the symbol of freedom, and the American occupation represented this. Everything American was special and treasured—their music, fashion, language, chewing gum, and wearing shirts out of the trousers instead of tucked in. The Americans were our protectors and our friends.

My Friend Edith

Sometime during the early part of the summer I met Edith through a classmate of mine. She was almost two years older than I, but we became friends and did a lot of things together during the next few years. Initially, she introduced me to the Salvation Army where she attended Sunday services. Edith was a Catholic, which was unusual since fewer than two percent of the North German population are Catholics. Edith had a brother and a sister who were quite a bit older than she, and were no longer living at home. Her mother was nearly bedridden with arthritis and her father had not returned from the war, so Edith was growing up somewhat unsupervised.

We both became extremely active in the Salvation Army, learning how to play the guitar and singing at street corners on Sunday afternoons with the Salvation Army brothers and sisters—mostly old ladies, actually. Mom was not happy about my dedication to this organization for fear that they might hook me. Tante Ella, a cousin of my father's, never married and spent her life in the service of the Salvation Army. Singing at street corners and in effect begging for money was not what Mom had in mind for my future. However, for the time being she let it go since we had a warm place to go to in their meeting hall, and a little dose of religion was not likely to get us into trouble.

The Salvation Army's doctrine did not permit its members to go to movies or dances. Women must wear only plain clothes and not curl their hair or wear jewelry. Any of those worldly enjoyments were considered unsuitable for a religious life. Mom wanted me to dance and have fun. The war had already deprived me of a normal childhood, and she did not want me to waste my youth by singing at street corners and being limited in my selection of a future husband. The Salvation Army also had strict rules in that regard. Three years later when I had become too serious and was ready to formally join the ranks, Mom did not give her permission and outright forbade my going to the Salvation Army services. This caused my first teenage rebellion against Mom's authority.

On the positive side, the Salvation Army songs use the melodies of folk songs and are more cheerful than church hymns. My guitar and the Salvation Army songs kept Mom, Peter, and me happy during many evenings when we were sitting in our dark room, being hungry and cold.

Swimming

Edith and I were good pals and we spent our time together whenever we were not in school. During the summer we went swimming a lot, ei-

I was nearly 14 when this picture was taken.

ther at one of the lakes or at the swim stadium. Edith was a good swimmer and diver. She had been taught by her older sister. I could not swim at all, but had always loved water and wished that I could swim. I would watch Edith dive off the five–meter diving board looking very elegant and professional, and I wished so much that at least I knew how to swim.

One day we were on our way to the swim stadium again and I told Edith that I was going to learn how to swim that afternoon. "How will you do that?" she asked. "Well, I'm going to dive off the five–meter board," I told her, "and then I am either going to swim or drown. And I am planning to swim because my life depends on it," I said. Edith thought it was a good idea, but suggested that I jump feet first rather than try to dive like she did. She also suggested the three–meter diving board to start with.

When we got there, I watched a couple of Edith's dives before I climbed up to the high platform. I had no fear of water and did not hesitate to jump. However, Edith had not thought of telling me to take a deep breath first—and to hold it! When I got into the water, it was a long way down to the bottom of the pool and it seemed to be an even longer way back up. By then I was swallowing water and surfaced coughing, spitting, and thrashing, but still not scared. I forgot about swimming and thrashed to the edge of the pool where a very angry lifeguard met me and helped me out. He yelled at me for awhile, then told me to get out of the stadium and go home. So much for my learning how to swim—for the time being at least.

Later that summer when we were at one of the lakes, Edith watched my attempts to imitate her as I was trying to swim. At that time she noticed what I did wrong, and the problem was breathing. Once she told me when to breathe and how to coordinate my breathing with the strokes, it worked like a charm. I was delighted when I was actually swimming the breast stroke, which was the common swim stroke in Germany at that time. From then on it was hard to keep me out of the water no matter how cold it got later in the summer and early fall. I practiced my swimming whenever I could and had no trouble swimming for long periods of time without stopping. To this day I can easily swim for an hour without stopping to rest.

Becoming a Teenager

I celebrated my thirteenth birthday on September 13. Having always considered thirteen to be my lucky number, I firmly believed that it would be an unusually good year for me. While looking back today, nothing stands out in my memory that was especially happy when I was thirteen, the fact that we survived one of the worst post war years was itself a happy event. We were living in an extremely difficult time and thought it could not possibly get worse. Little did we know then that much worse was still to come. "Enjoy the war—peace will be frightful" said someone not so many years ago when we sat in our air raid shelter and bombs were whistling on their way down.

As far as celebrating a birthday—well, there was no cake or even a special meal. We were fortunate to have something to eat at all. Inviting anyone to a birthday, either friends or relatives, had been out of the question for years. No one had food to share, and nobody expected anything. Besides, people lacked the energy to make a trip for just a visit, even within the city.

I did receive a very special birthday gift, and I wonder what my parents had to trade to get it. It was a silver charm bracelet with three charms on it. One of them was a horseshoe with a red heart in the center, another was a key. Perhaps the key to a lucky future? The third charm was a number 13, my lucky number! I felt really grown up because I owned a bracelet. Two of the charms survived, but I don't remember what happened to the bracelet or the number thirteen.

Recently I asked a jeweler to make a number thirteen for me, and to attach it and the two original charms which I had treasured throughout the years, to a new bracelet. I was happy to present this charm bracelet to my granddaughter Meagen on her thirteenth birthday on March 13, 2004.

Domestic Problems

Our living arrangements were adequate by the standards of that particular time if people got along with each other. Grandma's apartment in this more than seventy–year–old building consisted of a fairly good sized kitchen of about eight by sixteen feet, and one room about sixteen by sixteen feet. The kitchen had gas lighting and a brick cook stove which was fired with coal. The old–fashioned kitchen sink was the only source of water in the apartment. A toilet for use by all four families living on that floor was located on the landing above us, between floors. Originally the building had no plumbing. There were outhouses then and the plumbing had been added when the building was modernized around the turn of the century.

Daytimes we lived in the kitchen. It was the warmest and most cheerful room. Grandma's former living room/bedroom was now the bedroom for all five of us, plus storage for what was left of our furniture that had been saved from the burning building in which we lived until 1943. Mom, Papa, and Grandma slept in the bed in which normally a married couple would sleep, i.e. two single beds moved together. I slept on a couch at the foot end of those beds, and Peter on a sofa a little ways away by the window next to the displaced dining room table. The only thing wrong with this sleeping arrangement was that Grandma insisted on sleeping between Mom and Papa. What made Mom angry was that Papa allowed his mother to separate them.

Needless to say there were a lot of arguments between the three of them, and especially between my parents. At some point during the war years when things were not going well between them, Papa had been seeing another woman. From something that Grandma said, Mom found out that he was now seeing her again. She confronted Papa, and after that day he often did not come home at night. Mom and Grandma, having to spend the daytimes together in the kitchen, argued more and more.

Frau Schult, Grandma's neighbor for over forty years, had an identical apartment next door and could not help but overhear the arguments. One day she mentioned to Mom that with winter approaching she was planning to move her bed into her kitchen where it was warmer, and that she could let us have her other room. The idea was that Mom and Papa would have their own bedroom next door, and that Peter and I could sleep at Grandma's. It did not work out that way. Papa refused to move out of his mother's apartment, and Mom decided to move next door with Peter and me. This was the beginning of their separation. From then on we were a separate family living next door to Grandma, and we knew that Papa was not living there most of the time.

A Room of Our Own

It was a feeling of freedom to have a room of our own rather than being unwelcome guests at Grandma's. The room was bright and cheerful because it still had a fair amount of glass left in the windows. We enjoyed living there. For just the three of us it was a very spacious place. We had no kitchen, but our old faithful hot plate served us well once again. While officially we still had the use of Grandma's kitchen, Mom chose not to cook there. She decided to go next door only whenever we needed to get water. This cut down on encounters and thus minimized arguments.

I came up with the grand idea one day that I wanted Mom to have a baby so that I could have a little brother or sister to take care of. Mom told me this was impossible because we needed a father for the baby. She did not explain why, and I saw no reason for a father. After all, so far Peter and I had mostly grown up without one.

Just about that time I made another friend at the Salvation Army whose name was Ursula. She could sing beautifully and I admired her. Ursula was seventeen years old and an orphan. I had always wanted an older brother or sister. Since we could not have that baby I wanted Mom to have, I tried to talk her into adopting Ursula. I was convinced that Mom would like the fact that Ursula was already grown up and this would save Mom all the work that comes with taking care of a baby. To my disappointment she did not go for it. Mom loved children and had often said that if times were different she would have wanted more. Now she tried to reason with me, pointing out that she had plenty of worries trying to secure enough food to get the three of us through. These were difficult times and she just did not have the energy to take on the responsibility of having another mouth to feed. Mom's answer to my bright idea was "absolutely no."

It did not occur to me at the time that I may have subconsciously tried to get a fourth member for the family. In my mind four was a family, and now that we no longer had Papa it left only three of us. Previously when Papa was absent all throughout the war years, it had been only temporary and most kids had no father at home. As I began to realize that my parents' separation was permanent, I needed to find a fourth person to make the family whole again. I was hurting because of the separation.

Fall 1947

During the summer and fall Mom did a lot of sewing for other people. Fearing another cold winter, people wanted to have warm slacks and jackets made out of blankets, curtains, and any fabric that was not absolutely needed somewhere else. No work was done for money, of course. The hard currency was food or other needed goods such as clothes.

Mom did some sewing and alterations for a family by the name of Zabel, whom she had known for many years. The Zabels were upper class by the old German standards. They had American acquaintances and were getting used clothing and fabrics through them. In exchange for her work, Frau Zabel gave Mom clothes which she no longer wanted or her children had outgrown. Their daughter Ursula was about my age, but taller, and their son was a year older than Peter. I received a nice summer dress, a suit, and two years later a winter coat which no longer fit Ursula. While this winter coat was not a very warm one, I was delighted to finally retire my patched and already too–small–again "fur" coat, which by that time I had worn for nearly ten years. Frau Zabel approved of my association with Ursula and we became friends for a couple of years. However, I could feel some of the snobbishness of the elevated class come through and I was never quite comfortable with this friendship.

At one point the American family which the Zabels knew, was in a jam. Their German maid had to be away for two weeks and the American lady needed someone to clean the house in which she and her husband lived in Berlin–Dahlem. Frau Zabel asked Mom if I could go with Ursula to keep her company, and maybe help a bit. This was during summer vacation, and it turned out to be an interesting experience. Ursula had no idea how to go about cleaning anything, so I did most of the work and taught her a few things. She was quite willing to learn. We had a lot of fun and Ursula seemed to enjoy this new experience. The lady of the house was not at home, and when it came to the vacuum cleaner we had fun trying to figure out how it worked. At my home we owned neither a vacuum cleaner nor a rug to be vacuumed, and I had never seen a vacuum cleaner up close.

In return for our work we received food. At least I did get some. Ursula was paid with dollars besides the food, but those were not shared. I was happy with what little food came my way and enjoyed bringing it home to Mom and Peter, for all of us to share. I remember some Milky Way candy bars and a partial jar of peanut butter. Peanut butter was unknown to us and we thought it was delicious. Ursula and I did the job twice a week for two weeks, and I was delighted to have had the opportunity to participate and to contribute some extra food for the family to enjoy. Every bit of food helped to get us farther down the road in our fight for survival.

More Trips to the Farmers

In early winter Mom took her now obsolete wedding ring to the farmers and traded it for bacon and sausage. On another trip, as a last desperate measure, Mom traded her sewing machine for a sack of potatoes, perhaps thirty–five pounds, and a baby rabbit which we had to raise before we could eat it. Peter and I were enchanted with the rabbit. It instantly became our pet and little friend. We had much fun with our new pet. When the time came where Mom thought the rabbit could provide us with a couple of good meals, she was not able to kill it. She took it to the butcher who, for a piece of it, killed and skinned it for us.

Mom cooked a rare full meal for Sunday dinner. It was to be a special feast. When the three of us sat around the table, one after the other broke into tears. We could not eat the rabbit. It had been our little friend, and as hungry as we were we had to give the food away.

Christmas came and we had a tree and some happy hours, though mostly sad ones since Papa chose not to be with us at all. I had learned a long Christmas poem in school, and Mom enjoyed it so much that she invited Frau Schult, in whose big room we lived, in to hear it. Frau Schult spent some time with us that Christmas Eve since otherwise she would have been alone also. Her only daughter lived in Cologne with her family. We were happy to have Frau Schult join us. It was a distraction from our sadness about Christmas without Papa. She loved my poem and asked me to recite it a second time. I felt honored to do so.

Tante Ella

Tante Ella was a first cousin of my father's. She lived in Berlin–Schöneberg, was unmarried and had spent her adult life in the service of the Salvation Army. I remember her as being a very kind soul, positive and cheerful at all times. Tante Ella visited us frequently after we had moved out of Grandma's apartment. I had the opportunity to get to know her better than Peter did because of my involvement with the Salvation Army. Tante Ella and I occasionally went to special Salvation Army services in the evening, and afterwards I was invited to spend the night at her apartment. This was always a special treat, though I was painfully aware of the fact that she shared her food with me which meant that she had less to eat. She did it happily and was always delighted to have me stay with her. Such was her way, all kindness and goodness.

Tante Ella was like a bright light in the darkness of misery. She was always cheerful and sang happy songs all of the time. It was fun to be with her. After Mom and Papa had split up, she visited us regularly in an effort to console Mom.

One particular thing I learned from Tante Ella, which later became a part of my life, was how to set the table beautifully. On the few occasions when we did share an extremely meager meal together, Tante Ella always had the most wonderful, simple and unique ideas for making the table look beautiful. One time she placed salt and pepper shakers as little individual flower vases with each place setting. The flowers were dandelions which she had picked by one of the city trees out on the street. They looked like sunny little faces in their vases and brightened the whole room, as well as our spirits.

When Tante Ella married her deceased sister's husband, Willi Sprittulle in 1952, they gave a home to his grandchildren who were war orphans. The girl, nine, and the boy seven years old at the time, had been in an orphanage since they lost their parents during the war. Both Tante Ella and Onkel Willi, then in their mid–sixties, took on the challenge of raising those children until they could be on their own. My hat is off to them! I know Tante Ella found the strength in her faith and her joyful spirit and song to enjoy every moment of raising "her" family.

I feel honored to have had a special connection with her.

Tante Ella in her Salvation Army uniform. She devoted her life to helping others.

10

1948
The Blockade, Airlift, and Bare Survival
Age Thirteen

When we "celebrated" the arrival of the new year, we did not dream that it would be another fateful one, bringing unbelievable hardships. Each time we thought that it could not possibly get any worse—that we were at the bottom and things could only get better—it got worse instead. Here it was nearly three years after the end of the war, and *peace* had not yet come to us.

Life Goes On

All through the winter and spring there had been other warm places besides the Salvation Army meeting hall. Those warm places were the movie theaters. Reopened at first to play American films with German subtitles, they soon ran an occasional old German film as those became available after being censored and cleared. There were some marvelous musicals. I remember *Wiener Blut*, a musical film with the exhilarating Johann Strauss waltzes which everyone loved. Although money was nearly worthless, people found that it could buy them two hours of warmth and entertainment in a movie theater. Not that the theater was heated—it was the body heat which warmed it—and the illusion of the movie put us into a world of comfort and luxury. The price one had to pay was to stand in line for several hours to get a seat.

One cold and snowy afternoon while standing in such a movie line, I was absent–mindedly watching the streetcars pass by in each direction. One streetcar train that came along looked odd. Something seemed to be wrong with it. A moment later, I, as well as others, realized that all three cars of that particular streetcar had glass in *all* windows. A collective exclamation of awe went through the waiting crowd as everyone pointed at the phenomenon. Pedestrians on both sides of the wide avenue stopped to admire this "wonder" of a streetcar. We were so used to seeing our war–battered streetcars with a couple of tiny pieces of glass inserted in a sheet of cardboard or masonite, and with only an occasional whole pane of glass. This one had glass in every window, and we could not believe our eyes—it looked so beautiful. It was a symbol of hope for better times to come.

In the next two hours while waiting in line for the movie tickets, this wonder of a streetcar went to its destination at both ends a couple more times, and we could admire it each time as it passed. The sight was so awesome that it in itself was entertainment, and it made people in line forget the cold and the unpleasantness of the long hours of waiting.

Thanks to the initiation of the Marshall Plan, some of Germany's industry had started to revive. Glass was a top priority item because of the dire need. Seeing this wonderful glassed–in streetcar gave us the hope that we would soon be able to have glass in our apartment windows again. This meant not only more warmth during the cold winters, but also light in a country that has gray skies during a good part of the year.

My Confirmation and Start of Adulthood

Coming up at this time was a milestone in my life which was noteworthy. I was in eighth grade and would be graduating from elementary school at the end of the school year. For the past year, I had been attending the required lessons in Religion once a week. These were given by the minister of our local Evangelical Lutheran Church, Pfarrer Moldaenke, who was old and blind. A generation ago, he had confirmed my father, later married my parents, and christened me. From observing our blind Pfarrer, I learned the useful lesson of how to write in the dark, or without looking at the paper that I was writing on.

Sunday, April 4, 1948, was a big day for me. It was the day of my Confirmation in the Lutheran Church. During the winter months Mom had made a black dress for me, having to stitch it by hand since her sewing machine was gone. The dress was partially made from a satin coat lining and from another black fabric. Mom had received this fabric in exchange for doing sewing for people. It was a lovely dress, and I wore it for many years, even to school and later to work.

It was the custom to invite all relatives for the Confirmation Day party, but the problem was that there had to be a meal of some kind. Mom decided that this important milestone needed to be celebrated for the sake of tradition and remembrance. She talked the grocer into giving her the potato rations for the entire month of April. In addition, she bought potatoes and flour for all exchangeable ration coupons, such as those for bread and starch items. Then she baked a cake for the party, and made a big bowl of potato salad. To flavor the potato salad without mayonnaise, Mom got two herrings in exchange for meat rations at the fish store. She even boiled the heads of the herrings to add to the flavoring. This prompted nine–year–old Peter to compose a song about the

My confirmation picture. Mom made the dress from two different fabrics, the shiny one being satin coat lining.

boiled herring heads. He understood that these herring heads were somewhere in the potato salad, and he thought that he ought to warn people.

The first guest to arrive was my home room teacher, Frau Crohn. She had arrived quite a bit ahead of time and Peter volunteered to entertain her while Mom and I put the finishing touches on the table. Tante Ella, the Salvation Army aunt, had bought several sets of plain glass salt and pepper shakers to use as vases. Household items made of glass had just started to become available. We put several small flowers into each of those shakers and placed them at people's place settings. They were a lovely addition to the table and became the hit of the day. The little wildflowers from the lawn of the nearby public park were just the right size for our miniature "vases."

Soon my aunts, uncles, and cousins arrived. At one point, Frau Crohn who sat next to Tante Lotte, entertained her with the story about Peter escorting her to the toilet, which was located on the stairway landing above, between floors. Earlier, Frau Crohn had asked Peter where the toilet was and Peter said he would show her up the stairs. On the way, Peter asked: "Frau Crohn, do you need to go number one or number two? We put lots of paper up there, but be sure you don't forget to flush!" Everybody roared with laughter. My teacher thought that Peter was the cutest little boy she had ever met. She loved his polite manners, and realized that his reminder about being sure to flush came from Mom instructing us not to forget, since the toilet was being used by all neighbors living on our floor.

Everybody had a great time and it was wonderful to share a meal for once, even though we did not know what we would be eating the rest of the month. Mom was always confident. *Ach, es wird schon wieder Rat werden—* we will be provided for—was one of her mottos of faith which let her believe that a Supreme Being is always looking out for us. Tante

My brother Peter at age 9

Lotte and Onkel Martin who owned the butcher shop, had brought some wieners to go with the potato salad. Peter had been instructed not to sing his song about the herring heads. It was an unforgettable feast. There had even been the traditional afternoon coffee and cake. A party like ours, at that particular time, was quite rare. Mom had thought of everything, including the need to find some candles for the time after dark since our room had neither electricity nor gas lighting. Most of all, Mom had created for me a lasting memory of an important event in my life, and Peter had done his part by seeing to the entertainment.

The only cloud on this sunny day was that it hurt me to have Papa present because I could feel his discomfort about being with the relatives. Most of them knew that he had chosen to no longer live with us. He did not stay long.

Deciding my Future

On several occasions during the past year Mom and I had discussions about what kind of a career I would like to pursue that was within the range of possibilities. The school system was still semi–chaotic. It was said that whoever was then in high school was allowed to finish. However, no new students were starting high school because the whole school system was in the process of being revised. Everyone was confused, even the school officials. There had already been several "revisions" and "revised revisions," and still nobody knew exactly what was going on. The Soviets had their hands in this. In communist fashion they had started a "unified" school system in their sector and insisted that the West Berlin sectors follow suit.

I liked school very much and loved children, so the final result of my talks with Mom was that I wanted to become a schoolteacher. In Germany this would be a good job, and teachers were badly needed. Being a teacher used to be predominantly a man's job. With so many men not having returned from the war, women were taking over at this point in time, some of them even without specific training for it.

There were forty–one girls in my eighth grade class, and two of us wanted to become teachers. Not only our teachers, but the school's principal who was a woman, were overjoyed and promised to do everything they could to help Regina and me along. They found a place

My eighth grade class picture, September 1947. I am in the center of the second row with Frau Crohn, our teacher, looking at me. My friend Brigitte who lives in Missouri, is the dark haired girl directly in front of me.

for us in a middle school which agreed to admit us after we extended our knowledge of English and Algebra. Being in the American occupied sector of Berlin, we had been learning English. Early in the summer, Regina and I started on lessons to catch up in both subjects. We passed our tests and were officially admitted to this middle school, to start after summer vacation.

During school vacation in August, Regina and I went to the usual summer day camp in the *Grunewald* forest, this time as helpers rather than as kids. One day after we each had escorted our assigned group of children back to the school building, the principal called us into her office. In all of our previous dealings she had started to treat us as future colleagues, she was so proud of us. This time she could not even speak because of her tears. The school system had been changed—once again—to *Einheitsschule* or unified school. Middle school, high school, and vocational school, were being eliminated and the students absorbed into the now unified school system. At this time, she could not tell us where this would leave Regina and me, but she promised that she would work on it and let us know.

Next we received "great news" from the principal. Teachers were so much in demand that the Teachers College would take us after summer vacation without having been to middle school, and for us to report to the college and take our routine admission tests. Again, Regina and I went there, took the tests, passed them—except for one: age. We had to be seventeen years old to be admitted. Absolutely no exceptions. Regina was fifteen and I was not even going to be fourteen until September. Totally deflated we went home. I had to somehow "kill" three years. By then who knew what stage of revision the school system was going to be in.

Mom, according to her own story, liked to have fun rather than study. She said she did not do especially well in school. But she was absolutely brilliant in solving the problems of real life situations. So I could not go to Teachers College until three years from now. No problem. How about going to Business School in the meantime, was her suggestion. Learning bookkeeping, typing, shorthand, and business procedures would not hurt a teacher, and should the plans change, I would have an education with which I could enter the business world. I was happy about this solution, especially when we found that for the first time the Business School was offering a three–year program as a trial. It was a perfect use of this three–year period for me. Regina's parents liked the idea so much that they sent her to the three–year program also, instead of the normal two–year one.

Together we started Business School in September and were in the same class with two other girls from our eighth grade class. One of them, Brigitte Schulz, eventually immigrated to the United States and married Herbert Sieg. They live in southern Missouri with their children, and we have kept in contact throughout the years.

Another Move

Mom found out from a friend that a family who lived in a large apartment had a room available. Because of the vast destruction in the city of Berlin, people were required to sublet space in their apartments if they had more room than was allocated for the size of their family. The number of square meters of living space per person was determined by the housing authority. This family, whose name was Klemm, lived in one of the large old apartments in a lovely area quite near us.

Dr. Klemm was a scientist and had been well off before the war. He and his wife, three sons, and his mother, lived in an apartment which consisted of five bedrooms, a large living room, a sitting room, sun room, dining room, and a large kitchen. This was a lot of space, even for a luxury apartment in Berlin.

At this time, the Klemm family with their three boys had been allocated three bedrooms and the sitting room and sun room as their personal quarters. The mostly bedridden grandmother lived in one small room next to the living room. A further bedroom was occupied by a university student whom the motherly Frau Klemm had taken under her wing. The large formal living room was the music room, in which piano lessons were given by the grandmother. This left one room, the former dining room which, according to regulations, still had to be shared. The Klemms were looking for some "nice" people to occupy this room, and friends of theirs helped them look out for someone suitable. If they did not find anyone on their own, then the housing authority would arbitrarily assign people to move in.

Our present room had no electricity, and the winter nights had been long and dark. Candles were not available. We had an old kerosene lamp, but could get only a very limited supply of kerosene, and no wicks. All winter long we had been nursing this old, dying wick. Mostly we sat in the dark, using the lamp only when Mom was cooking, and for some atmosphere during meals. Ours being a former living room, there was no water and we had to get it at Grandma's next door. When Mom heard about the availability of a room at the Klemm's, she jumped at the chance to solve this problem.

The other reason for wanting to move was to get away from the close proximity of Grandma Stanneck's apartment. Mom and Papa were hurting each other with occasional verbal interchanges. Papa was no longer living with us; he had moved in with his lady friend by that time.

With a borrowed handcart, Mom and I carted our beds, table, chairs, and personal belongings to our new room which was only a mile away, and still in the district of Berlin–Steglitz. Mom had to take drastic measures to get the wardrobe and a few of the other furniture pieces we needed which were still stored in Grandma's apartment. Grandma had told Mom that none of our furniture was to be moved out of her apartment because it belonged to her son. Well, midnight moves were Mom's specialty. We had the key to Grandma's apartment because of needing access to water. We also knew on which day Grandma would not be home until late at night, and on that evening Mom just went in and took some of our things. I did not like it, but I had to help Mom carry the heavy pieces of that big wardrobe down the three flights of stairs and load them onto the handcart. To move all of our belongings, we had to make numerous trips to our new place during that night.

We could not then imagine that the darkest hours of our survival, as well as the most delightful interludes awaited us at the Klemm's cheerful household. What a blessing it was that we happened to live there at that particular time. Mom and Frau Klemm became fast friends and supported each other with their humor during another extremely difficult time in our lives.

More about the Klemm family later in the story.

The Berlin Blockade

West Berlin's Fight for Freedom

All during the winter and spring months we had been aware of more and more tension among the Allies, with the Russians being the contrary ones. The Western Allies—Americans, British, and French—suggested introducing a new currency and devaluation of the old Reichsmark to stop the runaway inflation caused by the Black Market. The Russians, as always, said "Nyet." They wanted to weaken the economy of western occupied Berlin to the point of total collapse so that the West Berliners would have no choice but to surrender to Communism. In any case, the Russians insisted that whatever measures were taken in West Germany, there would be only *one* currency in Berlin—theirs.

The Currency Reform

The Western Allies saw the urgent need for a currency reform, but not being able to come to a satisfactory agreement with the Russians, went ahead and printed the new currency so that it would be available whenever the time came. History says that the Russians agreed to the new currency, but only for West Germany, not for Berlin. We West

Berliners, as well as the Western Allies, knew that if Berlin were left out of the currency reform West Berlin would eventually be absorbed into the Soviet system of administration.

There were many diplomatic discussions with the Russians but no agreement could be reached. Each proposal submitted received the by then infamous answer "Nyet."

On June 20, it was announced that starting the next morning there would be a new currency in effect—the Deutsche Mark (DM)—in the three zones occupied by the Western Allies in West Germany. Berlin was not included in this announcement. For the first sixty old Reichsmarks, each citizen would receive sixty new Deutsche Marks. In time, all remaining Reichsmarks would be exchanged at the rate of one new Deutsche Mark for ten old Reichsmarks, which would amount to a ninety percent currency deflation. This announcement was a shock to people who had some savings, and even more so to those who had made a lot of money with black market activity. The currency reform was undesirable for the elderly who lived on savings and who saw their money decimated overnight—as well as for students who depended on grants or army gratuities. However, for most of the population there was a resurgence of hope even as they spent six or eight hours in lines at their local food offices to exchange their Reichsmarks.

Berlin, as always, was a special problem because of the city being divided. Secretly and at the last minute, the Western Allies flew a plane load of the new currency into Berlin. They then announced that as of June 25, each West Berliner could also convert sixty Reichsmarks to the new Deutsche Marks on a one–for–one basis. This was an interesting time. The exchange of people's savings of Reichsmarks on the ten–for–one basis did not happen until many months later. During that interim period all of us were equally rich and equally poor. We looked at this important event as the start of a new life. It gave us the courage to think of the future. It gave us hope.

The Soviets, wanting to "unify" all of Berlin and get it under their rule, reacted to this currency reform with drastic measures. Beginning earlier in the month of June, the Russians had stepped up their slow tightening of the noose around West Berlin. By the middle of June, at first military convoys, then all vehicles trying to leave Berlin for West Germany, were turned back at the Soviet checkpoint. The Autobahn (equivalent to our interstate highway system) between West Berlin and

West Germany was closed for repairs—so the Soviet administration announced.

Berlin's Lifelines are Cut

At the end of World War II, Germany had been arbitrarily divided up among the four powers. It so happened that the city of Berlin—Germany's capital—was located within Russian occupied territory. The Western Allies accepted this only because Berlin itself was also divided up into four sectors, each governed by one of the four powers. By Autobahn and by rail, the shortest distance to West Germany was one hundred ten miles. West Berlin was rightly referred to as an "Island in the Red Sea." All of the Allies including the Russians had agreed that there would be free access by road, rail, and shipping channels to West Berlin. Until that June, the Western Allies had no reason to think that any of this access would ever be cut off.

However, as the month of June wore on, measures were taken by the Soviets to cut off *all* access to Berlin, using whimsical excuses such as an announcement that:—the Autobahn between Berlin and Helmsted has to be closed because it is in urgent need of repair—the Soviet Military Administration is compelled to

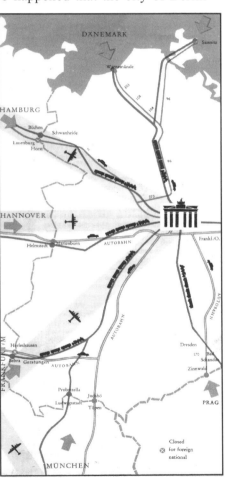

Map showing transportation routes into Berlin. All were cut by the Russians during the Blockade—the first battle of the Cold War.

halt all passenger and freight traffic to and from Berlin, and it is impossible to reroute rail traffic since such measures would cause technical difficulties—water traffic will also be suspended—coal shipments to Berlin from the Soviet zone are halted—the Soviet authorities have ordered the central switching stations to stop the supply of electric power from the Soviet sector of Berlin to the Western sectors because of "technical difficulties"— and so on.

For us, the phrase "technical difficulties" had become synonymous with the Soviet administration, harassment, and their effort to make all of Berlin Communist.

West Berlin has been Blockaded

Officially the blockade started June 26. As the news spread, there was disbelief and despair. We cannot survive this, people exclaimed. Even in prewar years Berlin had never been self–sustaining. It had heavily depended on supplies from the outlying farm areas, or, as in the recent past, supplies from West Germany. Each week thousands of tons of freight had to travel over a single track railroad that ran one hundred ten miles through the Soviet zone of occupation from the Helmsted–Marienborn border crossing to Berlin. Nearly every item consumed by the 2.2 million West Berliners, as well as by 6,500 Allied troops, their families, staff, and technicians, had to be imported along a lifeline that the Russians could cut at the border at any time. Now they had done it.

Ashen–faced people walked aimlessly about the streets hoping to hear bits and pieces of "news" as to what was to happen next. The fear of the Russians and their Communist system was worse than the fear of death—but a quick death, please, not starvation. People were tired of living because it seemed that there was nothing left to live for if there was no freedom. Mom was frantic. I think she was at the end of her strength and started to break. I remember Frau Klemm coming into our room and Mom asking her if they perhaps had a gun, or knew of someone who had one—and Peter and I started begging Mom to let us live— and Mom saying "not for Communism." Luckily, nobody had a gun in those times. All weapons had been confiscated at the end of the war.

It was devastating for me to see Mom "at the end of the rope." She, who was always optimistic and "found a way" saw this new crisis looming over us, and this time she thought that there was no way out. But Frau Klemm turned out to be a wonderful friend in need. She loved Mom's sense of humor and had a good portion of it herself. It did not take her long to talk Mom out of this gloomy moment. Just hearing her speak with her heavy Russian accent always made us laugh because she often used the wrong words or pronounced words strangely. We would sometimes imitate her way of speaking, and then she'd laugh about it herself. Now she described to Mom in humorous detail how her family and ours were going to "gang up" and fight the Communists together. After all, the Klemms knew the Soviets from firsthand experience and wanted no part of Communism.

The Klemm Family

The Klemm family had escaped from Russia in 1917 to get away from Communism. They had nothing good to say about the Communist system and would have picked up pitch forks to fight the Soviets with every ounce of strength. In fact, a year later when the first free election took place in West Berlin, Grandma Klemm, being bedridden, called for an ambulance to take her to the polls so that she could vote. She was not going to let the Communists count her vote as theirs. According to the Communists, every West Berliner who did not vote, did not dare to vote because he really wanted to vote for Communism and was not permitted to do so. Therefore, the Communists counted each uncast vote as theirs.

Living with the Klemm family was a great experience for us, besides being a lot of fun. Frau Klemm loved Mom's sense of humor, and the two women had many fun times and good laughs during our darkest hours of survival. Whenever things were especially rough, either with her family or with our present situation, Frau Klemm would stick her head into our room to see what was going on with us. Before long we would all crack up with laughter.

Dr. Klemm was a quiet man. We hardly ever saw him. Peter and I kept imagining that he lived in a separate room with all his mice. He was a scientist and did some kind of research in biology. The boys always had several cages filled with mice which multiplied quickly, and just as quickly they went to the laboratory with Dr. Klemm. In the meantime, the three Klemm boys, Vladimir (11), Nikolai (9), and Peter

(7), as well as my brother Peter (10) had a lot of fun with the mice. Mom was not quite as enthusiastic about the little creatures, especially when Peter let them out of the cage in our room and they walked all over the place—but Frau Klemm always put in a good word for Peter. Even though she had three boys of her own, she absolutely adored him. Peter was a cute little boy, fun–loving like Mom, and every bit as charismatic.

Then there was always music in the house. The Klemms were a musical family. Even Grandma, although being bedridden most of the time, still had several piano students including her grandson Peter. Vladimir played the trombone and the violin; Nikolai played piano and clarinet, and Peter was just starting to learn how to play the piano. I asked permission to use the piano because I wanted so badly to learn how to play. Frau Klemm gave me permission. The "music room" was next to ours, so that I could always hear when Peter Klemm had a lesson or was practicing. Whenever nobody was using the piano, I went and practiced Peter's lessons, and Frau Klemm told me that Grandma said I was doing it well. Grandma lived in a small room next to the music room which formerly had been the living room of this mansion–type apartment, and we visited her a couple of times. The first time we visited, she gave Peter and me each two little squares of chocolate, and we did not even know what it was. While we were holding it in our hands it was melting until Mom told us to eat it quickly. It was too late—we had to lick it off our hands.

We could not have lived in a more fun place during some of the

Frau Klemm and I, and her oldest son, Vladimir, during a visit to Berlin in 1960.

darkest times of our survival. Mom and Frau Klemm became fast friends, and they laughed and cried together. Herr Paproth, the student who lived in the room next to ours, practiced his Russian with Frau Klemm whenever they spent time in the kitchen. Each "family" did their own cooking, since rations were meager and nobody could share anything with anyone. Russian was one of the languages Herr Paproth studied at the university. Knowing that I had learned some Russian when we lived in the Russian occupied zone, Frau Klemm kept encouraging me to join them in their conversations. While I felt I did not know enough of the language to participate in conversations with them, I am sure they would have helped me along.

Later in life I regretted not having taken advantage of this wonderful opportunity. However, enthusiasm was often hampered by the lack of energy. It was hard enough just to get through the days. We lived (mostly existed) literally from meal to meal. In thinking back, I am amazed that we children were able to learn as much as we did in school, and especially considering that the teachers were also running on low energy.

With the house full of musicians, there was always music to lighten the mood and help us to forget our hunger. On many evenings when we were not busy with homework, Peter and I as well as Herr Paproth, were invited to join the Klemm boys in the family's small sitting room and play table games. Those were some of the bright hours of our existence then.

As in a protected little haven, the ten of us living in the Klemm apartment felt safe and content, as far as that was possible. Outside of our walls an incredible feat was being staged. To save the lives of more than two million Berliners, the city was being supplied by air! *Everything,* even the coal to create electricity for emergency use such as hospitals, and for public transportation, had to be flown into Berlin. It would take a whole book to describe the details of this tremendously detailed operation. The Western Allies did not move out and forget about us, but rather they and their families stayed; and they stood by us in our fight for freedom. To be hungry all of the time and barely survive on the number of calories counted out to sustain life, was a small price for us to pay. We were not alone in our quest for freedom. The Allies supported us 100%. Each airplane that flew in with supplies conveyed the message: "Hang on—you are not alone—we will help you all we can." This gave us courage and hope.

For nearly eleven long months, from June 26, 1948, until May 12, 1949, Berlin was blockaded by the Soviets and supplied by air by the Americans, British, and French.

Life During the Blockade

Although it was utter famine for 2.2 million hungry Berliners, we were all swept away by the spirit of the Airlift. To hear the planes' engines above us, continuously, day and night, was infinitely reassuring. It meant that the Allies were not letting go of West Berlin. They were staying here and were keeping their promise to help us fight for freedom. But, how long could this Airlift last? How long could they keep supplies coming at this impossible rate?

We did not complain about the low rations, much less about the nearly total absence of electric power. But recalling the last two winters, we began to wonder about coal for fuel to keep us from freezing to death, and gas for cooking. Needing to cut the city's gas consumption by 50%, gas had to be rationed, and this turned out to be quite complicated when several families had to use one kitchen.

During those days we read the gas meter at the start and finish each time anyone used the stove. If, let's say, three parties were cooking at the same time and one was finished, the gas meter was read and the usage divided by three. After the next party was finished, the meter was read again and the usage divided by only two. It had to be that exact. I had been given the tedious task of keeping track of everybody's gas consumption and making sure that we stayed within the allocation, or our gas would be shut off without warning. To avoid one party blaming the other for using more than their share—we were hearing some ugly stories on this subject—I tried to keep the records as accurately as I could. We never over used, but I had to mention a "caution period" for all of us when once we came close to our limit. It was a lot of work for me and sometimes frustrating when somebody had used the gas and forgotten to write down the meter reading while I was in school. However, we all got along so well and, as a team, we did whatever was necessary.

During the summer, the use of the city's power had to be cut by 75%. All streetcars and subways were halted by 6 p.m. Domestic electricity was limited to four hours a day, two hours in the daytime and two at night. Except for Sundays, we were gone in the daytime. Whenever the lights came on during the night—there was no set time when that would be—we got up and frantically worked on ironing, mending, darning socks, unfinished homework, and most importantly, cooking the next day's meal. As I mentioned, we had gas for cooking, but many people had to cook on hot plates in their rooms, as we had to do until we moved to the Klemm's apartment.

The Incredible Feat of the Airlift

Tempelhof Airport is located just south of Berlin's city center. With five–story apartment buildings located at the approach end of the runway, it was a challenge to fly into Tempelhof in good weather, let alone in fog and low visibility. While some radar was available, its usefulness was minimal in comparison to today's guidance systems. Extremely close spacing of the flights made the operation very dangerous. During April at the height of the Airlift, planes landed every sixty–two seconds around the clock. There was no room for a missed approach. If a pilot could not see the ground on final approach at the minimum altitude, he had to fly his full load back to the originating airport to be able to get back into line. The airlift pilots flew under tremendous stress. Flying three round–trips a day translated into fly—sleep—fly—and nothing else, seven days a week. They also had to fly exactly within the limits of the twenty–mile–wide air corridor, and even then harassment by Soviet fighter planes was quite common.

Could the Allies fly in enough supplies to keep the city alive during the winter? With greatest efforts the number of flights increased steadily, and the turnaround time decreased. While the planes were being unloaded with much haste, the pilots grabbed snacks at mobile snack bars, were briefed with the latest weather, and were ready for the next round–trip.

Hope falls from Heaven

There was one person who won the hearts of the Berliners—adults and children alike—and that was Lt. Gail Halvorsen who became known as the Berlin Candy Bomber.

One day during his time off duty, Lt. Halvorsen talked to a group of children who stood outside the airport fence and were watching the planes land at Tempelhof. He was impressed that they seemed to know what "freedom" meant and how important the airlift was.

The children were not begging for candy, as children everywhere else did when they encountered Americans. Wanting to give them something, Lt. Halvorsen found he had only two sticks of gum in his pocket. He split up the gum and distributed the pieces, with the promise that he would drop candy out of his airplane for them on his next flight into Berlin. Ingeniously, he made little parachutes from handkerchiefs onto which he tied Hershey bars and packages of gum, then dropped those sweet treats out of the cockpit window of his airplane to the waiting children just before landing at Tempelhof.

After several days of those candy drops, Lt. Halvorsen's "secret mission" became known to his superiors because the German newspaper pictured his airplane on the front page. The Air Force found that the thoughtfulness of this kindhearted man did more to cement relations between the Allies and their former enemies than any other attempt, and encouraged Lt. Halvorsen to continue. He became known as The Berlin Candy Bomber, and his idea turned into a large scale operation. Other pilots joined Halvorsen, and pretty soon thousands of candy parachutes had been dropped.

Peter, who roamed everywhere with his friends, found out before I did that there might be a chance to catch a parachute carrying a package of candy at Tempelhof Airport. Here is Peter's description of what he saw:

> On a sunny morning in early fall, my friend and I ventured first by streetcar and then by bus to the Tempelhof Airport. We were not allowed inside the airport, but watched the flow of planes coming in for their final landing across the last buildings and ruins, which were very close to the runway. It was at that time that I noticed white items which looked like snowballs coming out of one low flying airplane. I was not able to catch one of the flying objects that turned out to be little parachutes made by the pilots, with candy bars attached to them.
>
> I went home that night not knowing that one day, by the end of the year, I was going to be airlifted out of Berlin on one of those planes flown by my heroes, the men we called "supermen."

Peter excitedly told me what he had seen that day, and that he would return to Tempelhof again in the hope of catching one of the candy parachutes.

Colonel Halvorsen became the much admired hero of the Berliners. While all airlift pilots and personnel were heroes in the eyes of the Berliners, it was Colonel Halvorsen who put the *heart* into the Airlift. By sending gifts of candy down to the children, he told them that somebody cared about them personally. This great act of kindness gave them, as well as their parents, *hope*—hope for the future, hope for freedom, and hope for a better life.

Lt. Gail Halvorsen holding one of his candy parachutes before flying his plane to Berlin.

"Without hope the soul dies" Colonel Halvorsen said fifty years later, when I had the splendid opportunity to meet this kindhearted man and to finally thank him personally for what he did for the children and for all the West Berliners. Throughout the intervening years, and still at this time as I am writing this, Colonel Halvorsen flies missions to war ravaged countries and drops candy to the children.

I have often been asked if I caught any candy parachutes. The answer is that I did not go to Tempelhof Airport at that time. Peter is four years younger than I am and he did not have the responsibilities that fell to me. Besides going to Business School, I had to stand in food lines—often four to six hours at a time, several times a week—to get our rations. This took a lot of energy, and with the limited rations we were getting, there was none left for extra trips.

Fall and Winter 1948

With fall came shorter days and colder weather. The much reduced calorie diet did not do much to help keep us warm. While we were

While I did not catch a parachute during the Blockade, I received my Hershey bar in person from Col. Halvorsen in 1998.

fighting loss of energy and interest in life, our Allies were fighting to keep supplies coming in all kinds of weather.

Starting in mid November, the worst fog in years blanketed central Europe for weeks. I remember trying to catch the streetcar to go to school and not being able to find the streetcar stop which was close to the corner only a block from where we lived. Somehow the planes flew into Berlin. They had to, if the Berliners were to be kept alive. There were plane crashes which cost lives, but still the Airlift continued.

When we were not in school, we tried to keep warm under our featherbeds in the daytime. Our lives were inactive and uninteresting because we lacked the energy to go anywhere, except to school. Even school attendance was optional.

The Klemm's apartment had central heating, but this system had been shut down during and since the war because of extremely reduced coal rations. Obviously there was no coal for such a system during the Blockade.

Mom looked at our cast iron stove to see if she could rig up a way to use it to get heat. She decided that if she could get an extension for our stovepipe and run it outside through the plywood in the window, we could heat our room. Eventually, Mom found a source for a stovepipe and bought one. It was made of tin cans which were soldered together. The source of the cans, of course, was American. None of our foods ever came in cans. The basic idea of using tin cans to make a pipe seemed like a good one, however, the solder melted from the heat going through it. We lost most of the solder, but somehow the cans held together, though smoke would leak out and into the room. We could use the stove only for short periods of time until we got too much smoke into the room. Most of the time we had to open the window to let the smoke out, which defeated the purpose.

In school we read Mark Twain's book, *The Adventures of Tom Sawyer,* in German, and I thought it was the funniest book I had ever read. I was so happy when it was my turn to borrow the book and bring it home to read, so I could share it with Mom and Peter. When Peter fell asleep while I was reading, I got angry and could not understand why he was not interested enough in those wonderful stories to stay awake and listen. Mom loved Tom Sawyer. His tricks and his way of having fun were exactly up her alley.

With winter approaching, I had the great idea to knit socks and mittens for Peter. A number of years ago, Mom had knitted outfits for my five dolls from cotton yarn, which was then still available. I unraveled the outfits and started to knit. Mom looked very thoughtful. She was touched that I wanted to sacrifice my dolls' clothes to knit warm socks for my little brother, who always got such large holes in his socks that it was becoming impossible to darn them. Darning our socks was my responsibility. Although most people hated the tedious chore, I enjoyed it. Wool was rare at that time. It had not been available since before the war and any wool garments we had once owned, had long since worn out. Nylon had not been invented yet and cotton did not hold up well, so that darning became a never ending task.

Speaking of darning socks, I had my first paying job with the Klemms. With three boys in the family, continuous darning was necessary. Once or twice a week I sat in their warm room for a couple of hours and darned socks for the Klemm family, as well as for Herr Paproth. I enjoyed darning and even got paid for it. At that time, nothing could be purchased for money, but I saved it and also the money I earned from tutoring the Klemm's seven–year–old son, Peter, in arithmetic, German, and English. Many months after the Blockade ended and goods became available, I bought a fountain pen with this money.

The Klemms always spoke German around the house, except when Frau Klemm yelled at the boys. She did that in Russian, which amused us because the Russian language sounded more severe than the kind-hearted and fun loving Frau Klemm could possibly be, even if one of the boys deserved to be scolded.

Peter's Good Fortune

Peter was one of the lucky children to be flown out of Berlin during the Blockade. At a time of such political uncertainty, it was questionable as to whether or not our separation from Peter would end up being a permanent one. Here is the background of the agonizing question Mom and I faced.

The difficulty of feeding a city of 2.2 million people by air meant that everyone received barely enough food to stay alive. Many people starved during this period, and the humanitarian plight of West Berlin received worldwide publicity. At one point it was realized that the Airlift planes were returning to West Germany empty after unloading their inbound cargoes. It was suggested that the returning planes could fly out some of the children to lighten the burden of the Airlift.

That made sense, and large buildings with spacious grounds such as old mansions or castles, were hastily set up to accommodate children. In addition, some West German families volunteered to take Berlin children into their homes for the duration of the Blockade. It seemed feasible to fly as many of the children as possible out of Berlin so that the Airlift had fewer mouths to feed. Peter was then in third grade. The only qualification was to be lucky. "Lucky" because they could not take every child—only two children from his entire school could be selected, and all children were equally needy. To be fair straws were drawn, and Peter was one of the lucky two.

Mom agonized over the decision: Should we let Peter go? In the West he would have enough food to eat, get warm clothing, and have a much better life than the city of Berlin could offer at that time. But who knows what might develop with the unstable situation in Berlin— could we be sure the Americans would be able to stick to their promise to continue this incredible Airlift indefinitely to keep us alive? If the Airlift were to fail we would be absorbed into the Russian zone and cut off from the West. In that case we would be separated from Peter and might never find each other again. The Red Cross was working on millions of separation cases. Separations were a common occurrence near the end of the war when endless caravans of refugees moved to different parts of Germany while retreating from the Russian army. It was easy to get separated, especially from a child.

Mom was torn and in agony: "Shall I let my child go—to be spared the time of starvation now? But what about later? Will we regret it?" Mom and I had to count on the real possibility of a permanent separation from Peter. Yet, in the hope of a better future for her son she found the courage to send him. Such is the sacrifice that a mother's love for her child can make.

Christmas 1948

It was close to the middle of December and Peter was scheduled to leave a week before Christmas. Though sad that he would not be with us for Christmas, Mom and I enjoyed seeing Peter happy about his trip into the "land of plenty." While the West German people also lived on ration cards, they were much better off in comparison to Berlin. The needs of the airlifted children were going to be taken care of by the Red Cross, and by special food rations which would be equal to those allotted to people recuperating in hospitals.

On the exciting day of Peter's departure and his first flight in an airplane, Mom took him to the collection point at Gatow Airfield at the specified time. When I returned from school, Mom was back home with Peter. For a moment I thought she had changed her mind about letting him go. However, the weather was extremely bad. The cargo planes that were used to fly the children had only folding seats along the outer walls, and it was decided that with the bad weather it would be good to wait for another day. Peter's departure was therefore postponed for a week. We were happy to still have him with us for Christmas.

To keep the morale up, the Allies had flown in Christmas trees so that Berlin's children would not have to be without. We had a precious little Christmas tree, and it is amazing how much joy it brought into our otherwise dismal, cold, and hungry lives. I think it was a hint of "normal" times. Mom had even found a source for candles. Electricity was not available except for two hours at night, if West Berlin had enough coal to supply power for household consumption on any given day. Mom heard about someone who sold candles, having made them from collected old candle wax and mixed with other stuff—we found out later.

Exhilarated, Mom brought home six odd looking, mud colored candles and put them on our tree. We had a big disappointment when we lit them for the first time on Christmas Eve and they burned down extremely fast. By the time the last one was lit, the first candle was finished and about to expire. However, we were happy to have had candlelight for a few minutes, and we still had our beautiful Christmas tree. Mom and I enjoyed Peter's happiness about his Christmas present, an envelope of postage stamps and a little book in which to start collecting stamps. Peter was overjoyed and immediately spread out his stamps all over the bed. We were so glad to still have our sunshine boy with us. Christmas would have been pretty sad without our happy little boy.

Peter's Departure

Peter left Berlin two days after Christmas. At the collection point at Gatow Airport, forty–five emaciated looking children—some of them without shoes, others without winter coats—had congregated with a parent or a guardian. All were a sorry sight. Though the children were happy about their upcoming adventure, they were at the same time sad about the separation from their loved ones.

The plane did not have a heavy load. The little Berliners were almost as light as their meager baggage; and their cheeks were thin, as were their nearly worn out clothes. All children were needy. Each child was weighed in and progress reports would be received by us in time. There was a set of twin boys whom they did not want to separate, so both were being flown out. The boys were seven years old, and together they weighed a scant seventy–five pounds.

11

1949
Our Worst Winter Ever
Age Fourteen

We Miss Peter

Mom and I missed Peter as soon as he was gone, and we were happy about each letter we received from him telling us all about his new life, school, and his friends. While we were glad for his good fortune, doubts still plagued us about the weighty decision we had made to let him go. Each time a letter from Peter arrived, Frau Klemm could hardly wait to read it also. She was always anxious to hear how "her" boy was doing, and she often cried tears of joy about the good life he now had.

The following is partially quoted from accounts which Peter and others wrote home:

Peter described his first airplane trip to us:

> We flew high up in the sky across the Zone and the Iron Curtain. The plane's engines were noisy and the cargo area dark. We were sitting on benches made from canvas and wood that were attached along the walls of the plane.

After their memorable flight, the children went by train to the town of Melsungen near Kassel. From there they walked to their destination, the village of Walkemühle, in which the estate they were staying at was located.

When we got there everybody received some new warm clothes, underwear, and toilet articles. We were tired and went to sleep right away at night. There are nineteen bedrooms for the forty–five children. I share a room with two boys.

Some of the children slept in a bed of their own for the first time in their lives. Peter was happy there. He had always been an outdoor person and the large grounds in a country setting seemed like paradise to him. Mom and I were glad that he had enough food to eat, had warm clothes and housing, and enjoyed country life.

A few days after we arrived a Swiss Red Cross truck came and brought food and clothing. Each child received a pair of ankle–high walking shoes, clothes, and bed sheets. We were most interested in the impressive, huge wheel of Swiss cheese which two men struggled with trying to roll it down the ramp of the truck.

The food was a wonderful surprise for the children. As far as their ration cards, they were classified as recovering hospital patients and received additional allocations of milk and butter. Much more impressive than that were the potatoes. One message home read:

Peter (right) and another student with their teacher in Walkemühle.

There are even potatoes here, as many as we want to eat. Real potatoes, not dried sticks or powder. And you would never believe the big pile of coal we have, and we also have eternal electric light.

School was held at different locations depending on which grade the children were in. Grades one to four—which included Peter—had their classrooms right in the building in which they lived. Grades five to eight walked into the nearby village, and the high school kids rode the bus to the town of Melsungen.

"Klein–Berlin" causes Worries

The group of children at Walkemühle where Peter was, called itself "*klein–berlin*" (little Berlin). At one point untrue rumors started circulating in West Berlin about the "camps" the children from Berlin had been taken to. These rumors—started by the Soviets—said the children were in concentration camp type facilities, had to work until 11 p.m., sleep three in a bed, were being beaten, and got nothing to eat. Parents—including Mom—were in shock not knowing at the time where the rumors had originated. We should have guessed the source, but such was the uncertainty of the times that they created doubts. All the letters received from the children sounded wonderful and gave not the slightest indication of any mistreatment.

Mom received a notice in the mail one day telling her to appear at City Hall on a certain date regarding her son. She felt almost too sick to go, fearing that the rumors were true and expecting to hear that Peter was dead. Being weak from hunger to start with and sick with shock, she used her last energy to drag herself up the many steps at the entrance to City Hall fearing the worst. The other parents of Peter's group had also been called in, and when all were congregated they were reassured that the children were safe, happy, warm, and well fed. Except

Peter at *Walkemühle in 2000*

for the school homework and some minor chores such as helping to set tables, no child had to work. The parents saw pictures of their activities and the children sent letters and brochures home, too. Actually once the parents found out where the rumors had originated, they had no reason to doubt that all was well with their kids. However this episode had contributed a few more nails to Mom's coffin, as she used to say.

In August Peter safely returned to us in Berlin by train. The children had been kept an extra three months after the end of the Blockade to give the city some time to get stabilized after the eleven–month ordeal.

Employment for Berliners helps build Morale

West Berlin's two existing airports, Tempelhof and Gatow, were totally inadequate for the increased activity of the Airlift. An additional airport, Tegel, was built for which nineteen thousand Berliners were employed. This gave people work, a purpose, and most importantly, extra food rations.

Almost half of the workers were women, many of them wearing clothes quite unsuitable for the job. The same was true for the men. Some labored in their one–time best suit which had always been saved for festive occasions, but now had to be an everyday garment. It did not matter. Nobody cared. We were all in the same boat—we wore what we had, whether practical or not. It was the picture of the time. All worked to make Tegel a reality, and eight–hour shift followed eight–hour shift around the clock. The first runway of Tegel Airport—now Berlin's International Airport—was built in record time by the industrious Berliners. It was finished in only a little over two months. Incredible by today's standards, but the additional runway was crucial for Berlin's survival and provided an incentive for everyone.

All machinery and equipment had to be flown in by the Airlift. For this task, a C–74 with a twenty–five ton capacity was used. The bulldozers, graders, and crushers had been sliced into pieces to be flown into Tempelhof, then welded back together.

Early on during the Blockade, the Airlift flew in all parts, materials, and machinery needed to rebuild West Berlin's power station enough so it could operate. The Soviets had cut off electric power to West Berlin from the main power station located in the Soviet sector.

Berliners also did all of the unloading of the Airlift aircraft, and they did it in record time—usually under ten minutes—so the planes could be turned around quickly to bring yet another load of coal or food to the starving city. The Allies also found that former German aircraft mechanics were ready and anxious to provide their expertise to keep the planes flying.

Winter of 1948–1949 Seems Endless

We were surviving the darkest, coldest, hungriest time in our lives, dragging through the days from lack of energy. Our hunger was cumulative. In school, most of us had trouble concentrating and our reactions were slowing down. Simple math problems seemed to overwhelm us with difficulty. We had trouble staying awake. School attendance was optional, but I did not miss a day! Nowhere could it be any colder than it was in our room at home. I liked school and enjoyed learning new things. Besides, as long as we were going to be cold we might as well go to school and have something interesting to do to pass the time.

It is not known how many Berliners died from hunger that winter. It was estimated to be thousands. In our district, emergency vehicles were frequently called to homes where old and friendless people were found starved to death. While food rations had been somewhat increased in October to help us survive the winter, supplies could not always be flown in on time to cover the rations which were printed on paper. I recall it was the last day in November when we heard that because of the extremely heavy fog the Airlift might have to stop for a day or two. This meant that even the limited food supplies would not be available. Whenever food stores did receive rations for distribution, we had to stand in the grocery line for anywhere from three to six or more hours, or take a chance that supplies would run out before we got ours. The same "drama" repeated itself at the butcher and the baker. There were no supermarkets in those days. Standing in food lines took energy which we did not have. It was quite common for people to faint while standing in lines. I was one of those, being a teenager and still growing despite the lack of enough food.

Berlin winters are not mild by anyone's standards, being so far north. It could be well above freezing in the daytime, but at night icy winds came from the lake and the thermometer dropped, sometimes to ten degrees Fahrenheit—well below freezing. It was only minimally warmer in our room where the broken windows had been repaired with plywood.

It had been calculated that the coal allotment for every household could only be twenty–five pounds per person for the entire winter. Every ton of coal had to come from West Germany on the Airlift, and every ton of coal meant that a ton of food could not be flown. No Berliner would ever forget those bitterly cold months. We heard of people burning whatever was burnable, even their cherished parquet floors, treasured heirloom furniture, and books which had survived the bombings. Whatever would give them a few minutes of warmth was sacrificed.

Although it was icy cold in our room we had warm hearts, fun, and laughter, thanks to Mom's high spirits and her sense of humor. Whenever there was a moment of despair, Mom would not let it take hold. She would quickly suggest we find something to laugh about. Most of the time we stayed in bed to keep warm. As long as we heard the planes flying overhead we felt reassured and knew that we were not alone. The Allies were trying their utmost to keep us from starving and preserve our freedom.

Mom did her part in keeping us cheerful during this gruesome time. One day when eating the usual piece of dry bread, Mom told me to imagine that it is cake with raisins in it. While I was not sure I remembered raisins, Mom described them and talked me into enjoying our "cake." We laughed the whole time and kept imagining different kinds of fancy food. Frau Klemm often stuck her head into our room just to find out what was going on, and why we were laughing so much. Then she would join into our fun and contribute to it. Usually all she needed to do was talk with her heavy Russian accent and funny pronunciation of the words, and we would try to imitate her. The result was that the three of us were laughing so hard that tears ran down our cheeks.

Emergency Measures

In January 1949 we heard that coal stocks were dwindling, and would be exhausted within days. Then Berlin would begin to die. The most stringent energy cuts of the blockade had to be made. Even though the temperature often dropped to ten degrees, gas and electricity supplies had to be reduced to a new low. Cuts to conserve power were noticeable everywhere. Fewer streetcars were in operation, and the streetcars that did run and were meant to carry a maximum of one hundred twenty–five persons would be packed to suffocation with one hundred seventy–five.

One day West Berlin's power plant totally ran out of electricity because they were out of coal. As everything ground to a halt, so did the streetcar in which a classmate and I were riding to school. This was the cause for the only time I was late during the three years I attended Business School. My friend and I ran the rest of the way to school, but we were not able to get there on time. The lateness—six minutes—was duly recorded on our report cards. In Germany there is no excuse for tardiness.

Meanwhile time was working in the Allies' favor. Counter restrictions on shipments of materials needed by the Soviet controlled areas were starving them of vital West German products such as steel and machine parts. All trucks with supplies for East Germany were being turned back at the West German side of the checkpoint. This economic blockade was hurting East Germany.

Eventually the Russians agreed to some negotiations, and the Allies could see a light at the end of the tunnel. Still, the winter was not yet over, and with monumental effort the Allies stepped up the number of flights into Berlin. Planes were now flying in ten tons every minute around the clock, which amounted to nearly 13,000 tons a day.

The Airlift took its toll in lives. Sixty–five pilots, crew members, and ground personnel gave their lives to keep Berlin alive. It is amazing that so few died. The weather and fog were the worst in a decade, and by today's standards there were primitive navigation aids, especially the lack of instrument landing systems.

Spring 1949

There were more and more rumors about an approaching end of the Blockade. For Mom and me life continued as before, one day at a time trying to stay alive. We certainly missed Peter and his contribution to our little family. My parents' divorce had become final in early spring, and with Peter being gone we felt like the family was down to just the two of us. Nevertheless we were happy with the knowledge that he was spared the misery of this most difficult time.

Although all of our close relatives lived in Berlin, visiting family and friends seemed to be an activity that had died out. People lacked the energy for unnecessary travel, even within the city. Since we were all in the same miserable boat trying to stay alive, interest in others had become minimal. This was a time when one had to be selfish in order to survive. We were all clinging to our own lifesavers and no longer had the energy to worry about anyone outside of the immediate family.

It was therefore a special surprise to receive a visitor. One day early in the spring, Onkel Walter, as I called him, stopped in to visit us. He was a policeman, and his showing up at the door in uniform created a momentary shock for Frau Klemm who had answered the knock (no electricity) on the door. Onkel Walter was a former classmate and soccer buddy of Papa's, and he and his wife, Toni, were close friends of my parents. Peter and I called them "aunt" and "uncle."

The reason for Onkel Walter's visit was that he had heard about my parents' divorce, and he stopped in to pay a courtesy visit to see if Mom was doing all right. Somewhere in the conversation Mom casually mentioned that she needed to find work and asked him if he thought there would be a job for her with the police. She would be willing to take anything available. Onkel Walter told her he would check. A week later Mom started to work as a cleaning woman—broom artist, as she called it. As always, Mom had been thinking ahead. "As soon as the Blockade is over, consumer goods would become available and we would start needing money," she had told Onkel Walter. In the years to come Mom had more fun working at the police station. She always enjoyed her work regardless of what job she did because she performed it with a positive attitude, and she had a way of making everyone around her glad to be alive.

Springtime in Berlin

I had not really been aware of winter turning into spring, and darkness and despair into light and hope until one day in early May. With the weather getting warmer, I had convinced Mom that I could now walk to school even though it would be about a forty–minute walk each way. This would save having to buy my monthly ticket for the streetcar. Moreover, I loved to walk. One particular day was a bright and sunny one. My walk to school took me alongside the Berlin Botanical Garden, and I could see the spring flowers on the other side of the fence. The sight of those flowers, the warmth of the sunshine, and the talk that was going around that the end of the Blockade was in sight suddenly gave me "hope," and I felt I knew what "renewal of life" was all about. I felt as if I had just been reborn and had started a life in which everything would be OK.

The End of the Blockade

Several days later, vans equipped with loudspeakers announced that the end of the Blockade of Berlin was officially set for May 12. Vans with loudspeakers were normally used to make important announcements because most people no longer owned a radio. During the Blockade newspaper printing and distribution must not have existed. I don't remember anyone reading newspapers. All of our information came by word of mouth or, if it was important, from loudspeaker equipped vans which traveled throughout West Berlin for this purpose. We were elated by this announcement and were anxiously awaiting the magic day on which our ordeal would end.

May 12, 1949—the end of the Berlin Blockade—a day to remember, and the evening, too. There was dancing in the streets and everywhere people were hugging each other. We West Berliners were in a state of celebration as we realized that we had survived another life threatening time filled with extreme hardships. Now 2.2 million overjoyed West Berliners were celebrating their hard–earned freedom.

With the Blockade over, West Berlin had electricity again. In the Klemm's big apartment the electric lights went on. Some of us called to the others to try their lights, and to our amazement they all worked. In disbelief we kept switching them on and off like children, just for the pleasure of it. This was one of the things people did, delighting in little luxuries that had been so long denied them. The Blockade was over. Frau Klemm and Mom kept hugging and crying tears of happiness.

Around the corner in the Schloßstraße we could hear the crowds going wild, chanting "hurrah, we are still alive!" Little did we know at the time that our freedom would still cost us many years of fighting for it. The Cold War had only just begun.

Our heroes—the Airlift crews and support staff—had won the first battle of the Cold War without firing a single shot, and preserved the freedom of 2.2 million West Berliners. In total these crews flew two hundred eighty thousand flights go keep us alive!

For the moment everyone was ecstatically happy. To give us a glimpse into the future, the authorities were able to make available a couple of foods for purchase immediately without ration cards. The first item was canned codfish liver in oil. Mom bought several cans and we feasted on it. It was delicious with some bread, though that was still rationed. We did not have much bread and ate our fill of just the livers. Mom and I both got sick. We could not take the oily livers after our bodies had been deprived of fat for such a long time. Being so hungry, we had been wolfing them down.

It was not as easy as it sounds today to get to the point of "wolfing down" the contents of a can. We had not dealt with canned goods since before the war, and did not own a can opener. Mom attacked the can with a knife, then with a screwdriver and a hammer, all without success. Finally Mom gave up and asked Frau Klemm for help. After a seemingly endless search among unused kitchen utensils, she came up with a prehistoric version of a can opener, and the two women set out to mutilate the can while laughing hysterically. Eventually they managed to create enough of an opening to extract a few of the cod livers, one at a time. Frau Klemm joined us in taking the first delicious tastes. She then departed to rush out and buy some for her family before the supplies ran out. We were so used to limited supplies that we did not believe the authorities when they said there were plenty.

General Clay leaves Berlin

The United States military commander in Europe, General Lucius D. Clay, had been the pillar of fortitude and determination to keep West Berlin free at all cost. He took resolute measures to stay in Berlin, and lead the West Berliners through 328 days of famine and stress. This earned him their greatest admiration.

Before General Clay left Berlin, crowds gathered around the City Hall in Schöneberg to say farewell to one of their heroes. When General Clay made his farewell speech from the City Hall's balcony, he told the congregated Berliners that there were two kinds of heroes—that first there were the pilots who had flown the planes to Berlin in every kind of weather, and the mechanics and ground crews without whom the operation could not have functioned—but that no less important were the Berliners who had made the needed sacrifices to achieve the precious freedom they had chosen.

The crowd saying farewell to Gen. Clay. Without his leadership it is doubtful that the Blockade would have succeeded.

In honor of General Clay who had done so much for Berlin, the boulevard *Kronprinzen Allee*, one of the main thoroughfares in Berlin–Zehlendorf where the American Military Headquarters were located, was renamed *Clay Allee*.

At a later date a Freedom Bell was presented and hung in the tower of West Berlin's City Hall in Schöneberg. Its inscription reads: "That this Nation under God shall have a new Birth of Freedom." We listened to the ceremony and presentation on a radio at school and had chills running up and down our spines. We Berliners knew the meaning of Freedom.

Alice in Wonderland

Now came a time of discovery. Almost every day new and sometimes unknown goods appeared in the stores. Most of them were everyday household items—kitchen things to make chores easier such as sponges— but to us these were nearly unknown. We looked at them as if they were miracles. No, we did not need to own any of those items. We were happy to just see that they existed and we could admire them in the store windows which had been empty for so many years. Most of the store windows still had plywood instead of glass with only small glass inserts, like a mini window in the middle of a large piece of cardboard or plywood. These glass inserts were quite the fashion in those days. The precious piece of glass would have been taken out of a framed picture and installed in the middle of a plywood window where it was more useful. This started to change quite rapidly as glass became available again.

Eastmarks and Westmarks

During the time of the Blockade when we West Berliners were busy surviving, a new currency had been issued in the Russian occupied territory—which now called itself the German Democratic Republic—and marked the separation from the three western Allies. They called their new currency Deutsche Mark as well, and to distinguish the two—Deutsche Mark East and Deutsche Mark West—the currencies were commonly called Eastmark and Westmark. The difference was that the East had printed lots of Eastmarks which were worthless in comparison to the West's new currency. Within a short time the official exchange rate settled on one–to–ten. One Westmark became worth ten Eastmarks, even though the East denied this and insisted that their Eastmark was equal in value to the Westmark.

Berlin was now in a bizarre situation. One city, two governments, and two currencies. Goods had started to become available in East Berlin during the time of the Blockade, and the Russians had used that fact—unsuccessfully—to encourage West Berliners to move to East Berlin. Now with the Blockade being over we could shop in East Berlin—with our Westmarks, of course. We did. It took time before West Berlin's stores started getting goods, but East Berlin already had many things that we had not seen since before the war.

As goods became available in West Berlin as well, there was a lot of shopping being done on both sides, and an interesting thing happened. We paid with both currencies for one item. For example, if an item cost twenty Marks it might be labeled "five Westmarks plus fifteen Eastmarks." Sometimes it was half and half, but mostly the amount to be paid in Eastmark would be much higher. For a period of time, salaries in West Berlin were also paid partly in Westmarks and partly in Eastmarks. This created a lot of confusion. As the rate of exchange went up to twelve Eastmarks and higher for one Westmark, the multi currency arrangement was stopped and Eastmarks were no longer used or accepted in West Berlin. We could shop with them in East Berlin, but there they preferred to receive Westmarks since it was a hard currency. This stopped our shopping in East Berlin.

Food was still rationed in both Berlins, but a few food items were now available without ration cards in West Berlin such as cabbage, potatoes, carrots, or turnips, depending on availability. We no longer were so awfully hungry. Our long–standing prayers of having enough to eat were being answered. Occasionally now we had something to fill our stomachs with.

Mom loved her work at the police station and was glad to have a steady income. She owed this to her farsightedness, and to Onkel Walter for getting her the job.

The Hindenburgdamm apartment building. Our apartment was on the third floor, right.

Summer 1949

One day in early June we had a lucky break. An old family friend who was living in Cologne came to call on us in our room at the Klemm's apartment. She had come to Berlin to visit her mother and father–in–law, and looked us up to tell Mom that her father–in–law was required to sublet two rooms of his apartment. He would prefer to have someone whom he knew, even indirectly. The friend was aware that we had a right to more living space than our present single room, and thought that Mom might like to apply for her father–in–law's two rooms. Delighted with the prospect of more space, Mom promptly went to the authorities and received approval. Two weeks later we left the jolly Klemm family, borrowed a handcart, and moved once again. My shoulders and back were getting strong from the workouts during our many moves. Frau Klemm was especially sad to see her best friend move out, but at the same time she was delighted about our good fortune. We would be only half a mile away and could visit.

The location of the apartment we were moving to was on a major thoroughfare, the Hindenburgdamm in Berlin–Lichterfelde–West. The streetcar line No.74 ran past our apartment building, and the line No.77 was only a few blocks away at Gardeschützenweg. This helped me two years later when I needed to use the No.77 to travel to work.

Wow, this was grand! It was almost like having our own apartment. Herr Walther was a retired official of the BVG, the public transport system of the city of Berlin. His apartment was located in a block of twelve buildings which housed employees of the BVG. He was a widower in his late seventies, and he was not entitled to occupy such a large apartment all by himself. Consequently he moved into one room and we moved into the other two. The best thing for Mom was having the use of the kitchen. Herr Walther always cooked his main meal at noon, and Mom cooked late in the afternoon when she got home from work. Gas was no longer rationed. Mom had the luxury of having the kitchen all to herself whenever she needed to use it. This apartment was bright and sunny. There was a nice balcony off the kitchen, and all windows had glass in them by this time.

We could hardly believe the abundance of space. It was the first time that we lived in more than one room since our early days in Straupitz in the spring of 1943—six years ago.

Peter returns Home

Peter was due to return to Berlin soon after we moved in, and we could not wait to see his eyes getting big when he saw where we lived. We had been on a waiting list for our own apartment since 1943 when bombs had destroyed our apartment building. At this time Berlin's housing shortage was still critical. The wait to get an apartment of our own turned out to be eleven years—June of 1954. Mom and Peter moved into their own apartment two weeks after I had left for the United States.

Peter and the other children in his group returned to Berlin by train in early August. It was wonderful to have our sunshine boy home again. In our happiness to have him back safely, Mom and I could not do enough for our boy. Peter was in exuberant spirits! He ran back and forth in the whole apartment, admiring everything including the bathroom which had a bathtub with a shower in it. There was a hot water heater that could be used when we got coal. Peter even switched on the lights to make sure we really did have electricity again. He also loved watching the streetcars and traffic on this relatively busy street from the window. Mom and I enjoyed watching Peter in his delight.

In retrospect it had been a good decision to let him go and spare him the extreme hardships which the Blockade had imposed on us.

Life in Berlin after the Blockade

After the end of the Blockade West Berlin was starting to make giant strides towards economic recovery. The division of East and West Berlin seemed permanent for the foreseeable future at least, and we were the lucky ones to be *free* West Berliners, thanks to the Allies. We felt safe and secure under their protection.

Mom, Peter, and I were now occupying more than half of a beautiful apartment. We had two fairly large, sunny and bright rooms as well as use of the kitchen and bath. There was also a balcony off the kitchen where years later we could safely keep our bicycles. We lived as if we owned the place. Herr Walther was very kind to us. In a way he looked upon us as if Mom were his daughter and Peter and I his grandchildren. He seemed to be noticeably proud of us when introducing us to his friends. As for me, I felt that I now had a grandfather whom I really never had. I must have been about six years old when I last saw my grandfather Hinniger, and Peter had been too young to remember him at all. We never met grandfather Stanneck.

Herr Walther liked to tell me about the "good old times" when Berlin had horse drawn streetcars, and Lichterfelde—where we now lived—was a village near Berlin. I loved listening to his stories which he told with a good amount of humor.

There were twelve entrances to the block of buildings which were set in a horseshoe shape. This picture shows the courtyard inside the horseshoe.

There was a connection between us. Herr Walther's daughter–in–law grew up in the apartment next door to my father. She was two years older than Papa, and they went to the same school. She and her family now lived in Cologne. After we had moved into her mother's spare room next door to our Grandma, Frau Walther visited us whenever she came to Berlin to see her mother and father–in–law. She had been so kind to keep track of us and our situation, and it was she who looked us up at the Klemm's apartment to tell Mom about her father–in–law being required to take people into his apartment.

Now, whenever she and her husband or their son came to Berlin to visit, they would always stop in to see us in our section of their father's apartment. I remember the first time they came and brought some chocolate for Peter and me. It was such a treat. Chocolate had already become available in West Germany, but not as yet in West Berlin.

We still had ration cards. For several years to come West Berlin would lag behind in economic development because of its unique situation and isolation from the rest of the West. Before the war, Berlin's produce had come from the surrounding farmland which was now East

Germany. At this time everything West Berlin consumed had to come from West Germany. West Berlin was being referred to as an "Island in the Red Sea."

Peter in school.

My Brother Peter

Peter adjusted well to the new neighborhood. He always made friends easily being sociable and outgoing. Our apartment building was part of a block of twelve buildings set in a horseshoe shape. In the center of this horseshoe was a landscaped area which surrounded a fountain. There was a nice playground and a sandbox behind the buildings at the northeast side of the horseshoe. Peter spent a lot of time there with his friends. He still loved the sandbox even though he was eleven years old. We used to tease him about being a little too old for it, but his friends were right there with him. Years later on his Confirmation Day we took a picture of Peter in his first dark dress suit with the sandbox in the foreground.

Then there was school. Peter did not like school. As far as he was concerned, the world would be a wonderful place to live in if only there was no school. He has always been an outdoor person and was endlessly on the go with his friends. Sitting in a classroom seemed to Peter like serving a term in prison.

Mom had been the youngest of five children, and she grew used to getting away with things because parental supervision was scarce. Her parents had a store to tend to. This turned Mom into a wonderful, understanding and forgiving mother, although she was strict where it was needed.

When Peter was younger and we lived in the village of Straupitz, we used to have to go out and look for him when it was time to come home in the evening. Now he was required to be home at a set time, which he usually was. He knew what Mom's punishment for him would be and he did not want to invite it. The worst sentence Mom could give to Peter was "house arrest." To him it might as well have been capital punishment. Whenever Peter had house arrest he would stand by the window and longingly look out and watch his friends "be free." He would beg Mom to spank him or take away other privileges, including food, instead. Hard as it was on softhearted Mom, she would stand firm while silently she was suffering as much as Peter. Sometimes she could no longer stand the agony and would shorten the sentence.

One evening was a "heart attack producer" for Mom and me. Peter had not come home at the set time. As minutes turned into an hour, and then more, we were getting quite worried and were sure that something terrible had happened to him. At that time there were countless people disappearing from West Berlin who were kidnapped by the Soviets. Although we had not heard about children disappearing, there was always the possibility. Nobody trusted the Soviet regime. Then there were other awful things that could have happened to Peter. We did not have a radio, nor did people have telephones, and he had so many friends that we had no idea whom he was out with that day.

Finally, nearly two hours late, Peter arrived at home and told us his unfortunate story. He and a couple of his friends had found out that the escalators were now in operation at the Schöneberg interchange station of the *S–Bahn*, the electric elevated city train. The highlight of a trip to Grandparents Hinniger for me as a young child had always been the treat of riding the escalators when Mom and I were changing trains at that station. Peter is four years younger than I am, and he had never seen escalators in operation anywhere. Naturally the boys considered it a "must" to go there and experience the miracle of "riding on stairs." Peter and his friends spent the afternoon at the Schöneberg Station and forgot about the time while having fun riding up and down on the escalators for hours. It was summer and still daylight, so they did not notice when it got late. Just as they realized that they would be late getting home, the Railroad Station Police caught them and held them for an hour, and lecturing them on being a nuisance.

Our first reaction, of course, was relief to have Peter home safely. His story was amusing as he described to us all the fun that he and his friends had. While they were having a lot of fun "riding on stairs" without having to walk them, they were also clowning around after the novelty of just riding had worn off. They deserved being lectured by the Station Police about how dangerous it was to run up a down–escalator, and down on an up–escalator, and how easily someone could get hurt. Mom felt that this was not a time to punish Peter. He had already served his sentence in being frightened by the Station Police. We were amused about Peter telling us that it was not his fault for getting home so late, but rather the police's. Mom and I were just happy to have our boy back.

School

There was still a critical shortage of school buildings. Going to school in shifts continued to be routine. We switched weekly. One week we would go to school from 8 a.m. until 12:50 p.m., and the next week from 1 p.m. until 6 p.m. This meant that every other week we had a short weekend when we got out of school at 6 p.m. on Saturday night and had to be back at 8 a.m. on Monday morning. School was in session six days a week. I attended Business School from September 1948 until June 1951.

Soon after we moved to the Hindenburgdamm apartment, I started out for school one morning and met one of my classmates who was just walking out of the apartment building next door. Her name was Gerda Dietrich. From that day on we always walked to and from school together. Both Gerda and I were fast walkers and we could get to school in twenty to twenty–five minutes. These walks together started a lifelong friendship for us. Before I emigrated to the United States, Gerda met and later married Gerhard Strecker who worked as a plumber at Tempelhof Airport for thirty–seven years. They still live in Berlin with their family. We stayed in contact and see each other every time I am in Berlin.

Margot König was another friend I made while in Business School. She was a war orphan and grew up with her aunt's family. A year after I left for the United States she moved to Hamburg to take a job there. We are still in touch by mail and telephone, although we have not been able to see each other more than three or four times over the years. My many visits to see older relatives in Berlin never left time for a trip to Hamburg.

Things I Remember About School at that Time

Business School was fun. I loved learning about bookkeeping, and I especially liked typing. Shorthand was a challenge, as far as working up to a certain speed with those peculiar little symbols. The problem with typing was that no practicing could be done except at school during the lessons. Nobody had a typewriter at home. Paper to write on was precious and of poorest quality. Pencils were "nursed" along until they were down to the last three centimeters or less, if possible. Books were not available and only the teacher had one. The study texts were read to us and we had to take notes. This gave us the chance for practical application of our shorthand skills immediately.

While this was called a business school, it can be compared with a high school in the United States, but with specialized courses for students expecting to become secretaries, bookkeepers, or going into business administration. In this school I was taught office skills and procedures, as well as typing, shorthand, bookkeeping, office management, economics, the use of then existing office machines, business correspondence, and business administration. In addition there were the general courses such as mathematics, history, geography, home economics, calligraphy, and a foreign language—which was English since we lived in the American sector of Berlin. Unlike the grade schools at that time, this school was coeducational.

Normally it was a two–year program. In 1948 a three year program was offered for the first time as an experiment. I had enrolled in it because at age fourteen I was too young to go to Teachers College, and I was also the youngest of the forty–seven girls in my class. No boys had enrolled in the experimental three–year program. Our teacher was Herr Berndt, who was in his mid–forties. I remember him as being a cynical and unhappy man. At some point we learned that he had lost his wife and two children in the air raids, and we could understand his unhappiness, though not his antagonism and unkindness towards us.

Our five–hour school days were divided into three ninety minute sessions with two breaks. During the longer, fifteen–minute break we devoured our half liter of hot soup which was dispensed in all schools every day. Then we were required to walk around in the school yard, rain or shine, to get some fresh air for the balance of the break. We were in the American sector and the soup we received reflected this

Class picture at Business School—1949

since the food was donated by the Americans. Cookie soup was everyone's favorite without exception. We were children and liked sweets, as all children do. The wonderful cookie soup often had chunks of cookies in it. We loved it! Every Friday we received a one and a quarter ounce chocolate bar in addition to our soup. This had started before the end of the Blockade and was the highlight of the week for us. Chocolate had been a faraway memory until then.

Four of the girls in my class lived in the towns of Teltow and Mahlow which are located just outside the Berlin city limits in the Soviet occupation zone. The *S–Bahn*, Berlin's electric elevated city train—managed by the Soviet administration—still traveled freely to all areas of the lines' network. The girls had special permission to come to our school in West Berlin, even during the Blockade.

One of our courses in home economics was a cooking class. This required us to provide the ingredients for the dish to be cooked. None of the girls' families could spare any of their still rationed foods. We were able to bring to class some flour, milk, and an egg from our rations for the Swedish pancakes that were on the menu for our first week's lesson. Another time we cooked a simple soup. However, dishes requiring meat were impossible, and the cooking class had to be abandoned for lack of food to cook.

After the doomed cooking class, our home economics course went on to sewing. Here I was in my element. When we had a needle threading contest, my friend Brigitte and I were the two fastest ones and had to compete against each other. I won, and Mom was so proud of me. Some fabrics had started to become available. After the inevitable simple project of making an apron, we then were taught how to make a blouse. Having inherited my aptitude for sewing from Mom, it was difficult for me to understand why most girls had trouble. I was working on a second blouse when some were still struggling with the apron.

Shorthand was fun and became quite a challenge. We had to master the interesting little symbols, one for each individual letter at first, and later one symbol representing a word or a whole phrase. Simultaneously we needed to pick up speed. Our teacher, Herr Dross, dictated at different speeds and one had to be able to write, and read back perfectly, whatever had been dictated. It took a lot of practice to get up to the speed that was required of us, and I felt that I did not get enough practice during classes.

This gave me an idea. I could probably coax Mom into reading some text that I could use for dictation practice. It would help me work up to a higher speed level. When I asked her, my ever accommodating Mom said she would do it, and she even agreed when I wanted to invite three of my friends to our first session. Mom did not dictate the text I had given her with the even speed that we were used to from Herr Dross. Poor Mom, she had no experience with this and I criticized her for not dictating exactly as Herr Dross did. Later in the real world I learned that no boss dictated with Herr Dross's evenness, but rather in spurts, as the thoughts were coming to him. At the time I did not know any better, and Mom was happy to be "fired" from the dictation job.

Life Improves

Money had purchasing power again as consumer goods slowly became available. Mom had purchased a used sewing machine, and both of us were starting to make some clothes which we urgently needed. Everything we owned was worn and patched, though usable, which had been most important in this "land of nothing." Now we were on the threshold of better times—we hoped.

A favorite pastime for people who live in cities was, and still is, to go window shopping, especially now that store windows were made of glass again and there were goods being offered for sale. It was wonderful to go looking, and to find out that money could actually buy merchandise once again. After so many years of consumer goods being unavailable, everybody needed everything. All we needed now was enough money—I mean lots of it! To put this statement into perspective, one pair of shoes cost more than an office secretary's monthly salary was at that time. I had almost two more years of school ahead of me before I would be able to work and earn anything. That would only happen if I could then find a job. Jobs were scarce and people worked for extremely low wages just to have work.

One of the items we needed to purchase immediately was another bed, although it had to be on credit as was customary. The three of us were still sleeping in the king–size bed, which was all we had. We did not even own a sofa. Mom and I decided that we would buy a wall bed which could be folded away in the daytime since it had to be placed in the living room. During the day it was like a narrow cabinet against the wall with a shelf on top, and at night the bed could be folded out. The king–size bed was actually two single beds put together, so we then really had three single beds. Peter and I fought over the new foldaway bed, and ended up taking turns.

Winter 1949—1950

While all winters in northern Germany are cold, dark, and dreary with only about seven hours of daylight, this one promised to be a better one than the many previous winters. Not that anything had changed about the weather or the number of daylight hours, but rather our general condition had changed so much for the better. We lived in a comfortable apartment, had rations for coal and a stove to burn it in, had almost enough food to eat, and we even had electricity so we did not have to sit in the dark. What else could we ask for?

Christmas was approaching and we could even buy or make little presents for each other. In school we were allowed to bring in a candle and some greens to put on our desks, and as a special treat on Saturday afternoons we were allowed to light our candles. At that point our teacher knew what was coming: "Please, Herr Berndt, tell us about America."

On Being a POW in America

Herr Berndt had been one of the lucky people who became a prisoner of war of the Americans. He had been shipped to the United States to work in orange groves in Arizona. One afternoon in the winter during the Blockade when it was too dark to read by 3:30 p.m. and there was no electricity, Herr Berndt had volunteered to tell us about America. It was Saturday, and he felt we had earned a treat.

He did not realize what he was starting. We were absolutely spellbound by all the wonderful things he told us about. Oranges—the prisoners were picking oranges. Our expressions were question marks. Many of us looked at each other, but did not want to interrupt the spell of the tale by asking questions. As Herr Berndt went on talking about picking oranges and being allowed to eat all he wanted, one girl finally had the courage to interrupt. She raised her hand, then asked the crucial question: "Herr Berndt, what are oranges?" He had forgotten that we were too young to remember, and he tried to describe to us what oranges looked like and how they tasted. When I got home that day I asked Mom if I had ever eaten oranges. She said I had when I was about two years old. It has to be pointed out that Germany cannot grow tropical fruits, and imports of that kind must have been discontinued long before the war started. I was fifteen years old, but some of my classmates were sixteen and seventeen, and they did not remember oranges either.

Herr Berndt told us about the climate in Arizona, how it is a desert and sunny all of the time, even in the winter. Sunny days sound wonderful to northern Europeans. He then told us about some marvelous inventions of technology—air conditioning—and heat which turned on automatically when it was cold. In the summer it gets so very hot in the daytime that the buildings have to be cooled. We could not even understand the concept of air conditioning. He told us that both the cooling and heating functioned automatically. Our eyes nearly popped out of our heads from astonishment—"automatic" heat? We were teenagers and had chores to do at home. One of the more unpleasant ones was to go into the dark basement of the apartment building and carry buckets of coal up three or four flights of stairs—and we thought that we were lucky because we had coal at all.

We could almost not believe Herr Berndt's amazing stories. Some of them may have been made up later on when we kept begging him to tell us more. To us they were a special treat, and a glimpse into a land of endless space and the freedom to explore that space.

Our Papa, by contrast, had been a POW in Russia. He was so starved when he returned home that he was lucky to have reached home at all. To hear Herr Berndt tell it, the American POWs were allowed to eat all the oranges they wanted and received regular good meals as well. Meanwhile in our world—with Berlin being blockaded at the time Herr Berndt told us this particular story—all of us were ready to sign up to become POWs in America.

12

1950
School and the Start of Normal Times
Age Fifteen

When we returned to school after the new year had started, our teacher reminded us that this was not only the beginning of another year but also of a new half century. The previous half century had not been a good one for Germany. It had brought us two disastrous world wars, a horrible depression, runaway inflation, as well as hardships, sorrow, and starvation after each war. While we were not out of the woods yet, we schoolgirls were young and filled with hope for the future. We could not then imagine that Germany and Berlin would stay divided for thirty–nine more years, and that both parts of Germany would recover from the war and its aftermath at a shockingly uneven pace.

At the time of this writing another half of a century has gone by, and I often think back on that first day of school in 1950. We reviewed all the developments in the different fields of science, medicine, and technology that had been a part of the first half of the twentieth century, and we could not imagine the changes that would take place in the second. I am writing this book on a computer which superceded the electric typewriter a quarter of a century ago. It, in turn, superceded the manual typewriter on which I was taught how to type. I cannot help but reflect on the most recent fifty years and the giant strides that have been made in every field.

Back then at the beginning of 1950, the West Berlin economy was making tremendous progress. Businesses sprouted out of the rubble as more and more merchandise became available. Even some foods could now be purchased without ration cards. In school we still received our half liter of soup every day, and a small chocolate bar on Fridays. We thought we were in heaven.

Personal Problems

I have always been very shy, and I blushed easily. In school, when the teacher asked the class a question we raised our hands if we knew the answer. When called on to speak, the rules were to stand up out of respect for the teacher. Whenever I stood up to answer the question I would always blush. I don't know why, other than being shy. The kids would then laugh and tease me about it. This blushing has been a curse all of my life and it may account for my lacking in verbal skills.

Naturally I preferred not to participate in school plays, but if I was asked to do so, I would try for a role that required no talking, or as little as possible. Our school put on a short Christmas play even during the Blockade, and I remember that one vividly. Since there was no electricity, the only light in the auditorium came from candles that rows of angels were holding both on the stage and around the perimeter of the auditorium. Hurrah for me, the angels were silent. All they had to do was stand there wrapped in a white bed sheet, hold a lit candle, and look decorative. The difficult part about being angels was having to stand up for a long time. We were all emaciated angels, and some of us fainted from lack of nourishment. I was one of the angels they lost, and I remember that I did not even blush with embarrassment.

One of the other shortcomings I have is that I cannot sing. Some of the girls in my class could sing beautifully, and I admired their talent. Throughout my school years I suffered tremendously from this lack of ability. I hated report card time because we were always tested for singing. This meant that each of us had to stand up in front of the teacher and the whole class, and sing a song. For me it was agony of the greatest proportion. Not only did I suffer humiliation when some classmates already laughed before I started to sing, but I never got very far into a song before the teacher could no longer stand to listen to me and waved for me to stop. One of the worst things about this testing was that the teacher called on us in alphabetical order. With my last name being Stanneck I had to wait until near the end, which prolonged my suffering.

As was the case with most classes of school children after the war, we were a motley bunch of recent origin and ages. Most of the children had been from Berlin originally, but were evacuated sometime during the war and eventually returned to Berlin. While Mom, Peter and I returned from the Russian occupied territory at the end of 1946, others were not so lucky. We still had new girls come into class occasionally who had just now returned from the eastern territory given to Poland. They had not joined the refugee trek in time and were then held back as prisoners. The arriving girls always wore kerchiefs because their heads had been shaved to control lice. Most of them had not been to school in several years, and they were therefore two or three years older than everybody else in our class.

My problem was the opposite. I had skipped the sixth grade and was almost a year younger than everyone else. This has hurt me during my teenage years. While I had no troubles with my school work, I never adjusted socially. Being barely fifteen when all of my peers were anywhere from sixteen to nineteen was an awful spot to be in. On top of that I was very shy, and I was really still a child. It was difficult for me to understand why my classmates were so keen on silk stockings, hairdos, male movie stars, and impressing boys. Consequently I was left out of their conversations about those subjects on the grounds that I was not yet grown up enough. This experience hurt me at the time, and I never overcame being uncomfortable in social situations. I always felt that I did not belong, especially when people were talking about things that I was not knowledgeable about.

Problems with my Teacher

Another problem I had was that Herr Berndt, our homeroom teacher, did not like me. This was obvious not only to my peers, but also to other teachers. The latter I did not know until my shorthand teacher told me that he and other teachers had been comparing notes. They were wondering why I got only mediocre grades from Herr Berndt when I was getting excellent grades in all subjects which others taught. Herr Dross, my typing and shorthand teacher, asked me what was going on, but I only shrugged my shoulders. Herr Dross said he would have a talk with Herr Berndt.

I knew one of the reasons. When giving the answer to a question, whether the answer was correct or not, Herr Berndt always made a cynical remark. This bothered most of us, but I must have been more sensitive about it, and I resented the way he treated us. When he also made snide remarks about my blushing—which really hurt and embarrassed me—I stopped giving answers. Whenever I was called on to give an answer, I would stand up as was required, but would say nothing no matter how sarcastic his remarks were. Out of respect for the teacher I could not defend myself. Silence was my only weapon for most of the three years. In his sarcastic manner Herr Berndt labeled me the "Great Silence."

The other reason did not come to me until forty–five years later, when Margot, a close friend and former classmate, and I discussed it. Herr Berndt had named her Silence Number Two because she had been rebelling for the same reasons. Margot had asked me in a letter: "Why would you not talk when everybody including the teacher was aware that you always knew the answers to the questions that were asked?"

I thought about this question of hers for days after reading her letter. Suddenly I knew. The answer came to me like an enlightenment, so that I picked up the phone and called Margot in Hamburg. The answer to Margot's question was so obvious now that I was forty–five years older.

Herr Berndt was then in his mid–forties and "reigned" over a class of forty–seven teenage girls. Most of the girls had a crush on him, which he enjoyed, and he resented anyone who didn't. Some of the girls might even have had more than a crush. I remember Alexandra going to pieces when he announced that he had remarried—he had lost his wife and children during the war. I had been puzzled about Alexandra's reaction at the time.

At the age of fourteen when I first met him, I was still a child in that respect. To me Herr Berndt was my teacher and to be respected, but I also expected to be treated as a student and not be bombarded with his cynical personal comments. In other words, even though he did not like me—which did not bother me—he could at least have been polite. Margot agreed with me in all aspects and the "light went on" in her mind as we talked. She was surprised that it took us all those years to figure out why the two of us, plus a few others, were at such odds with the teacher. To prove that our conclusion was pretty much on target, I reminded Margot that Herr Berndt had given a photograph of himself to each one of us at graduation time. How could we forget him?

Then in 1951 the culmination of this battle came when it was time to issue our final report cards before graduation. Under pressure from the other teachers Herr Berndt was more fair with my grades, except for one. He just had to sock it to me in some way. Even now I laugh out loud every time I think about it. Just before the final exams were to start, Herr Berndt said to me one day in front of the whole class: "Stanneck, I am going to give you one D. In which subject do you want it?" The whole class gasped. I chose Politics which I disliked, but he insisted that I was good at that and suggested Geography. I did not care. Either way I had enough A's and B's to keep up my average. That D in Geography certainly has not kept me from finding my way around in many places of the world. Over the years I have had many good laughs about my three–year battle fought with silence.

West Berlin Recovers

We were having more food to eat now, and our bodies as well as our spirits recovered. Our horizons started expanding beyond the boundaries of just survival and staying alive.

By now Mom and I had been to the theater and the opera, and we had become aware of the rest of the city again. It still looked dismal in East Berlin. The mountains of rubble in the streets and on the sidewalks were just as much a part of the scene now as they had been five years earlier at the end of the war. Most of the rubble in West Berlin had been cleared, and ruins which were beyond repair had been taken down.

We could shop in East Berlin because they wanted our Westmarks. However, none of the police or other government employees were allowed to go into East Berlin. The East Berlin police was a part of the military, and they resented the West Berlin police. If given the chance they would find an excuse to lock up a West Berlin employee or official. It was not safe for Mom to go into East Berlin because she worked for the police. Mom's two brothers lived over there. She asked her younger brother, Helmut, to buy her two oriental rugs. They were imitation, but we were happy to have these beautiful rugs in our living room. Eventually they even traveled to the United States with Mom. She was so proud of them. They were lovely and of good quality.

Other than being at odds with Herr Berndt, I enjoyed school and learning business skills in preparation for getting a job and earning money. The idea of adding three more years of studies to become a teacher had been scrapped. I needed to earn money to help Mom. She was struggling with supporting both Peter and me while we were still in school. Peter was not due to graduate from elementary school until 1953. Because of the large percentage of unemployment in West Berlin, a ninth grade had been added to elementary school.

We took two class trips while in Business School. One was a nature trip early in the summer on which we hiked, roamed, marched, and sang our way through what was left of Berlin's beloved forest, the *Grunewald*. The other trip was in the fall when the big Industrial Fair was held at Berlin's Fairgrounds by the *Funkturm* (Berlin's Radio Tower). It was informative to see new developments in Germany's reviving industry, and each of us hoped to find employment in some part of this industry in the future.

Mom was proud of me for doing so well in school. She felt reassured that with this education I would be well equipped to get a good job some day. Knowing how much I liked my typing classes, she surprised me with a used typewriter for my birthday. I was elated. Owning my own typewriter would enable me to practice my typing and gain more speed.

My First Trip to West Germany

My friend Gerda belonged to a youth activities group at church. She had talked me into participating, and we had some fun times in discussion groups, playing table games, and going on hikes. This church group also arranged for a trip to the island of Sylt in the North Sea during the August school vacation. Mom was delighted and wanted me to go even though I insisted that we could not afford it. The trip was actually quite inexpensive because it was a group trip and subsidized by the church. Somehow Mom scraped together enough money for me to go. Now that life was getting back to being more normal, she wanted me to participate in such special events to somewhat compensate for the deprivations which had been so much a part of my young life.

The Island of Sylt consists mostly of sand dunes. Pictured is the church in Hörnum and a part of our camp—visible are two of the tents to the left of the church tower.

It was a sixteen–day trip. We went by bus through the hated Russian occupation zone without abnormal delay, then north via Hamburg and into Germany's northernmost province of Schleswig–Holstein, Germany's dairy land. I loved riding on the bus and seeing what this country we lived in looked like. At a little town close to the Danish border we boarded a train. It was fun to ride across a causeway to the town of Westerland on the island of Sylt, and on to Hörnum, the southernmost town on the island where our church camp was located. We enjoyed sun, sand dunes, and swimming in the sea, as well as boat trips to nearby little islands. At night we slept in tents on beds of straw, and I loved it, especially when it rained. All too soon it was time to return home with a big collection of wonderful memories.

Christmas Trees and The Cold War

Christmas was near and this year everyone was excited about it because we could buy little gifts, or materials with which to make gifts for our loved ones. We were all looking forward to the happiest Christmas we have had in many years, or in memory, for the younger children.

However, it turned into another story of the Cold War. We West Berliners on our "Island in the Red Sea" saw once again how fragile the threads of peace and hope were. We had survived the war and the Blockade, but little things did mean a lot, especially to children, as our world was very small having been confined because of deprivations. We still had ration cards for most food items, but some clothing and household articles had become available. We could even buy candles for our Christmas tree. However, there were no Christmas trees. This time the Cold War seemed to be directed at the children!

About two weeks before Christmas, vehicles carrying Christmas trees to West Berlin were turned back at all border crossings. Whoever had purchased a Christmas tree earlier was the lucky one. Living in apartments, most people did not buy their trees until about a week before Christmas unless there was a balcony to store the tree and keep it cool until it was time to decorate it on Christmas Eve.

When the news of "no Christmas trees" got around, the then still remaining ones were sold out within minutes. It was a devastating blow to us children to think about Christmas without a tree. In school we talked about how we could build a Christmas tree by drilling holes into a broomstick and inserting pine boughs. Unfortunately, while we may all have owned a broom, not enough boughs existed in all of Berlin to provide a Christmas tree for each family with children. Our beloved Grunewald forest needed many more years to recuperate from the devastation of the bombs and the pillage during some record cold winters. People who owned homes and had "Christmas trees" or other evergreens growing in their yards found that these disappeared overnight.

We children had missed out on so much in our short lives without ever complaining. We accepted things as they were, mostly because we did not know any better and there was no choice. But to purposely blockade Christmas trees from being brought to Berlin was incomprehensible. It was an intentional attack on innocent children.

As the time of the Christmas holiday came closer we became more restless. We dreamed about Christmas trees and in school we talked about not much else. "Of course, the trucks with the Christmas trees would be permitted to pass the border at the last moment. The Soviets just could not be that cruel." Unfortunately we children trusted in vain. This was the Cold War, and Stalin had no heart for children.

Peter and I pestered Mom about a Christmas tree. We knew from experience that Mom would do her "magic" once again and somehow come up with a tree. She always knew a way out, or she invented something. Unfortunately this time even she, too, believed that nobody could be so heartless, and that the borders were sure to open at the very last minute. When this did not happen and it was three days before Christmas, Mom promised Peter and me that on the day of Christmas Eve she would bring home a tree for us. Our question as to where she would get one was answered with "trust me, we will have a Christmas tree." Afterwards Peter and I realized that Mom did not want to disclose her idea as to the source lest we talk about it in school and ruin her plan. Her mind had obviously shifted to Plan B.

Only our Mom could have Done It!

Mom had promised to bring home a Christmas tree in the early afternoon of Christmas Eve. School was out early that day and Peter and I stood by the window waiting with much anticipation. Eventually we sighted Mom as she rounded the corner two blocks away. She was walking and pushing her bicycle with a precious Christmas tree on it. A miracle had happened. We were not going to have Christmas without a Christmas tree after all! Mom had to literally fight her way through crowds of people who wanted to know where they could buy Christmas trees at this time. They assumed that the borders must have opened for the trucks loaded with Christmas trees for West Berlin.

Peter and I raced downstairs and nearly carried the tree, bike and Mom up the three flights of stairs. We had a Christmas tree! When the precious tree was safely in our room, Mom told us her story.

At the time Mom worked at Berlin–Steglitz Police Precinct 193 as a cleaning woman. In early December the Police Station had purchased a very large Christmas tree. Their tree was usually placed in a big room with a high ceiling on the ground level of the building where the policemen spent their off–duty hours during work time. Also located in the downstairs area were a number of cells for people who had to be locked up temporarily, as well as a kitchen which was Mom's domain. The offices were upstairs.

Starting at lunchtime on Christmas Eve there was a Christmas party going on at the offices and everybody, including Mom, was upstairs. While the office staff and off–duty policemen were busy celebrating, Mom went downstairs to "take care of" the Christmas tree. She removed the ornaments from that huge tree, sawed the tree in half, decorated the bottom half of the tree with all of the ornaments, and took off with the much nicer looking top half which was big enough to be a regular size tree for us, reaching from the table nearly to the ceiling of our apartment.

Who can steal a Christmas tree from the police without getting caught? To solve this case did not require the involvement of the crime department at Police Precinct 193. Everybody figured out immediately that it was one of Mom's pranks once again. She had a tremendous sense of humor and was always up to practical jokes. Everybody loved her. Now some were angry. After all, they did not have a Christmas tree for their children. But most of the policemen thought it was funny and so typical of Mom's spirit and finding a way to cope. She needed a Christmas tree for her children and decided that half a tree was adequate for the off–duty policemen. Consequently she took it upon herself to help them share their tree.

Mom, of course, was the only one who could get away with it because she was just the cleaning woman and not a law enforcement officer.

One of the policemen, the old family friend who hat gotten the job for Mom, even came to visit us during the holidays to see what the other half of the tree looked like. He worked at a different precinct but had heard about it there. The following year they were teasing Mom, saying that they had better put their Christmas tree on chains and post a guard because certain people had the nerve to steal the Christmas tree right from under the nose of the police.

Our Christmas was wonderful, though marred by thoughts of the many children in West Berlin who had no Christmas trees. Even during the Blockade the Allies had flown in Christmas trees for all families with children.

I received a pair of ice skates for Christmas and I thought I was in heaven. Along with the ice skates were a pair of ankle high shoes which were needed to screw the skates onto. The ankle high shoes got a lot of wear in the years to come, but never with the ice skates. They were my first pair of new shoes since early in the war. Unfortunately in early February I severely sprained my right wrist, and I had to have my right arm in a splint for several weeks. I was warned by the doctor that I had to be careful because the next time I sprained my wrist in this manner it would be much more serious. This made me realize how much I needed my wrists for shorthand and typing in school. After I finished school the following summer, I had to find work and help Mom by earning some money. I could not take a chance on messing up my arms. The family's welfare was at stake. Reluctantly, but probably wisely, I gave up any thought of ice skating for fear of again injuring my wrist.

Peter immediately appropriated my ice skates when it became apparent that I would never use them. He put them to good use playing ice hockey, and eventually he became a member of a team playing not only in Berlin but also in West Germany.

13

1951
My First Job
Age Sixteen

Many good things happened during this year. The most important one was that Germany was making giant strides towards getting back to normal. Rationing stopped in West Germany in March, except for milk and sugar. West Berlin, by contrast, was taken off rationing in stages, and the last of rationing did not end until 1953. East Berlin continued to ration some foods, including meat and bread, until May of 1958. West Berlin was always a special case because of its isolation from West Germany. Everything good during the recovery period happened in West Germany long before it happened in Berlin.

In order to help West Berlin's economy get healthy again, West Germans had to pay a 2% hardship tax (*Notopfer)* for Berlin, plus two pennies extra postage on each piece of mail which amounted to an extra 10% of the regular postage. This tax created animosity in parts of West Germany, particularly in Bavaria. Berlin had formerly been the capital of Prussia, and the Bavarians and the Prussians have hated each other since the beginning of history. There was a lot of hostility reported at times when Berliners traveled to Bavaria because the Bavarians felt that their hardship taxes were paying for the Berliners' vacation trips. Was this peace? Had they forgotten so soon?

My Ski Trip

In January an opportunity came to go on a two–week ski instruction trip in the nearby Harz Mountains. A group from the older classes at school was going, and our physical education teacher offered to let anyone from our class participate. I was one of three from my class who went. Mom had had a memorable trip to the Harz Mountains in her youth, and she really wanted me to go. The total cost was only twenty–six Westmarks. We didn't have the money to spare at the time, but Mom borrowed it from her sister Lotte who had the butcher shop.

I have always loved winter, snow, and cold weather, and I was overjoyed at the prospect of learning how to ski. I was also anxiously looking forward to seeing mountains. Berlin is flat and I had seen hills before but never real mountains. The highest point in the Harz Mountains is only about thirty–eight hundred feet, but it sounded impressive to us flat landers.

The Harz Mountains by the most direct route are less than two hundred miles from Berlin. However, we had to travel nearly half again as far because of needing to cross the East–West German border at Marienborn/Helmstedt before we could proceed south.

Here is an excerpt from my diary about the border crossing part of the trip:

> We cleared Dreilinden, the West Berlin border into East Germany without much formality. Three hours later we arrived at Marienborn in the pouring rain. It was nice and warm in the bus and we hoped to be able to stay in it. No such luck. We were told to get off the bus and walk to a long military barracks building to have our passports and hand luggage checked. Meanwhile the bus was checked out separately, and with our baggage it then drove on through the barrier. Inside the building we waited in lines at different counters to have our papers checked, written on, and stamped. After the hand luggage check we had to walk out of East Germany and across the border to the checkpoint of British occupied West Germany for a routine stamp in our passports. Sopping wet and chilled to the bones we boarded our bus to continue the journey.

The crossing at checkpoints and the formalities were usually accompanied by unnecessary delays and often made very unpleasant—and even scary—by Soviet harassment. Security was constantly reinforced, and this went on until Germany's reunification in 1989. No wonder the poor "island–dwelling" Berliners became known as being a rude species. They were frazzled by years of having to endure those conditions.

Here are examples of some of the standard harassment techniques: Driving on the Autobahn through the Soviet occupation zone—a distance of only one hundred and ten miles—took more than three hours of driving time, not counting the time spent at the border crossings at each end. The reason for this were the speed limits. One would start out with a normal speed limit of sixty miles per hour and suddenly, unexpectedly and for no reason at all, find a twenty–five miles per hour sign. At that very point one had better be at the posted speed because the East German officials were waiting. The fines were stiff and had to be paid on the spot in Westmarks. For the entire one hundred and ten miles they had the speed limits alternating between fast and slow, always at different sections of the highway. People did not dare drive fast for fear of coming around a bend and finding a low speed limit sign without having time to slow down.

The other sure money maker for East Germany was the total absence of road signs when approaching Berlin. Here the Autobahn splits into several different directions. It was required to take the direct and only approved road to checkpoint Dreilinden to enter West Berlin. Taking the wrong fork resulted in people having to pay dearly for it, or they would go to jail for two weeks. This happened to my Uncle Martin one time. He was stopped immediately after having taken the wrong fork and requested to show the visa which permitted him to be on that particular section of the Autobahn. Of course he had no visa—he had no intention of traveling there. He was fined three hundred Westmarks, or he could have gone to jail for two weeks. Three hundred marks was a large sum, but traveling the Autobahn one needed to carry that much cash, just in case. People always paid the fine rather than go to jail—there was no assurance the East German police would ever let them back out. The East German regime counted on people paying. It was their way of raising hard currency. My uncle never drove to West Germany again after that incident. It was not the money as much as the fear of losing their freedom that terrified people.

Other harassment consisted of unnecessary holdups of traffic, slow-down of processing the passport checks, delays by checking every inch of every car, and opening all the luggage. The list is endless. My husband Mal, and I experienced this in 1960 when our car was selected for an hour long search.

Back to my ski trip. My diary continues:

> Our accommodations are at a charming youth hostel in the village of Torfhaus at about 2,500 feet elevation. Upon arrival it is snowing, and we no longer worry whether we will have any snow to ski in. It had been raining until we got to the higher elevation.
>
> During our tour of the hostel, disappointment takes over. The rooms are small and cold, and the water seems to come straight off of a glacier. We froze all night in the unheated rooms, then got smart and now we dress instead of undressing before going to bed.
>
> The hostel mother is amazed at how much food the Berliners devour. We do not yet have all the food we want to eat since most food is still rationed in Berlin. Here we are thriving on two weeks of plentiful food and fresh air.
>
> We had our first ski lesson and practice. The forest with the snow–laden trees looks like a picture postcard. All I can think of is the abundance of "Christmas trees," and that most of the kids in our group had celebrated Christmas without a tree.

Youth Hostel and view of "Brocken", the highest point in the Harz mountains, which is in East Germany.

There is lots of new snow and we enjoy our lessons, excursions on skis, as well as downhill skiing. During a couple of clear, sunny days we could see the highest peak of the Harz Mountains, the Brocken, and a big hotel near the top. An excursion to it is out of the question as it is located in East Germany.

Once a day we have a work session. This is not a school vacation. School is in session and the participants of this trip had to be good students if they wanted to be excused from classes. The only skill likely to suffer is our shorthand speed. One of the two teachers who came along has to give us forty minutes of dictation every day, dictating at the speed of a hundred and twenty syllables per minute. German words are long, and shorthand speed is measured in syllables instead of words per minute. We do not like having to take short-hand dictation each day, but it was the condition for being excused from classes.

Our group at Torfhaus. I am standing third from the left.

Summer and graduation time are not far off, and we cannot afford to lose any of the speed we have worked so hard to build up.

About a week after I returned from my trip it rained, and then the temperature dropped rapidly and turned everything to ice. On my way home from school I was telling my friends that I would go skating with my new ice skates later that day. In anticipation I was clowning around and pretending to be skating a waltz on the icy sidewalk. I fell and severely sprained my right wrist. The doctor said he wished it had been broken because it would have been less complicated, less painful, and would have healed a lot faster. He put a splint from my elbow down to my fingers to immobilize the wrist for a month. I did not know then that ahead of me lay several years of pain and problems with my wrist.

My Trip to Swabia (Schwaben)

I graduated from Business School on June 23rd and anxiously went out to find work. Jobs were exceptionally scarce at that particular time. I did not care much for bookkeeping, but rather hoped to do secretarial work, although with the job shortage I was open to both. As much as I searched I could not find a job. This was not unusual. Unemployment was rampant in Berlin at that time.

Despite weekly visits to the unemployment office I still had not found a job by early July when Mom suggested I defer the search. She wanted me to take advantage of a trip that was being offered by the church group which Gerda and I belonged to. It was a three–week trip to Swabia located in southwest Germany in the vicinity of Stuttgart and the Black Forest area. Mom's reasoning was that it would not hurt to have a vacation before life became really serious. I agreed, but I still had to continue looking for a job right up until a few days before the trip because the Employment Service Agency requires one to actively search.

The case worker at the Employment Service had no objection when I told her I would be taking three weeks off from my job searching to take this trip. I was not receiving unemployment money since this was my first job. If I were, they would have objected. The case worker actually seemed rather relieved not to have to worry about me for those three weeks.

The following is quoted from my trip diary:

On Tuesday, July 17, 1951, we left by bus from the Funkturm (Berlin's landmark radio tower). There were two other small groups traveling to different destinations so that we had a full bus. The border crossing was uneventful, which was unusual. After dropping eight boys off in the town of Marburg that evening, the singing stopped and everyone went to sleep. At four o'clock in the morning we arrived in Heidelberg where the other group left us.

Our bus had trouble negotiating some of the narrow streets in the old part of the city, but all fourteen of us fell in love with Heidelberg and wished we could get off the bus and stay there. Ursel, one of the women from church who was in charge of our trip, told us that we would have a chance to see a little of the city. Our return bus trip to Berlin was to start in Heidelberg.

Our arrival. I am on far left.

Finally, after twenty–three hours of travel we arrived in the town of Kleingartach in the province of Swabia, our destination for the next two out of the three weeks.

Upon arrival the housemother of the Church Youth Center made a little welcome speech and we just looked at each other with question marks on our faces, then asked Ursel for a translation. Even when the housemother tried hard to speak high German instead of the local dialect called *Schwäbisch*, we had a lot of trouble understanding her Swabian accent. We felt as though we were in a different country. The Swabian and the Bavarian dialects are the most difficult ones for the northern Germans to understand. While only spoken and not written, these dialects are like different languages.

Swabia is lovely country with mountains, forests, and rolling hills covered with grape orchards for the wine industry. We hiked to a different area every day loving the exercise and the fresh air, and when we got back to the Youth Center

Ruin of a Monastery in the Black Forest. I am on upper left.

we devoured mountains of the wonderful Swabian special-
ties which were served to us. Our housemother was delighted
about our appetites and could not do enough for us. Every
night she left huge bowls of *Kichle* (home baked sweet
snacks), another specialty of the area, on the tables in the
dining room in case anyone got hungry during the night. I
remember several nights when some of us spent hours in the
moonlit dining room talking and munching.

One of the highlights of our trip was a day trip through
the Black Forest. Ursel had found a local person who owned
a VW bus and would drive us through the Black Forest—
provided that the fourteen of us could squeeze into this nine–
passenger bus. Of course we could fit in! To make sure, Ursel
had us practice seating the day before to establish who would
sit where. We had to leave one whole seat for the driver and
the other front seat for Ursel and Hilde, our two chaperones,
to share. By careful placement of the skinniest girls (of which
I was one) between the larger ones, we managed to pack in
like sardines and had a great day. What a lovely area the
Black Forest is. No wonder there are so many vacation and
health resorts, as well as songs about the beauty of the Black
Forest.

The Big Scare

We stayed in the town of Kleingartach for two weeks and were
having an absolutely wonderful time. Ursel was allowing a week to get
from Kleingartach to Heidelberg. As part of the experience we were
going to camp, hitchhike, and take whatever means of transportation
we could get along the way. We started out by taking a bus to a small
town on the Neckar River, then walked on the road along the river, and
after a few miles a truck gave us a ride. It was an open bed truck and we
loved riding in the back and feeling the wind in our hair. At night we
stayed in youth hostel camps, and one night was spent in a rain shelter
building on top of a mountain where we experienced a fantastic—scary
to us—thunderstorm. Eventually we hitched a ride on a barge up the
Neckar River all the way to Heidelberg. The barge was continuing on
to Rotterdam and we wished that we could go there. The crew would

have liked the lively company of fourteen singing girls. However, our bus was going to be waiting for us in Heidelberg to take us back to Berlin.

The following is quoted from my trip diary:

> We arrived in Heidelberg later than planned and were sorry not to have time to see some of the city. Then, contrary to expectation, we were able to see a bit of Heidelberg after all. Ursel received word that the bus for our return trip to Berlin was delayed by a couple of hours. If we ran up the hill we would have enough time to see the renowned Heidelberg Castle and from there have a splendid view of the beautiful city below. We did run up that steep hill, saw the castle, and afterwards we still had time to walk through the city streets for awhile. Out of breath we returned to the meeting place and started our wait for the bus. No bus arrived. Ursel called Berlin again and was told that the Soviets had closed the borders once more for a day because of some festival they were having, or so they said. A bus would be in Frankfurt for us the next morning—the bus company hoped. So did we. Now we had to get to Frankfurt.
>
> Heidelberg suddenly lost its charm. All we wanted was to go home. It felt as if doomsday had arrived. We were separated from our families and did not trust the Soviets to open the border when they said they would. Our group must have been a sorry sight. People kept looking at us—fourteen gloomy souls sitting on suitcases at the curb where the bus

We took this picture in 1999 of the Marienborn checkpoint, almost ten years after the two Germanys were reunified. Now totally deserted, it remains a monument to this horrible earlier era, and even today gives me goose bumps to see it.

Marienborn checkpoint in 1999. My husband, Mal, is seen in the left center.

was to have come for us. Earlier we had been full of high spirits and were clowning around, but suddenly all energy had left us. From experiences with the Soviets and their lame excuses for border closings, there was the possibility of an indefinite time of separation from our loved ones. The months of the Berlin Blockade were still a vivid memory. Some girls started to cry. Even Ursel and Hilde were stunned into inaction. Some time went by while we were just sitting there staring into space, until Ursel suddenly jumped up realizing that we had better get on a train to Frankfurt.

We spent a horrible night at the Mission Hall of the Frankfurt Railway Station. The Mission Hall was a bunker from World War II days located underneath the station. It was a dreary, depressing, and extremely noisy place with babies crying, children running and screeching, people talking loudly, and the trains rolling into and out of the station above us all night long. We were too restless to be able to sleep, and long before eight o'clock in the morning we sat at the curb and looked anxiously for the bus from Berlin which would take us home. It did arrive on time and was greeted with cheers and tears of relief. We were the happiest kids.

In the afternoon we had some very anxious moments as we approached the border checkpoint at Helmstedt–Marienborn and saw the long line of trucks. We counted one hundred and seventeen trucks, and more joining the truck line constantly. By the stench from trucks carrying fish we could tell that they were food trucks bound for Berlin, and that a lot of them had been sitting there since the border closed two nights before. The East German border officials were not processing trucks for the time being because of "heavy passenger traffic." Hours later when we crossed the border into West Berlin we cried tears of happiness.

This incident was a classic example of the Soviets' infamous harassment techniques which were to last for decades to come.

Despite all the problems it had been a great trip, although I missed my friend Gerda who had already found a job before the trip started. At this point I really felt that I was well traveled having been to the northern, central, and now the southern part of Germany—all within one year thanks to Mom's insistence that I take advantage of the opportunities as they present themselves.

Berlin, I Love You!

The postscript of my diary reads:

> After nineteen days of adventure I am glad to be back in Berlin, and certainly ready to go to work. I had not realized that despite the beautiful country we saw, I had missed the hustle and bustle of the big city. Here the streets are crowded with people, the shops have exciting window displays, and there is traffic and noise. Unlike the laid–back people in the less crowded countryside, this place is alive. I am even happy to hear the streetcars clanking up and down our street. No matter how beautiful it was elsewhere, to us Berliners there is no place like our Berlin. Berlin, I love you!

No, there is no place like Berlin anywhere in the world. Despite the constant harassment from the Soviets, this city and the spirit of its

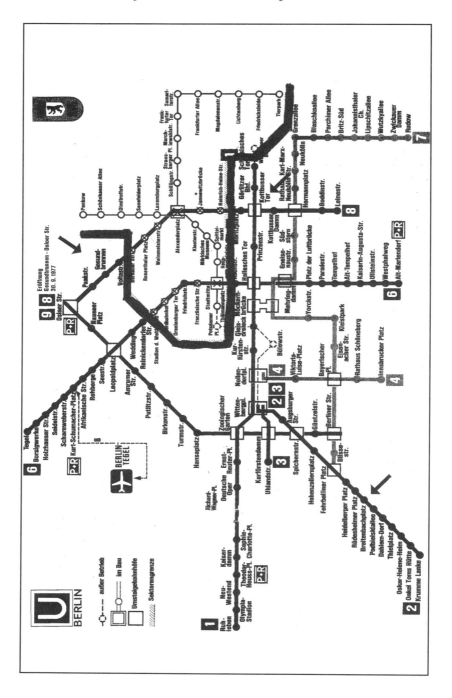

people cannot be annihilated. The Berliners and their city had risen from the ashes like the Phoenix—and having humor and freedom, nothing, no matter how annoying, was going to do them in. One of the songs that has been written about Berlin portrays the optimism of the Berliners in a humorous way: "Even if all the snow burns up, the ashes are still left."

There were incidences constantly. Until the infamous Berlin Wall was built ten years later, people could travel freely between East and West Berlin on the city's transportation system. However, certain rules had to be observed when traveling through the Soviet sector of Berlin. One day a friend of Peter's was jailed in East Berlin. He had been riding to work on the subway as usual. His place of work was in the extreme northern part of the city. On the way to work the subway line went through a part of East Berlin for about five or six stops before re–entering West Berlin. The friend was reading a newspaper and had not put his paper away when the train entered East Berlin. West Berliners were not allowed to read West Berlin newspapers while in East Berlin—they did not want East Berliners to glance at the newspapers and be politically influenced. Two weeks in jail was the punishment for the boy. His mother was frantic. Again, nobody trusted the Soviets. One never knew when they decided to have their legendary "technical difficulties" and therefore changed the rules or jail sentences.

Rules such as reading the forbidden newspaper were not posted. They were learned from bitter experiences. Eventually there were so many unwritten rules and resulting incidences that people avoided traveling through East Berlin altogether. There were two electric train systems that traveled through both East and West Berlin. The *U–Bahn*, or underground, was under West Berlin management, and the *S–Bahn*, or above ground city train, was under East Berlin administration. The *S–Bahn* was avoided altogether by West Berliners. It was run down due to lack of maintenance, and because it was under East Berlin control no one felt comfortable taking it. On the *U–Bahn*, travel through East Berlin could be avoided by changing lines once or twice to avoid going through East Berlin.

See subway map, left. Peter's friend worked at Gesundbrunnen (arrow, top right center), the second stop on Line 8 after the East Berlin border—heavy dark line. Coming from Steglitz (arrow, lower left), the shortest way was to change from Line 2 to Line 8 (arrow, right center) which travels through East Berlin for six stops. Circumnavigation was possible, but would have required several changes.

The other unique situation created by the East Berlin administration was with the telephone system. Not having a telephone when we lived in Berlin, I don't remember when it happened. The East Berlin telephone system was severed from the West Berlin system so that it was not possible to make a telephone call between the two Berlins. If a West Berliner really needed to get in touch with someone in East Berlin, he had to route the call through West Germany to East Germany and only from there could the call get through to East Berlin. The same was true in reverse.

However, nothing could kill the spirit of us West Berliners. Our "island" was our paradise of freedom. As long as we still had freedom we had hope, and hope is everything. As a dear friend of mine put it so accurately: "Without hope the soul dies." The Americans had become our protectors. They had helped preserve our freedom and were staying in Berlin to make sure that we got to keep this most precious of gifts.

My First Job

I resumed job interviews immediately after returning from my trip. Here I need to go into some explanations. We were recovering from the war and its aftermath. Berlin still had ration cards, and while more and more consumer goods were becoming available, the cost of these were way out of proportion to earnings. This meant that whatever few clothes people owned were close to being worn out, and anything new was worn continuously. I did not have anything suitable to wear to a job interview.

Mom owned one reasonably nice suit which she had taken in exchange for sewing she had done for a friend. Otherwise she still wore her old railroad uniform—now plain without insignia—to work when it was cold in the winter, and she had made some things to wear during the warmer seasons. Over the years when I was outgrowing my clothes Mom had used up her dresses and coats to make clothes for Peter and me. At this point all three of us needed everything. We had made do and stretched everything as far as was possible.

Mom felt that I needed a suit to look more businesslike to go to job interviews. The problem was that Mom's suit was too large and too short for me. I was even skinnier than she was and almost two inches taller. Mom promptly altered it to fit me. The suit was of a soft green color and she had to sew darts into the skirt waist with brown thread—the only color we still had left after so many years of nothing being available. Later I wore this suit to work every day, alternating it with my black confirmation dress until I could afford to make a down payment on an outfit of my own. I wore my brown boots all the time. They were the only shoes I owned. At times, especially for the job interviews, I limped along with Mom's good white shoes

My boss, Herr Heyn, owner of Parfumerie Royale and Alfred Heyn G.m.b.H.

which were one and a half sizes too small. Prices were so high compared to salaries that all purchases such as clothing had to be made on credit. Otherwise it would have been impossible for the majority of the people to make those purchases.

When the Employment Service referred me to an interview for a job as a typist in a cosmetics firm I was sure they would not even look at me. Most girls my age liked to experiment with lipstick and nail polish, and I had no interest in that type of thing. I was convinced that no cosmetics firm would want me and I would not even have bothered to go to the interview, except that I had to. To my great amazement I was hired—unpainted face, brown darts in the green skirt, and Mom's shoes which were too small and nearly made me limp. My salary was ninety Westmarks a month, to be raised to a hundred Marks after the three–month trial period. This was the going rate then, and people were happy to have work.

Starting to Work

My place of business, Parfumerie Royale, was an upstart perfume import business which had five employees in the office: Herr Müller, general office manager and in his early thirties was even tempered, always smiling, and painfully slow about everything. Frau Moritz was a paranoid woman in her sixties who made it her full time occupation to know everybody else's business when she was supposed to be doing the bookkeeping. We had many good laughs on her. She was a chronic complainer about just everything, particularly drafts, and she was forever yelling: "Close the door—I'm feeling a draft!" The times when we would really crack up with laughter would be when the door had not even been opened yet and Frau Moritz was already yelling: "Close the door."

Then there was Frau Ritter, the cleaning woman. She rivaled Frau Moritz in that she not only knew everybody's business, but had access to more information about the boss' private life to spike the gossip. Nobody except Frau Moritz was interested in any of that.

Out in the field were a staff of salesmen, both in Berlin and in West Germany, who brought in the orders. Herr Götz, a young man in his mid–twenties, was the driver who delivered the merchandise in Berlin. He saw humor in every situation and was the life of the office with his hilarious stories, all of which were true. He could tell us about some incident that happened to him while driving around the city in such a funny way that we all laughed hysterically.

Finally there was the newly hired office slave, Fräulein Inge Stanneck, who had spent three years majoring in Silence, and who was not interested enough in fellow human beings to want to know everybody's business but rather liked getting the work done instead. Above all of us was the almighty Herr Alfred Heyn, owner of the treadmill.

The location of the office was a few blocks from the *Kurfürstendamm*, West Berlin's once glamorous shopping boulevard which at that time was making progress in emerging from the ruins. With people still not having quite enough food to eat, I found it interesting to see a luxurious cosmetics store being the only business that was rebuilt in an otherwise bombed out building. To me such a store seemed unnecessary, and I wondered who could afford to buy cosmetics. However, I had a job because of clients like these.

Our office space was a large apartment on the street floor of a partially bombed old building. At one time it was an upper class apartment building with a desirable address. There were huge rooms with high ceilings and big ornate doors. Everything was now ancient and in need of repair and renovation, though the former elegance was still evident.

I started out spending my workdays in a dreary back room in which we stored some of the merchandise as well as miscellaneous furniture from the rest of the apartment. This room looked out on the ruin of a building located across a narrow dark space between buildings, which prevented daylight from coming into the windows. My job was to calculate and type all invoices for the orders which the salesmen brought in daily, or in the case of West Germany, mailed in. This was the top priority. Orders generated income, and the faster we could get the invoices typed and the goods delivered the sooner the money came in.

Next I was to take dictation and type all correspondence. The answering of the doorbell when someone came also fell to me, being the youngest and newest employee. This turned out to be a total waste of my time because Frau Moritz found a reason to walk out into the foyer every time someone came to the door.

Handshakes—"Shaking hands seems to be a national sport in Germany," wrote an American businessman after his first trip to Germany. Having grown up with this custom, it was nothing especially noteworthy to me until I worked at the office. Custom and good manners dictated that one always shook hands when greeting or departing. While in school I had been shaking hands with girls of my age, it was quite different when greeting people at the office. I found that there are many different handshakes, and some of them can be rather painful. There were men who seemed to feel they had to exhibit their strength by nearly crushing a girl's hand. Soft, almost lifeless handshakes can be unpleasant, too. I learned about people and their handshakes from experience.

Office Days

Our work day started at eight in the morning. Officially we worked a fifty–hour week, which meant nine hours daily and five hours on Saturdays. On my first day of work when I was trying to get ready to go home shortly after five in the evening, I was given more work to do which had to be done that night. When this went on every evening, I got the hint that I was expected to stay late. Everybody else did. Herr Müller was too timid to rebel against the system and Frau Moritz had nobody to go home to. We all needed our jobs so we stayed, usually until seven or eight o'clock. I was often kept until nine and sometimes ten o'clock at night without having had a chance to eat the sandwich I had brought along for lunch. In reality we all worked eleven to thirteen hours on weekdays, and eight to ten hours on Saturdays. In the nearly three years I worked for Parfumerie Royale, there were only about a dozen occasions on which I was able to leave the office before three in the afternoon on Saturdays instead of at five or six o'clock. Needless to say there was no overtime pay. People were fortunate to have jobs.

Being a small office, everybody took care of whatever work came along. There were no job descriptions. When a lot of orders had come in from West Germany, everybody helped pack the packages, and whoever left before the post office closed at seven in the evening, mailed them. Being the youngest—I had my seventeenth birthday a month after I started to work—and having an abundance of energy, I was working the hardest, and I really can say that I honestly liked it.

At the time I started to work there, the products sold by our company were perfumes and eau de colognes, lipsticks, nail polish, and soaps, all imported from France. Our ace at that time was a perfume and cologne called *Sortilege* by LeGalion, for which we had just received the distributorship. It was expensive. A small bottle of *Sortilege* cost more than I earned in a month, and it was incomprehensible to me that there were people who had money and spent it on stuff like that.

Only three years earlier there had been a currency reform and everybody had been equal, holding sixty Westmarks. Now some people were already more equal than others.

Business was good and we expanded the lines, eventually including American products. I remember Dura Gloss nail polish and Max Factor cosmetics, among others. Later on Parfumerie Royale expanded to include men's toiletries as well as baby products. This was how I first became acquainted with The Mennen Company of Morristown, New Jersey, which was to play a major role in my and my family's lives.

Dr. Adolf Burmester
I owe a great deal to this kind and thoughtful gentleman. He was a rare person who was genuinely interested in the people he met. Without his help I would probably not have gotten a job at The Mennen Company in the United States, and my life would have been very different.

Dr. Adolf Burmester

I had been working for the firm for about three weeks and was getting into a good routine as I got familiar with the products and their French names. It had taken some time to get used to deciphering the salesmen's handwritings when typing invoices. Herr Heyn seemed satisfied with my work and I started to feel secure in my job.

On one particular Monday morning I met the genius behind Alfred Heyn's Parfumerie Royale—his personal friend Dr. Adolf Burmester, who was also the contact person in Paris and later in the United States.

That morning when I answered the doorbell I nearly went into shock upon opening the door. There, filling out all of the space in that door was a colossus of a man who after a rather normal handshake for someone of his size, walked past me and went straight into the office. He seemed to know his way around.

Much later that morning when I had some business to go into the main part of the office, the huge stranger was still sitting there and chatting with everyone as if they were all old friends. When I entered the room he stood up, bent down from his great height to take a closer look at me, and asked: "Who is this little girl? She looked terribly scared when I came in. She must be new here." He had spoken kindly and was interested, and he seemed concerned about having scared me. At that point I was introduced to Herr Dr. Burmester. He looked to be in his early sixties, had a gentlemanly manner, a genuine smile, and a heart of gold, as I was to find out.

A brilliant person, he was educated in Weimar and Oxford and had earned his Ph.D. in Chemical Engineering. He came from an old upper class family and was a perfect gentleman.

Dr. Burmester was a close personal friend of the boss, Herr Heyn. He spoke several languages, had a lot of connections both in Germany and abroad, and a way of talking large name brand firms into supplying a nondescript upstart outfit. He handled major financial matters such as bank loans, and he also had a "foot in the door" at the fanciest cosmetic stores in Berlin where he often ironed out problems to keep them happy as our customers.

I did not know that this giant man was there to stay until a couple of days later when Dr. Burmester dictated a letter to me. Afterwards he made a comment to the effect that I would get used to his way of dictating after we had worked together for awhile. He admitted that he had a habit of using a lot of foreign words when dictating, such as Latin and French, and for me to feel free to ask him if I had any doubt about the spelling. This floored me and I saw a human side to him which I did not expect from a boss. In Germany at that time, if one had a job one was expected to have been trained to qualify for that job. Dr. Burmester's use of foreign words reflected his education, and his offer to help me with those foreign words spoke of his consideration for others, which was noticeable in all of his dealings.

Reassured about his offer to help but still intimidated by his great size, I thought: Oh no, he is going to stay? Being a friend of the boss, I had assumed that he was just visiting. He was actually working there and had been away on vacation when I was hired. As time passed, I found that he became a good mediator between this timid girl who needed the job, and the slave driver of a boss who could not get enough out of people.

Dr. Burmester was also an excellent typist, and there were countless times when he offered to finish up work for me late at night, insisting that I had been there too many hours and needed to go home and get some rest. After such kind acts of his I usually found out the next day that he had "lit into" his friend Alfred and urged him to be more human. One time Herr Heyn told me that Dr. Burmester said I was afraid of him because he yelled so much. Herr Heyn said he was sorry and would try not to yell, but his good intention did not last long. Actually he never yelled at me but at the driver, the salesmen, or whoever came in to see him. Herr Heyn just was not a tactful person, but I considered it to be my problem that I jumped every time he raised his voice.

Dr. Burmester, in comparison, was a soft spoken, good natured, grandfatherly friend to everyone. He always saw only the best in people and treated them with kindness and respect; he was understanding, down–to–earth, and had a terrific sense of humor. He took it in stride that he had no desk to his name. He found himself a cardboard box and put all of his office belongings including pending correspondence into it. He labeled the box "Burmester's Office" and kept it on the floor in a corner near my typewriter. Since my typewriter was in constant use, he always had to wait until I was away from my desk to be able to write a quick letter. Much of the time he typed his own letters after I left at night rather than dictating them to me, out of consideration for the workload I had and not wanting to add to it. Dr. Burmester usually came in just before or after noon and then stayed as late as he needed to at night.

Office Reorganization

The use of our office space was disorganized, at best. One Friday we were all asked to come in at seven the next morning and be prepared to work "extra long hours" to reorganize the office. As I said, Dr. Burmester really did not have a desk anywhere. Some of the time he was in the storage room where I sat and where he had a comfortable chair; other times he would be in the small office and use a corner of Herr Müller's desk. Herr Heyn decided that the small office room should from now on be for him and me. Herr Müller and Frau Moritz were moved into the room next door which until now was the warehouse and parcel packing space. The warehouse area was moved into the dark rooms in the back of the apartment.

I was delighted with the bright, sunny office after having sat in a dungeon like atmosphere. However, there were major drawbacks. Herr Heyn was a chain smoker. Poor Dr. Burmester still did not get a desk of his own and continued to use everybody else's. As before, he kept his "office box" on the floor near my typewriter. Dr. Burmester also smoked continuously, but differently from everyone else. Instead of inhaling he puffed the smoke out, with the result that after one cigarette there was so much smoke in the room that I could hardly see my typewriter. A window could not be opened because of the inevitable distress cry from Frau Moritz in the next room: "I feel a draft," even though the door was closed. By the way, in Germany all doors are kept closed at all times.

Frau Moritz was quite unhappy with this new office arrangement. She no longer was in the office in which "everything happened," and curiosity was killing her. Luckily for her, the safe had remained in the office which was now occupied by Herr Heyn and me. Since all office records and ledgers were kept in the safe at night, it gave Frau Moritz the opportunity to come in every morning to get her ledgers out of the safe and to return them before she left at night. This was not enough. Frau Moritz made countless trips to the safe every day, noticeably when a visitor, customer, salesman, or a friend had come to see Herr Heyn. She just had to find out who was there and what was being discussed. We could count on Frau Moritz using the excuse to come into the room to get papers out of the safe every time. Then she would stay and sort through things for as long as she dared, in order to be able to listen in on the conversations. This was quite conspicuous to everyone, and one day Herr Heyn asked me: "Why is she constantly coming in here?" I told him I did not know, but both of us burst out laughing because we both knew why.

At home everything revolved around my work schedule. Our meals on weekdays consisted mostly of different kinds of vegetable stew. Vegetables and potatoes were no longer rationed and there were no lines to contend with at the grocery stores. Mom's workday started at six in the morning and she was usually home by three in the afternoon. Any grocery shopping was done on the way. Then Mom cooked and she and Peter ate their supper at a regular time. My food was saved and heated up whenever I showed up at night. Mom did not like this crazy schedule of mine. She felt that I should have some free time to do things with other girls of my age. While I liked working, I did keep hoping that things would change as the firm grew, and that more people would be hired for the office. The firm did change as far as growth, but no additional people were hired to help with my workload.

Dancing School

Mom was the youngest of five children. She grew up during and after World War I. Her two older sisters and oldest brother had been sent to dancing school to take lessons in ballroom dancing when they were in their teens. By the time it got down to the last two kids, times were bad at the end of WWI and the family was struggling to make ends meet. Mom had always wanted me to have the things that she missed out on in her own youth. One of those had been dancing school. For her daughter it was going to be the best in Berlin, so she decided on *Tanzschule Hegenscheidt,* an old family business which had already been renowned before the war.

I had no interest in learning how to dance. At seventeen I was still a child and shy. When I asked Mom if I had to dance with boys and she said "yes," I became scared and told her that I was not going to any dancing school. This grew into an argument between us. Mom insisted and assured me that one day I would be thankful to her for sending me. Then I remembered how I had loved watching my parents during the "good old times," when they were playing records and dancing to the music. But those times were in the past. The war had not only de-stroyed factories, military targets, and people's living quarters, but it had also destroyed families and relationships. Wherever one looked, couples were divorced. I was still hurting from my parents' divorce and was not going to get married anyway, so there was no point in my going to dancing school. Mom insisted, telling me how much fun it would be. I argued, but she stood firm. I had no choice.

The first obstacle was to get home from work at a reasonable time so that I could plan on such an adventure. When I told my boss that I had to leave by six o'clock every Wednesday night to go to dancing school, his answer was: "Why do you need to learn how to dance? I didn't go to dancing school and I can dance." I then suggested that Herr Heyn take it up with my mother, but he did not want to do that. Mom had been in to see him once about my long working hours. As a result the hours were somewhat cut back for awhile, but then crept up again. Herr Heyn was amused when I assured him I had to go there only once. Mom had said that if I really did not like dancing school after I had tried it, I would not have to go. I was sure that I would not like it.

Then came the dreaded day. I don't remember whether I wore my confirmation dress or the skirt from Mom's green suit and a blouse. Those were the only two possibilities. It did not matter because the other kids were in the same boat. Nobody owned dressy clothes at that time unless they had been dug up in "grandma's attic." One memorable thing about the evening was that I was so reluctant to go that Mom walked there with me and waited—outside, thank heavens—to make sure that I stayed. To say the least, it was embarrassing to have been escorted to dancing school by one's mother.

The other memorable thing was that I liked it. First of all, the boys were sitting lined up against the opposite wall from the girls and looked just as scared as we did. Second, before we even learned the first step we were taught proper behavior and manners, not only for dancing, but also for other social occasions such as going out on dates. Only then were we ready to be taught how to dance the first simple steps. By then we had been given enough time to get reasonably comfortable with the surroundings—and the boys sitting opposite us—so that we were anxious to hear music, and the rest became mechanical. I was even asked to dance all of the time which surprised me as I had been sure that nobody would want to dance with me. There were a few more girls than there were boys. Dancing turned out to be fun!

Dancing is Fun

Mom did not have to escort me to my lesson the following week because I could not wait to go back. I loved the happy music, and dancing to it was fun. To properly execute the steps with style was a challenge. I liked dancing, and it did not take me long to excel in it. When the first set of lessons was completed and I wanted to sign up for the second set, Mom was delighted. After that some of us took advanced steps and style, joined the dance club and danced in competition with other clubs. This meant having a steady partner with whom to train for the contests. I usually danced with a young man whose name was Heinz. We did not date—it was my choice—and it was fun having an excellent dancer for a partner without being pressured into dating. We won a number of first prizes together.

Mom and I went to balls given by the police and by organizations to which my friends or their parents belonged. There were dances on steamship cruises on Berlin's rivers and lakes, and there were garden plot festivals—wherever there was a dance on Saturday nights, I was there and danced my feet off. A dance would normally start at eight in the evening and end at five in the morning, unless one wanted to catch the last train or streetcar after midnight, but that was not even up for consideration. Only old people left at that hour, or girls who were bored because they did not get asked to dance very much.

The most fun dance was the semiannual police ball at the *Lichterfelder Festsäle* (Festival Halls in Lichterfelde). The Berlin Police had an excellent band which played at most major functions all over Berlin, such as outdoor concerts, symphonies, musicals, and of course, at the annual Police Sports Show held at the *Olympia Stadion*. For avid dancers the police ball was tops. There the band split into two and took turns playing so that there was never an intermission. Because of Mom's work, we always received tickets to the police ball which were in great demand. If I was lucky, I was asked for every dance and never sat down all night long. Being there with Mom was my protection when it came to not wanting to accept dates or offers of being walked home. I really loved to dance, but I was not quite ready to date yet.

After I had signed up for the more advanced dancing lessons, Mom insisted that she make a dress for me which was a little more fancy than my everyday clothes. I remember a pale blue dress with ruffles and bows, and once again—as in my childhood—I dreaded going to the next lesson because nobody else wore such a special dress. Once we started attending balls, I made a couple of gowns to wear for different occasions.

Christmas 1951

This was a special Christmas. Mom and I decided we would buy a Christmas present for all of us—a radio—and surprise Peter. As usual, Mom received some Christmas money for Peter and me from our Papa. We could use it for a down payment, and since both Mom and I were working we figured out that we could pay off the radio in four months. We loved surprising Peter because his happiness and enthusiasm always showed. Together Mom and I picked out the radio in the store down the street, had the room antenna—a wire going part way around the room near the ceiling—installed, and were anxious for Christmas to come. We kept hoping that Peter would not notice the antenna and were relieved when he didn't.

In Germany, the main celebration of Christmas is on Christmas Eve. We usually went to church for the candlelight service at six in the evening. The church would have two large Christmas trees decorated with nothing but white candles, and there would be more candles on the altar and around the nativity scene. It was always special to hear the traditional Christmas story being read from the Bible. During our fifteen–minute walk home, we would enjoy looking at the windows of the apartment buildings along the way and see many Christmas trees with their candles lit. Upon returning home, Mom would light the candles on our tree while Peter and I waited in the foyer. Then we were called into the living room and exchanged our presents. Peter was absolutely awestruck with the radio. Our surprise was a huge success, and it was a perfect time to have our radio. Now we had Christmas music in our room, and we no longer needed to eavesdrop on Herr Walther's radio in the room next to ours. Last year we had asked him if he would turn his radio up so we could hear the music better. He had even been so kind to leave the radio turned on for us when he went out to be with friends, so that we could have Christmas music for the whole evening.

We each had a new piece of clothing. Mom and I had decided on a red corduroy skirt with a vest type top and a white blouse for me. It was a stunning outfit and became my office "uniform" for the next two years, as well as a new dancing school dress. The black confirmation dress was still in service, and so were the boots—originally meant for the ice skates—which were still the only shoes I owned.

For the celebration of the holidays, Mom had baked some cookies and I had helped her by licking the bowl and the spoon, plus a little extra dough. Consequently, I had an upset stomach and as far as I remember, this was the end of my liking sweets for many years, except for chocolate.

Herr Heyn had been able to purchase a whole case of canned pineapple in West Germany. He gave everybody at the office a can for Christmas, and we thought we had received a bucket of gold. Somehow he noticed that I did not seem to know what pineapple was. It had not been available since before the war, and I had never even heard of pineapple. When everyone else was out of our office, Herr Heyn gave me another can. I was so proud to bring two cans of this tropical fruit called "pineapple" home to my family for Christmas. What a feast we had with this delicious treat!

14

1952
The Salt Mine
Age Seventeen

We had many reasons to be thankful as we welcomed the new year. There was progress in every aspect of our lives. We had music in our home, some new clothes to wear and enough food to eat, but most importantly, we were living in West Berlin and had freedom.

My Job

There was never a dull moment at the office—the salt mine—but I loved it. I was a very efficient worker, conscientious, and trustworthy. Occasionally even Herr Heyn hinted that he appreciated my work, and one day he gave me a raise of ten Marks a month.

Our top priority every day was to process the invoices and to mail or deliver the merchandise. The quicker this happened, the faster the money came in. The salesmen who were covering Berlin stopped by the office daily, sometimes twice a day, to drop off the orders they had written. Our men who worked parts of West Germany sent their orders by mail. The firm did not cover all of West Germany at that time, but Herr Heyn did have a small branch in Hamburg. It was a two–person office which took care of the city and surrounding territory.

After each salesman had come in during the morning and Herr Heyn had looked at the orders, I typed up the invoices in record time. A short time after starting to work for the firm I had memorized the addresses of at least two hundred perfume shops and drug stores which carried our merchandise. Not having to look them up saved a lot of time. The salesmen seldom wrote full addresses on their orders. I had also memorized the prices per piece, half dozen, dozen, three and five dozen for most items, and did not have to spend time calculating them. This baffled my coworkers and kept the slave driver happy. I did have quite a good memory. Perhaps those forty–stanza poems we had to memorize in school served a purpose after all. At the time I could see no practical use for long poems. In the beginning Herr Heyn always checked my price calculations on the invoices, but he soon gave up when he never found a mistake.

Herr Heyn seemed to be a skeptical person but he became more considerate as he began to trust and appreciate my work. I did not waste any time socializing with the salesmen or customers, and I was not interested in them and their personal business. Instead, I was my usual unsociable self who thrived on hard work. Not long after I started to work for the firm, I had been given the task of typing five hundred letters to our customers, promoting the expensive French *Sortilege* perfume and eau de cologne. All five hundred letters were originals. Each typographical error meant an erasure and that looked untidy, so I was extra careful with my typing. Dr. Burmester and Herr Heyn were surprised when it took me only three weeks to complete the job in addition to doing all of my regular work.

Fun at Work

Funny things happened at work all of the time. These were really everyday life things that turned out to be comical. Shortly after moving into the small room which was now our office, Herr Heyn was bothered by a particularly large dirty spot on the wallpaper and he made a comment to that effect. The old wallpaper should have been replaced about twenty years ago. Being my mother's daughter in that I was seldom lost for a solution, I told him I would take care of it in no time. I took an eraser out of my desk and went to work on the dirty spot. Within a couple of minutes the dirt was not only gone, but the spot had turned into a large clean one without damaging the wallpaper. Herr Heyn looked at it for a moment, surprised and pleased, and then asked me to take care of a few other spots elsewhere. Before long I had cleaned up so many spots that he started to help, and we both enjoyed the results. The more we looked the more spots were evident, so that soon we were working here and there all over the room. The problem with that was that the freshly erased spots now stood out bright and clean in the ancient and overall yellowed and dirty wallpaper. Suddenly Herr Heyn had "the" idea. "The whole room needs to be erased," he said with a big grin. Immediately he yelled to call in the driver who occasionally was around while waiting for goods to be compiled before he could deliver them: "Götz," he ordered, "stop at the stationery store and buy the biggest eraser you can find—we are going to erase the whole room." Herr Götz had a way of staring at a person as though he was looking at a ghost. He could not believe what he was hearing or seeing.

What Herr Götz did not realize as yet was that he was about to be entrusted with the task. For the next six weeks, whenever he was not delivering merchandise Herr Götz stood on a ladder and erased wallpaper. The room started to look noticeably brighter, as if it had received a fresh coat of paint. We had quite a few good laughs during those weeks. Herr Götz muttered many a choice word as he went through countless super–large erasers. Those big erasers were expensive, and it took two dozen or more to erase the whole room. Herr Heyn began to wonder about the cost of cleaning up the wallpaper, but he certainly liked the result. Had wallpaper or paint been available it might have been cheaper to redecorate the room, but those were still the times when we had to make do with what we had. Erasers were available— paint and wallpaper were not.

The weeks during which Herr Götz worked on erasing the wallpaper became quite entertaining for me. He had a terrific sense of humor and we laughed all the time whenever "the boss" was not there. Not only did Herr Götz swear in the funniest way about the seemingly endless and insane task of cleaning the walls of a whole room with an eraser, he also had some funny stories to tell about his job of driving and delivering goods. He saw most of the incidences from a humorous point of view, whether with customers or other drivers on the road.

I remember two of the funny incidences that happened when Herr Götz gave rides to our Dr. Burmester. An extremely large man, Dr. Burmester was in his mid–sixties, and walking long distances was often difficult for him. He did not like to bother with public transportation, especially between his home and work, because the distance was too short to utilize it. His apartment was less than one kilometer away and he usually walked to the office in the morning. However, when he needed to go on business errands during the day, or went home in the afternoon or evening, he would try to catch a ride with Herr Götz.

At that time our "delivery van" was still a VW Beetle. Just watching Dr. Burmester as he tried to squeeze his bulk into the VW was enough to get anyone hysterical with laughter. After Dr. Burmester was seated, Herr Götz, despite being exceptionally slim, had hardly any space left to sit, let alone room to handle the stick shift on the floor. The really funny part was Herr Götz's description of how as soon as he was seated in the car, Dr. Burmester would start digging in his pockets to find his cigarettes. At that point Herr Götz had to get back out of the car and wait until they were found. This happened every time without fail. When they finally got underway, Dr. Burmester would puff out the smoke as he was enjoying his cigarette. Soon Herr Götz could no longer see anything through the smoke and had to open the window, no matter how cold it was outside.

One day Herr Götz burst into my office laughing, and he could hardly wait to tell me the latest funny story. Dr. Burmester had a sweet tooth. He knew a bakery that was occasionally selling cake and even had whip cream for the cake. On that particular day Dr. Burmester bought some cake and whip cream for the traditional "afternoon coffee and cake time," and intended it to be a special surprise treat for his wife. When Dr. Burmester tried to get out of the car with his sweet load he needed help. Herr Götz took the cake from him and walked him into the apartment building to the elevator. At that point he handed the cake back to Dr. Burmester. This was an old building and the elevator was a tiny one with a three–person capacity. There was a spring–loaded folding seat on one wall. Dr. Burmester folded the seat down and put the cake on the seat. Just as the elevator door started to close, Herr Götz watched Dr. Burmester's horror–stricken face when the seat snapped back up and smashed the precious cake and whip cream all over the elevator's wall. Poor Dr. Burmester. He was always so happy when he could surprise his little doll, as he called his wife. This time his surprise was ruined, and the office had a good laugh about the humorous way in which Herr Götz told Dr. Burmester's story of woe.

My Boss—Herr Heyn

Herr Heyn traveled a fair amount. Not only did he have the branch office in Hamburg which he personally supervised, but his official residence was in Braunschweig, about one hundred twenty–five miles west of Berlin, where his wife and young son lived. He owned a Mercedes and traveled home on most weekends. Eventually he was able to rent a couple of rooms in an apartment building next door, and he moved his family back to Berlin.

The Heyn family's living quarters in Berlin were an extremely inconvenient setup. During this still critical housing shortage, it was a minor miracle to have been able to get two rooms, and not just anywhere, but in the house next door. These two rooms, however, were only bedrooms and did not have a kitchen. Frau Heyn had to use the kitchen in the apartment where our offices were. There was no living room for the Heyn family as the business took up the rest of the space in the apartment. Frau Heyn and their seven–year–old son, Peter, spent their days in our kitchen which was quite small.

I was glad to be relieved of the coffee–making duty. It was his wife's job now. When I started to work I had been told that it would be my responsibility to make the coffee for the boss. Initially I had assumed that meant making a single pot in the morning, but Herr Heyn drank coffee all day long in between smoking cigarettes. Making four or five pots of coffee every day was another burden which was disruptive. It took time away from my work.

Whenever Herr Heyn left the office for awhile, his son Peter would come in to see me and ask me to help him with his homework. He was petrified of his father, and asked me to please not mention to him that I was giving him some help. The poor boy seemed to have a lot of trouble keeping up in school. It looked to me like he needed much more help than I could give him during occasional short periods of time. I lost sight of Peter several months later when Herr Heyn moved his family into a nice house in Berlin–Dahlem.

After they moved, the responsibility of making the coffee came back to me. However, I was so glad for Frau Heyn. She had always been unusually quiet and looked unhappy. Having her own place without the boss being around during the day would be much better for her and Peter. His fear of his father told me that he must be quite difficult to live with.

Some of the other "office" services I provided were anything from sewing a button back on a salesman's coat to taking Frau Moritz's bookkeeping home with me to do it on Sunday. She could often not get it done during the week and saw no way she could ever catch up. I knew a way—stop wasting time trying to keep track of other people's personal lives. Being much younger, it was not my place to tell her the obvious.

On many evenings, by the time I finally got out of the smoky office I would be so starved for fresh air that I preferred to walk home instead of taking the streetcar. It was more than an hour's walk, but I enjoyed it after being cooped up in the office for ten or more hours. Even when it was raining I would sometimes walk at least part of the way. My walk took me along major traffic arteries. Street crimes were virtually non-existent at that time so that safety was not an issue, even after dark.

Springtime in Berlin,
and a Bicycle

Berlin is a beautiful city, but especially so in the springtime. A number of songs have been written about "Springtime in Berlin." Many of the city's trees that did not survive the war had been replaced so that once again we Berliners could sing about our green city and blossoms in the springtime. Berliners love their city trees so much that during especially dry summers the fire department goes around and waters trees.

I just had to be outdoors more than my work schedule permitted. My solution was a bicycle. I gave all of my earnings to Mom except for five Marks a month personal allowance and fifteen Marks for my monthly streetcar pass. She and I together always made the decisions about necessary purchases. One day I presented my plan to Mom. I wanted to buy a bicycle with which to ride to work. By using it I would save the fifteen–Mark streetcar fare, and depending on how much a bike would cost, I could probably pay it off in about a year.

Mom approved of my plan wholeheartedly and we went shopping for a bicycle. There was one which I liked especially well. It cost three hundred thirty Marks, and it was a shining beauty with a light blue frame. I bought it. My new bicycle was cleaned or dusted after each use, and for the time being it spent the nights next to my bed. From then on I had to ride my bike to work, rain or shine. There was no money for the streetcar, but I did not mind and loved riding in the rain. The first time I visited Papa with my new bicycle he was sad that I had purchased it on credit. He did not approve of this method of acquiring possessions. I can still see his sad face and hear his voice when he asked: "Did this really have to be?" Enthusiastically I explained to him the details of my financial justification, and that I planned to have the bicycle paid for in about eighteen months, or much sooner if I got a good raise. He looked happier then. Mom and I knew that he was struggling financially and could not offer any help.

Now I had a bicycle, and like a wild Indian on a Mustang I was tearing through Berlin on my wheels. I could easily beat the streetcars as they had to keep making stops. Soon I lost interest in them and concentrated on racing with the cars instead. When I was not at work or dancing, I was on my bike exploring Berlin.

Herr Heyn was not happy about my bicycle when he found out that I was racing. One morning he saw me arrive at the office at high speed, my face red as a lobster, and he seemed upset. In my exuberance I told him that I could get to work in nearly half the time that it took the streetcar. "How long is the streetcar ride?" he asked. I said: "twenty–seven minutes, and it takes me only sixteen minutes by bicycle." "If you keep racing like that I will take the bike away from you," he threatened. He looked so grave that I wondered why he would be so upset. I asked Frau Moritz who knew everything about everyone. She told me that he used to participate in motorcycle races, and that after an accident he had been paralyzed and spent two years in a wheelchair. This explained his distress about racing, and it let me see that he was human and had some concern for others. To avoid getting caught again, I made it a point to slow down a block before I got to work.

Herr Heyn did take my bike away from me one night in the winter when the roads were icy, and he gave me money to go home on the streetcar.

Life at Home

It was interesting to note how my horizon expanded once I started to work. I was no longer a child but was becoming a member of the adult community. I left the family circle and ventured out into the world, but at night I returned to the protective haven of my family.

I kept a record of each week's top hits selected by the RIAS Berlin radio station.

Mom was a wonderful mother to grow up with. Every night no matter how late I got home, she would sit with me while I ate my dinner and listen to my telling her everything that happened during my day at the office. She knew all of my co–workers by name as though she had met them. Mom was my best friend and confidant. Her understanding and support were boundless. She loved fun, and with her humor we turned even the most unpleasant of the day's happenings into a story that we could laugh about.

We appreciated and enjoyed our radio which cheered us up with music and stories. One night a week I listened to the hit parade on the radio. Being a teenager and dancing, I loved to hear the latest hits, or dance music of any kind. Those were the days of Tangos and Viennese Waltzes, Foxtrot and the romantic English Waltz, the Rheinländer, Quickstep, Polka, and some of the Latin dances, such as Rhumba, Samba, and Mambo. The hit parade also brought quite a few American hits which were quickly becoming popular. This led to the Jitterbug.

At times I needed someone to practice my dancing with, and by and by I taught Mom many of the advanced dance steps which I had learned in dancing school. My attempt to teach her the Jitterbug resulted in more laughter than dancing. This just was not Mom's style and she didn't see how anyone would want to hop around like that. I pointed out to her that the Charleston of the 1920's was not so different, but she insisted that it had more class.

There were several programs that we loved to listen to on our new radio. A weekly series called *Der Insulaner* (The Islander) was most popular with all West Berliners. Created during the Blockade, it was still running at this time and remained by far the most favorite radio program. West Berlin being an "island in the Red Sea" had given inspiration for a program series of comedies about West Berlin's grave situation in general, infused with quite a bit of sarcastic humor about the Communist regime which was attacked in a humorous way. The program reflected the Berliners' legendary ability to cope with anything, and making fun of the most desperate situations on top of it.

One of our favorite evenings together would be *Schokoladenabend* (chocolate evening). Chocolate was now available. Occasionally for a special treat Mom would buy a whole chocolate bar (3½ ounces) for each of us. Then Mom, Peter and I would sit in bed before going to sleep, and while eating our chocolate bars we would talk, laugh, and exchange stories and funny happenings. Some of it would be reminiscing, such as: "Remember during the bad times, when we had to stay in bed to keep warm, and were happy to have one piece of dry bread to eat?" Those times seemed so far in the past, yet only three years had gone by since then. Now we were each eating our favorite kind of chocolate for dessert instead of dry bread for dinner. Mostly we had fun and we laughed a lot. Spending an evening with a chocolate treat while talking and laughing was special and memorable. Such times together were immensely valuable and bonding!

Ice cream had also become available. The restaurant across the street sold ice cream because the Americans liked it, and they had money. We often saw American military people stroll down the street. They liked to talk to children, and particularly liked Peter who was a friendly and outgoing kid. Many times Peter would come home and tell us about having received a treat of either an ice cream waffle (two small waffles with ice cream in between like a sandwich) or chewing gum from American soldiers after he had run an errand for them or helped them find a street, or whatever. They always called him "Pete." We did not abbreviate names in such a way, and when Peter told us it was pronounced "Pit," the family and friends started calling Peter "*Pittchen*" (an endearment), and still do so to this day.

Fireworks at the Funkturm

As West Berlin's economy recovered, our range of activities expanded. The city was really coming to life now considering what Berlin had been through. There were going to be fireworks at the *Funkturm*

Funkturm and Messegelände (fairgrounds)

(radio tower) by the lake on the fairgrounds, and Mom thought we should go. Everyone else was going. It was May first, Labor Day in Europe, and big fireworks were advertised. I did not want to go. Fireworks meant noise like bomb explosions, and I cringed at the thought of it. Peter was excited. Being four years younger than I, he did not remember the bombings as I did. Mom described to us the most beautiful fireworks she remembered ever seeing in her youth, where there had been displays looking like suns and windmills, hoping to make it more desirable to me. I went along, of course, but not happily.

When we got off the subway at the *Funkturm Messegelände* Station we joined the mass migration of bodies headed for the fireworks. All of Berlin seemed to be on foot. I was ready to turn around when we got into that mayhem. It reminded me of the lines of people during the days of long food lines, and of overcrowded trains and streetcars.

Next came the fun of finding a good place to stand where we could hopefully see more than only the high shots. The little lake at which the fireworks were to be shot off was no longer approachable. Mom noticed a place between walkways at which a small area was staked out with wires around it to keep people from stepping on the new grass.

Mom suggested that we stand immediately behind that area so that nobody could get in front of us and we would be able to see better. It was a good place to stand and the fireworks were beautiful, although I was startled and jumped or shivered at the noise of each shot. In between whenever there was a lull, I had time to tease Mom because there had not been any of the suns and windmills she had described to us earlier.

During each small pause, people were shifting in hopes of finding a better place to stand in order to see more. Noticing the empty space directly in front of us, some headed for it, tripped over the low wires, and fell onto the damp "to–be grass" area. Mom was the first one to notice this and we tried to warn people, but most were so concentrated on watching the fireworks that they paid no attention to our efforts. Soon we gave up trying. As we watched them fall we laughed at their surprised reactions. Others followed as if in a stampede, and while the fireworks were going on and people looked up instead of at the ground, more and more tripped and fell into the soft soil and on top of each other. We, as well as others who were standing near us, were no longer watching the fireworks but rather watching the people either fall, or do all sorts of last–second acrobatics while trying to keep from falling. Some got angry when they heard us laugh, others joined in the laughter. Mom, Peter and I remembered that episode more than the fireworks. We still laughed all the way home, and for a week thereafter.

Summer 1952

Berlin's largest lake, the *Wannsee*, has two islands—*Pfaueninsel* (Peacock Island) and *Schwanenwerder* (Swan Island). Army tents and cots had been donated by the Americans to set up summer camps on those islands for West Berlin school children. Peter had been to one of those camps the previous summer. He had enjoyed it tremendously and was going again. Mom found out that children under eighteen years of age were entitled to go to camp regardless of whether or not they were still in school. She suggested that I go since I liked camping. Having missed out on so much earlier in our lives, Mom was always looking out for Peter and me to take advantage of any experience possible. I was not going to be eighteen until September. This would be the last summer in which I would be entitled to participate.

Another one of Mom's motives was to have concrete plans made to sort of force Herr Heyn into giving me a vacation. I had heard from the older employees that it was extremely difficult to get time off for any vacation at all. Herr Heyn balked, of course, but he was in no position to argue that I was not entitled to a vacation after a year of working there. Being under eighteen I was entitled to four weeks by law, but was asking for only three weeks to go to this camp. He did not really understand why I wanted to go to a camp, but on the other hand he did not want my mother to come in for a confrontation again. Consequently, with or without his blessings I was going to camp.

I was sent to beautiful *Schwanenwerder* in Lake *Wannsee* with kids in my age group. It was like being in paradise, living in tents in the forest with water all around, hiking and swimming every day, as well as having plenty of good food and fresh air. The camp even had access to two small rowboats, so that once during the stay everyone had a turn to be taken out on a little cruise after dinner. Camp was a lot of fun and I was so thankful to Mom for insisting that I go.

Afterwards came the treat for Mom. I had learned an American line dance in camp, to the tune of "she'll be coming 'round the mountain when she comes." I loved this dance and wanted to teach it to Mom but we needed lots of people. One day when we were visiting at my friend Alice's I rounded up Mom, Peter, Alice and her Mom, her brother, and even the grandma plus a few "ghosts"—and tried to teach them the

dance. To my dismay they just didn't get it. All they wanted to do was to sing "yippi, yippi" and clown around. Alice caught on and thought it might be fun, but noone else appreciated what teenagers liked. So much for "yippi, yippi," as Mom liked to call this favorite dance of mine. She seemed to like the word "yippi". Later in the 1960's when the Hippy era started, Mom always referred to them as the "Yippies."

Mealtime at camp. I am sitting at this end on the left.

Back to the Salt Mine

Herr Heyn must have missed the services of his office slave while I was away. Upon my return I received a raise, having worked there for a year by then. This brought me up to one hundred and twenty Marks a month. After the invigorating camp experience I plowed into action with an overabundance of energy.

As the company expanded to include more and more cosmetic lines, additional people were hired to help with the extra workload. There were two drivers now, as well as a person who compiled the orders in the stockroom. We were also looking into the practicality of bottling certain eau de colognes. It was expensive to import heavyweight goods, and bottles could now be manufactured in Berlin and filled by us. Herr Rattay was hired to corroborate with Dr. Burmester about the feasibility, and then to put the plan into action. Our ace, *Eau de Sortilege* by Le Galion was doing quite well in the market and was also under consideration to being bottled locally. My five hundred letters to market *Sortilege* were paying off even better than expected.

My workload of typing all the extra invoices and additional correspondence was enormous, yet there was no sign of extra help for me despite Dr. Burmester's hints to his friend Alfred. As the nine and ten o'clock quitting times became the rule rather than the exception, Herr Heyn occasionally gave me an unexpected bonus of fifty or even a hundred Marks. This helped the family finances but my social life was nonexistent.

With ration cards nearly gone now for Berlin, we could buy some special treats for Christmas. There was chocolate and candy, oranges, and other foods which we did not remember existed. Except for chocolate and fruits I was not at all keen on sweets. I loved pickles and told Mom that I really wanted a dill pickle for Christmas—a whole pickle to eat all by myself without having to share it with the family by getting only a couple of slices at dinner time. I did get my pickle and I still remember the joy of biting into that crunchy, tasty treat.

Mom bought half a duckling for Christmas dinner, which made a mouth–watering meal for us for the two days of Christmas. The traditional German Christmas meal is goose, but it cost more than our budget could afford. We had entered a time which we thought we would never see, when food was available and money was scarce. Until recently it had been the opposite.

15

1953
Normal Life and Great Changes
Age Eighteen

New Year's Eve was really festive for us because we had a radio and could listen to some good programs for entertainment. To celebrate, Mom had made a traditional dish for us to eat now that the ingredients for it were available. It was new to Peter and me, and brought back pleasant memories for Mom. She felt like normal times had returned. Since I had no memory of *normal* times, I was delighted with the present. It was a remarkable time to be living in this city. The progress in the quality of life was amazing.

When a new year is about to start one always wonders what it may bring. This turned out to be the beginning of a year that would bring great changes for us which were to affect the future of the whole family.

Peter's Confirmation and a Job

On the first of April we celebrated Peter's confirmation. Mom and I were happy to present him with a bicycle, and Papa outfitted Peter with two suits, a trench coat, and a pair of shoes. Wow! Did our little boy look grown up in his first suit! We could even invite our relatives and friends to Peter's confirmation party, and feed them properly, too. What a difference from my confirmation five years ago, and how much had happened since then.

Peter on his Confirmation Day. He is all dressed up in his first suit.

Peter graduated from ninth grade in June. The school system was still undergoing changes, eight years after the end of the war. Last year because of extremely high unemployment, it had been decided to add a ninth grade to elementary school. This would keep the young people in school rather than sending them out looking for jobs which did not exist.

The whole education system had changed—once again. College, high school, and business school were done away with after they had been reinstated just a couple of years earlier. Instead it was now a *united* school system which was divided into three branches—the scientific, technical, and practical branches. I do not see much difference except that it was fashioned after the Soviet system, where the individual branches were not called "high school, college, or business school."

Peter had previously been placed in the technical branch where he spent grades six to nine. Since he was not going on to any further studies after graduation and jobs were hard to find, he was initially hired by a little grocery store across the street from us as an apprentice. There he worked long hours for minimum pay. The owner, Herr Havranek, had a terrible temper and Peter was afraid of him. He rarely gave Peter the time off to attend vocational school twice a week for half a day. This was required in order to learn business management, and was a part of the agreement when taking on an apprentice. It was not until Mom stopped by and had a few words with the man, that he complied—though reluctantly.

Peter Works with Papa

Mom watched this for a short time, then mentioned to Papa one day that Peter was not being educated properly to learn business management. Instead he was being used as a handyman for everything in the store and around the house, including helping the owner's daughter with her homework. Mom felt that Peter was being taken advantage of. Papa said he could use some help and suggested that Peter come and work with him.

Papa had been working as a salesman for a tobacco goods company, a family–owned business called *Tabak Erbach,* since before I was born. With tobacco goods now available and the company being back in business stronger than before, Papa was able to work as an independent supplier. This meant that he had his own customers whom he supplied directly. He had to go out and get the orders, write his invoices, compile the orders, and deliver the goods, which he did by bicycle. It was a hard job. There was no way he could afford to buy a car.

On several occasions Mom had commented to me that Papa looked tired and not at all well. Feeling that the job was getting too hard for him, Mom had suggested that he at least buy a motorized bike. With a tall load on the back of the bicycle, even a small hill in a basically flat city seems like a mountain. Papa was glad when Peter came to work with him and took over the job of making deliveries to his customers as well as getting new orders. This meant carrying heavy loads on the bicycle, but Peter enjoyed it. He had a new bike and was young and strong. Many of Papa's good customers had been loyal to him since before the war, and Peter could easily get orders from them. They liked Peter. He was polite, friendly, and outgoing.

For Peter this was a time of getting to know his father and starting a good relationship with him. Frau Wilde, the woman with whom Papa now lived, was wonderful to Peter. She adored him and could not do enough for him. Frau Wilde was an exceptionally kindhearted person.

Peter with his bicycle on a typical cobblestone street in rural Lichterfelde.

In the tumultuous time at the very end of the war she had taken in a baby girl which she had found abandoned in the street, and raised her. Frau Wilde had lost both of her sons as well as her husband during the war, and this girl had given her a lot of joy and a purpose for living. Papa was so happy to have his son spend weekdays with him. The separation and divorce had been devastating to him, too.

I made it a point to visit with Papa, and also with Grandma Stanneck, as often as I could get out of the office at a reasonable hour. This was getting easier lately. Under pressure from my self–appointed protector, Dr. Burmester, Herr Heyn had finally hired a girl to help me with my workload.

I enjoyed visiting Papa. Frau Wilde was always kind to me and tactfully withdrew so that I could have time alone with my father. Papa and I were just starting to get acquainted as adults, and it seemed to be difficult for both of us. He always appeared extremely sad to me. I knew that he had memories of horrible experiences from fighting on the Russian front, and especially of his POW time in Russia. He never wanted to talk about these experiences which had changed him so much. The breakup of my parents' marriage had not been entirely his idea either. I always had the feeling that he would have liked to have mended things despite of all the differences. Mom could be quite stubborn, and she had become an extremely independent woman during the war, albeit by necessity. To be sure, Grandma had been the wedge that really doomed the marriage, and Mom never had a chance from day one.

Many years later I understood. Frau Wilde had been a godsend to our Papa during an extremely difficult time in his life when he needed a lot of understanding to heal the wounds of his past experiences, just as the abandoned baby girl she had picked up in the street was healing hers. I made contact with Frau Wilde during my visit to Berlin in 1980 and we had a heartfelt talk. She was so happy to hear about Peter's family and mine, and was hoping to meet my family during a future visit. I promised to keep in touch with her. In 1982 I took my husband and children to meet her. She was delighted with my family.

A year later Peter and I surprised Frau Wilde with a visit when we were both in Berlin for the occasion of Tante Lotte and Onkel Martin's fiftieth wedding anniversary. Peter bought a huge bouquet of red roses for the woman who had been so good to him, and especially to our Papa during a very difficult time. Frau Wilde was undeniably delighted to see Peter again, and she enjoyed looking at pictures of his children. It was our last visit together. She was eighty–six years old at the time and her health was failing. She died within a year. Peter and I were glad that we had included her in our lives. It was a good closure for her as well as for us.

The Happy Life

Goods became more and more available in West Berlin, and Mom and I had a lot of fun buying a piece of clothing now and then. Living on a major business street, we watched several new shops open up. One of those was a small boutique for which the owner, Herr Hannemann, did all of the designing and sewing himself. His prices were quite reasonable. Mom and I loved to look at Hannemann's window displays. We were attracted by his unusual designs and were dreaming that some day we could afford to buy more of his creations. My red corduroy outfit had come from his shop, and I received compliments all of the time.

As jobs became more plentiful and salaries increased—I was now earning one hundred thirty Marks a month—we were able to afford the luxury of an additional piece of clothing occasionally, or some fabric to make a dress or a blouse. I owned a regular pair of shoes by now, and with gladness I gave my boots to Peter to wear with his ice skates.

Mom and I wore the same size and we shared some of our clothes, although I was two inches taller than she was. We also had a lot of fun designing dresses for me to wear to the dances I participated in. Mom never bought a pattern. She was a tailor and could make her own patterns and designs. I inherited some of her aptitude and was learning much from her.

At this point I owned several outfits to wear at work, and I could at last retire my confirmation dress—which I had worn for more than five years. With two outfits, one could alternate every week, wearing one outfit one week and the other one the next. My red corduroy outfit with the white blouse was still so becoming that I did not mind washing and ironing the white blouse every other day. But now I had a summer dress as well, and a skirt to wear with different blouses in addition. By winter time I would be able to make another dress.

Life was really good now. I enjoyed my dancing, both social and competition, dated now and then, and life had stabilized after so many years of turmoil. We had not even moved in almost four years! After ten years we were still on the waiting list for an apartment of our own although where we lived now was almost as good as having our own apartment. Mom and Herr Walther were not in each other's way in the kitchen because of having different schedules. I can honestly say that things were going exceedingly well for our little family.

In the Aftermath of War

Not that the awful war and the damage it had done could easily be forgotten. There were daily reminders of the horrors it had bestowed on us. The Russians had taken prisoner 3.3 million German soldiers, of which 1.1 million died in captivity. At the end of the war the Russians did not release all of these prisoners, instead keeping many of the healthy ones as slave labor in Siberia. It was not until 1955 when Germany and the U.S.S.R. reestablished diplomatic relations that the last prisoners were finally released.

Numerous times we would hear of the heartbreaking story of a POW in tattered clothes finally arriving from Russia after all these years to find that he had been given up as dead, and his wife remarried. Life had started anew, which did not include him. This was a fairly common occurrence, tragic as it may seem. The lists of POWs and of those missing in action were endless and incomplete, so that it was not uncommon for a man to show up after many years of not having been heard from. The Red Cross did what it could to get people back together. Unfortunately many tragic fates were a part of everyday life then.

The divorce rate was shocking, but on reflection, hardly surprising. Men who had seen war at close range had changed so much as a result of the horrible experience that many of them had difficulty fitting back into society. At the same time, the women had been coping with life and their young families at home as best as they could. They had become independent, were the heroes in their children's eyes, and were accustomed to being the bread winners. For many women it became impossible to readjust to married life. It was often no less difficult for the children to adjust to having the father at home without seeing him as a rival for their mother's attention.

The population of Berlin, and most likely of all other cities that had experienced heavy bombings, could not tolerate certain noises which were reminders of the air raids. In Berlin the sirens of fire engines and ambulances had to be changed to play a different tune. The oscillating whine of the regular sirens struck people with terror.

A Visitor from America

My Grandmother Stanneck was the third–oldest of ten children. Her sister Martha, the youngest, had emigrated to the United States in 1929 when she was twenty–seven years old. She was the one who had sent us CARE packages in 1947 and early 1948. Now in July of 1953 she came to visit Germany for the first time since she had left.

The first time I met Aunt Martha was at her brother Karl's apartment in Zehlendorf where there was a gathering of relatives. Mom took Peter and me to visit, to thank Aunt Martha personally for the CARE packages she had sent. Some of Aunt Martha's other brothers

Valten Family Reunion in Berlin

From left: Martha Valten, Marie Valten Stanneck (Grandma), Berta and Reinhold Valten, Paul Valten, Karl Valten and Martha Valten Timmann from the U.S.A.

and their families had come from East Germany for the occasion. We did not know any of those from East Germany except for Onkel Wilhelm, the youngest of the brothers, who had stayed with us in Straupitz at the time we were invaded by the Russians at the end of the war. It was an awkward gathering. I felt as if we had all come to stare at some kind of a monument—Aunt Martha. Only her brothers and sisters were old enough to have known Aunt Martha before she left Germany many years earlier.

The second time I met Aunt Martha was at Tante Else's apartment on the last night of her visit in Berlin. It was an evening gathering with more relatives from East Germany, all of whom I also met for the first time. Neither Papa nor Peter were able to attend because of work. With so many people competing for Aunt Martha's attention, I really did not have a conversation with her, but I did notice that she kept looking at me as if she liked me, or perhaps wanted to say something. That was the end of her visit.

As the summer went on I enjoyed many trips to some of Berlin's lakes for swimming. I loved to swim. Now that I had a bicycle I could ride to one of the lakes on a hot evening after work and cool off.

Papa's Death

On the evening of August 19, Peter came home from work while I was sitting alone eating my dinner. Mom was out on some errands. I thought Peter looked white, like a ghost. He sat down at the table across from me, but he did not say a word. Wondering why he was home later than normal, I offered to get him a plate of stew, but he just shook his head. He was strangely quiet and kept watching me—staring at me without seeing me—for a short time. Suddenly he said in a grave voice: "Inge, Papa died this morning." I went into shock.

Papa had died of a heart attack, and was dead before Peter could go for a doctor. He had been alone with Papa at that time, and saw him fall down and die. This experience would cause him many years of nightmares. Peter had just turned fifteen and Papa was only forty–seven years old.

All the East German relatives who had been in Berlin just a few weeks earlier for the happy occasion of welcoming Aunt Martha from

America, were now back to say a last farewell to our Papa.

Peter worked Papa's customers for a few more weeks to get things wound down, then Herr Erbach, owner of the firm, hired Peter as an apprentice to learn the wholesale business. Along with his apprenticeship, Peter went to vocational school twice a week for the next three years.

Although I had made a couple of dresses for myself by now, my black confirmation dress had to be pressed back into service. It was customary in Germany to wear black clothes for a year to mourn the deceased. After a few weeks of seeing me in black Mom said I was too young to walk around in mourning clothes any longer,

Erich Stanneck

and I agreed. The color of the dress did not change how I felt inside, and I did not need to put on a show for other people.

At the office, Herr Heyn had become thoughtful after I lit into him a few days after Papa's death, telling him that he would also die soon if he kept drinking so much coffee all day long and smoking nonstop, as Papa had done. He immediately cut down on both, but not for long. Herr Heyn also started to become somewhat protective of me in a fatherly way.

My Friend Evelyn

Life went on at the office. Herr Heyn had recently hired a girl to help with the office work. Her name was Evelyn Lesch and eventually we were to become lifelong friends. It was now her first priority to type the invoices every day as the volume had increased, and I was being kept too busy with typing correspondence.

On a beautiful sunny September day about a month later, Evelyn and I took our lunch bags and went out to sit in the little park above the subway station *Hohenzollernplatz* which was across the street from the office. During our conversation I mentioned to her that I was delighted to have someone about my age working at the office, and that it was my nineteenth birthday that day. Evelyn told me that she would be nineteen in two days. Years later after we had become fast friends, we adopted each other as twin sisters.

Even though Evelyn's desk was in the next room where Herr Müller and Frau Moritz had theirs, we did not see much of each other. There was hardly ever time to exchange a few words. Lunch in the park that one day had been a rare occasion because Herr Heyn was away and we took time for a lunch break. Mostly we either ate while working or, more often than not, we did not eat at all.

We did not have time to see each other socially until months later when Evelyn and I went to see a movie together one day. She lived in Berlin–Zehlendorf very close to where Onkel Karl and Tante Martha lived, near the subway station called *Onkel Toms Hütte*. Evelyn invited

*My favorite subway station **Onkel Toms Hütte**. There are shops on the left all along the station platform, and again on the other side of the train. Fences separate the station from the shopping areas.*

me to her apartment to introduce me to her parents. Her father liked books. I remember Herr Lesch sitting at a big desk and behind him was a whole wall of bookshelves filled with nice books. I was so impressed. Only once before had I met a person who owned a large desk like his. All the other people we knew, including ourselves, had just the bare minimum of furniture left after the war. No luxury items.

The subway stop *Onkel Toms Hütte* is a unique one. Because my aunt and uncle lived near there, I had known it since I was a young child, and always loved it. There was an underground shopping street, the *Ladenstraße,* parallel to the tracks on both sides, which was divided from the station with fences. Whenever the train pulled into the station, I used to enjoy seeing the shops, and I always wished that we lived there and could shop in this unique underground street. There even was a movie theater. After the end of the war, American families lived in that area and they also occupied the shopping street at the subway station. For a time it was off–limits to Germans.

At the time I met Evelyn the area was open to Germans again and I was as excited as a little kid to go to the *Ladenstraße* for the first time. Evelyn had troubles getting me to go into the movie theater—I was happy to just walk in that street and look at the shops. They were nothing special really, just a variety of general merchandise shops such as baker, butcher, greengrocer, drug store, housewares—the kind of shops we had where we lived. But these were special to me because they were all next to each other, concentrated in one street and under one roof like a miniature shopping mall. That evening was an experience—I was elated to finally have been in the quaint little shopping arcade which I had been admiring all of my life. Little things do mean a lot!

There was only one other occasion on which Evelyn and I went out together, the following Feb-

Evelyn Lesch

ruary at Mardi Gras time. The *Freie Universität von Berlin* (Free University) sponsored a student ball and it was quite a nice affair. The lecture halls were decorated in different themes and each hall had a band playing a different type of music. People were dressed up in Mardi Gras costumes—or supposed to be—but we did not really have anything to wear to this affair. I borrowed a pair of blue jeans and a plaid shirt from a friend, and Evelyn also wore blue jeans and a shirt. Those were special clothes for us. I did not own any casual clothes at the time, let alone any dress–up clothes to wear to a Mardi Gras ball. A close family friend of Evelyn's parents who was going to be there, had been given the job of keeping an eye on Evelyn and me. We were amused about having a chaperon.

Grandma Stanneck

After Papa's death I started visiting Grandma regularly once a week in the evenings after work. I knew how devastated she must be after her son's death, and I wanted her to have something to look forward to every week. Mom had encouraged me to do this.

Grandma, who normally was a fighter, had become quite subdued. I had the feeling that she had no appetite and was not preparing any food for herself. Soon I went there twice a week and took food to her so we could eat together, but she just nibbled and said she was not hungry.

On October 25, Mom called me at the office to tell me not to stop at Grandma's on my way home that evening. Grandma was dead. She had given up on life and died of a broken heart. With her son no longer living, she felt that she had nothing left to live for, and her heart stopped.

Marie Valten Stanneck, my Grandmother

A Letter From America

Late in the fall of 1953 I received a letter from America which would change the direction of my life, and play a major role in determining my future and that of my family.

Aunt Martha wrote and invited me to immigrate to the United States. She wrote to tell me that she and Uncle Adolph would do the necessary sponsorship if I wanted to come. Aunt Martha went on to say that they would be happy to have me live with them—they lived in northern New Jersey—and that close friends of theirs had a daughter who was my age, hinting that I would have a friend when I came. Aunt Martha also wrote: "If you don't like it here, you can always return to Germany." These words helped immensely in making this most difficult decision.

Mom was ecstatic—I was numb. While Mom was dancing around the room with the letter in her hand and singing "pack the bags, you're going to America," I was totally speechless. At last I found enough words to say: "No, I am not going." Mom could not believe it. My reasoning was that we were doing fairly well at that time. I was earning a little more money so that I could be of help to Mom with the finances. Although Peter was working, he was far from being able to be on his own. As an apprentice he earned only fifty Marks a month during his first year of apprenticeship, and would be paid at the most seventy–five Marks in his third year. I needed to stay around to help Mom. She had struggled enough throughout the years we were in school. Now that things were getting better for us I was not going to abandon my mother and brother.

Mom's reasoning was that West Berlin was a time bomb which could explode at any moment. "There is no future here in Berlin," she said, "so get out of here while you can. This is your once–in–a–lifetime opportunity, and it must not be passed up." When I argued some more, Mom came up with the deciding trump in that she said: "Look, you can go over there and try it, and, as Aunt Martha writes, if you don't like it you just come back. In that case you will have had a great trip and have seen America."

Little did we know how big America really is. Now fifty years later, I am still working on seeing it! Mom also pointed out that this move of mine would benefit the whole family in one way or another. It was her belief that we would all have a better life if I decided to emigrate, which came to be true in the years to come. At this point her reasoning finally made sense to me, although I was sure that I would return. Remembering my five weeks in Saxony as an eight–year–old, I just knew that I would get homesick.

I had to admit that a trip to America sounded wonderful, but I could not get enthusiastic about leaving Mom and Peter—and Berlin. With my bicycle I had been discovering what a beautiful city Berlin is with its lakes and forests, parks, rivers and canals. I also remembered how happy I had been to be back in the city after we returned from Straupitz.

Then there was my dancing. I was about to sign up for training— over Mom's veto—to participate in ballroom dance endurance contests. Mom did not want to hear about that at all. She felt it was too rigorous and that I had enough stress at work. With Mom being totally against it, I now had the feeling that she wanted to ship me off to America which would automatically end my fighting her about the endurance dance issue. She knew how strongly I disagreed with her on that.

"My Fate is Sealed"

Mom had me sit down and write back within a couple of days to tell Aunt Martha and Uncle Adolph that I would happily accept their offer, and to ask what the next step would be. Before mailing the letter I kept it with me at the office until the end of the workday. I well remember my feelings and my hesitation before I dropped my letter into the mailbox. Holding it in both hands, I looked at it and expected it to talk to me and reassure me that it was the right thing to do. Then, as I dropped the letter into the box, I said: "My fate is sealed." I still see myself standing there and staring at the mailbox. My letter was inside it.

What a weighty decision for a nineteen–year–old to have to make! Was I joyously happy about it? No.

It took probably a couple of weeks of walking around as in a daze before I fully realized what I was about to do. I clung to Aunt Martha's words "you can always go back." On the other hand, I felt a sense of responsibility with the realization that "the whole family will benefit"— if I go—and if don't? It just took time to get used to the idea. I remembered our teacher's stories about his POW days in Arizona. I had seen a movie of huge cattle drives in Texas, and seen a slide show about

Niagara Falls, Yellowstone Park, and the Grand Canyon. Now I would travel to that fantastic, faraway country.

Here I have to make an important observation about Mom's strong suggestion that I leave despite my reluctance. Mom was the most unselfish person I have ever known. She had a traumatic childhood having grown up during and after World War I, and had lived through its aftermath of deprivation and starvation, as well as runaway inflation. Then came her marriage, the Great Depression, and World War II where she found herself fighting for survival once again, this time with her two young children. Up until now her life had been one big struggle.

Mom wanted Peter and me to have a better life than she has had. Her intuition and long range vision were astonishing. She intuitively knew that her big decision to let me go would be for the better. America was a safe and stable place to be. It was the number one world power. I knew how hard it was for Mom to send me away, and I also knew that she would have to struggle again to make ends meet. However, she felt that it was best for my future, if not for the future of all of us.

Applying for U.S. Immigration

The next few months were extremely busy ones. There was ongoing correspondence with Aunt Martha, and collecting the necessary papers required for immigration into the United States. In addition I was working long hours, dancing, sightseeing in Berlin, and sewing clothes for myself.

Last year, Parfuemerie Royale had become the distributor for the products of The Mennen Company, a family–owned business located in Morristown, New Jersey, which manufactured men's toiletries and baby products. We had just received authorization to bottle Mennen Skin Bracer, an after shave lotion, in Berlin. For the time being we were doing this in the basement of the old apartment. We had also hired several more people for the office and were now renting an additional apartment in the building adjacent to ours. The whole office moved to the other building, except Herr Heyn and I stayed put. He had asked me where I wanted our office to be, either next door or where we were. I told him that I did not care where I sat, as long as it was as far away as possible—and when I hesitated, he finished the sentence for me—"from bookkeeping." When I looked surprised that he knew, he said: "I know what's going on around here. That Moritz woman is going on my nerves, too. I'd just as soon be some distance away from her." We both laughed. That settled it and Herr Heyn and I kept the little office with the painstakingly erased and now clean wallpaper. The rest of the old apartment was turned into manufacturing and warehouse.

Of course I had a secret—I did not need to put up with Frau Moritz or anyone else there much longer. For the time being I did not say anything to anyone at work about my invitation to emigrate to the USA. While I was beginning to get used to the idea, I still had mixed feelings, and at times I wondered whether it all was reality. However, at work I was too busy to think much about it.

A couple of weeks before Christmas, Herr Heyn asked me to come and work at his house to help him with a special project of record keeping. This included an invitation to join the family for a wonderful Sunday dinner. Frau Heyn was an excellent cook, and the delicious roast was a special treat for me and something we could not afford at home. Herr Heyn paid me three hundred Marks for working that day and as additional Christmas bonus. We had already received a small Christmas bonus at work, and I was not to mention this special one to bookkeeping because our Frau Moritz would become hysterical. Herr Heyn feared the outbreak of a civil war at the office.

Christmas 1953

The holiday season this year was both joyous and bittersweet. We had so much to be thankful for. We had jobs, enough food to eat, a warm room, and all the necessities we needed for a reasonably comfortable life. In addition we had luxuries: two rooms in a nice apartment, a radio, bicycles, some nice clothes, and even a Christmas tree. But most importantly, we had freedom and good health.

I had been invited to immigrate to the United States. This meant that I had to leave the family, and my Berlin.

Papa was gone. Grandma Stanneck was gone.

It was Christmas—the festival of light and love, of anticipation about the future, and of hope for a peaceful new year. Christmas 1953.

It was impossible not to get carried along with the Christmas spirit. Having received the generous Christmas bonus from Herr Heyn, Mom and I could now go to that favorite little boutique of ours and buy the two winter coats we had so admired in the window. We were going to buy them for ourselves anyway, but we would have had to pay them off in a number of installments. I was still wearing the lightweight, and by now shabby, winter coat which Mom had taken as payment for sewing work five years earlier. Mom owned only a jacket of medium weight. Two years ago she had given her winter coat to someone on the street who was freezing and had no coat. Mom wore her new coat only that one winter. When I left for the United States, she insisted that I take her coat with me. She felt I ought to have two winter coats so that I would have a good start as far as my wardrobe was concerned. This unselfishness was so typical of Mom.

We did have a wonderful Christmas. Nevertheless, the realization suddenly hit me that if proceedings for my immigration to the United States continued to move along as smoothly as they had been so far, then this would be my last Christmas in Berlin.

16

1954
Breaking the Ties
Age Nineteen

Quitting my Job

At the beginning of the new year things were moving along quite rapidly with my immigration procedures. Once I had passed my physical examination at the American medical facility it looked like my visa for the United States might be issued within a month or two. With this news I finally got caught up in the excitement about my upcoming adventure.

Until now I had not said anything to anyone at the office. I was required by law to give three months notice, so it was time to inform my boss of my plans for the future, and to quit my job. Once I received my visa I had to use it within four months or it would become invalid.

Herr Heyn was shocked when I told him that I was emigrating to America. He could not believe that I wanted to do such a thing and go so far away from home. After thinking about it for a few minutes, though, he admitted to me that if he were as young as I was and had the opportunity, he would take advantage of it, too. He had just raised my salary to two hundred Marks a month to be more competitive in the job market, and now he instantly raised it to two hundred and fifty Marks—perhaps hoping that I would change my mind and stay.

At this point I found out that I had a very valuable ally in our dear old Dr. Burmester. First, he rubbed it in by asking his friend Alfred whether he was aware that he was about to lose his best worker, and prophesied that he would have to hire three people to replace me. Dr. Burmester was genuinely happy for me and wished me good luck. He immediately offered to write a recommendation for me, in English, when the time came for me to leave. It was he who kept encouraging me during the next few months whenever I expressed doubts about my venture. As my self–appointed mentor, I turned to him with questions about the USA, since he had been there several times before the war. If he could not answer a question, he would go to the trouble of finding out.

Evelyn, who was a big fan of everything American, wished that she could go in my place since I did not seem too enthusiastic about it. Before I left, I had to promise her to write and tell her all about my life in America. Those long letters to each other were the beginning of our lifelong friendship. With the help of my husband, Evelyn immigrated to the United States in 1959, and she still lives in northwestern New Jersey.

Frau Moritz assured me that I would not like America because her son had emigrated to Australia and returned a few months later. He did not like Australia. I failed to see what Australia had to do with America, but one did not argue with Frau Moritz. I just "closed the door" on her.

Herr Müller smiled in his quiet way. He said he was happy for me and wished me good luck for the future.

Herr Renner, one of our salesmen in Berlin, called me up on the phone and spoke to me in fluent English. I had no idea who was calling or what he was saying, and thought that perhaps it was a phone call from The Mennen Company. Herr Renner then switched to German and told me he just assumed I could speak the language. He wanted me to be able to practice by having someone to talk to, and he offered to be that someone.

The whole staff was in a turmoil and more excited about my upcoming trip than I was. The crew in production who were bottling not only Mennen Skin Bracer but also the luxurious French Eau de Cologne *Sortilege*, poured some of that expensive stuff into their tea and toasted my obvious good fortune. Herr Götz, the driver, henceforth had permission to give me rides whenever I needed to go to the different authorities to collect some of the required papers. I promised to send him wallpaper from America if he ever got stuck with a nasty erasing job again. He had really disliked that chore, but we still laughed every time we talked about it.

A Job in the USA

Whenever people asked me if I knew English, I had to answer "very little." Living in the American sector of Berlin, English was required in all schools. Theoretically I could have had nearly five years of English lessons, but through circumstances, I started to learn English from the beginning five times during that period. The longest cumulative time of English instruction I had was during the last year and a half of business school. Under more normal circumstances I would have had three years in total. Those were still unstable times back then. Refugee families continued to arrive from the eastern regions given to Poland where they had been imprisoned. Each time there was a new girl in class, the teacher had to start from the beginning to accommodate her.

How would I get a job with so little knowledge of the English language? Well, I had it all figured out, of course. I would try to get a job working on a production line in a factory, and when I had learned enough English I could get back into an office job. For simple, everyday conversation I could get along from the start—or so I thought—until I found out that I had been taught British English, and that American English seemed to be quite a different language.

When filling out a questionnaire for immigration I had to cheat a little, as per suggestion from Aunt Martha. Unskilled workers such as manual laborers who worked on production lines were plentiful in the United States. Aunt Martha found out that farm workers were in great demand. It just so happened that Uncle Adolph's brother, Bill, lived on a farm in Pennsylvania. It was not a crop raising farm—Bill had farmland and a few domestic animals, but he actually earned his living by being a painter. According to Aunt Martha's instructions I was to write on the questionnaire that I was going to work on the farm. With that statement I would have a better chance of being granted a visa within the current year's immigration quota.

A Visa and a Trip to the USA

Everything worked out better than expected, and one day in early spring I was asked to appear at the American Consulate to receive my immigration visa for the United States of America.

Now it was real and I was excited, especially about the ship voyage. Immigrants then still traveled by ship. Flying was much more expensive, and the baggage allowance was too limited. Mom and I had already decided on the *M.S. Italia* for the voyage to New York, and had picked up a brochure at the travel agency. The *Italia* was an old ship of the Hamburg–America Line, and the first ship to sail under the German flag again after World War II.

To pay for the visa—twenty–five dollars or one hundred Marks—and for the ship voyage—one hundred eighty–five dollars or seven hundred forty Marks—I had to take Aunt Martha up on her offer and borrow the money from her. It would otherwise have taken me several years to save this amount, and the visa was valid for only four months. I planned to travel as inexpensively as possible, and Mom and I selected an outside cabin—I wanted a window—which could accommodate four people, for a sailing from Hamburg on May 22 and arriving in New York on June 2.

I quit my job at the office as of April 30. Mom felt I should have some time to make farewell visits with relatives and friends, and to go through all of my belongings and decide on what to take. She also felt that I needed some rest from the treadmill I had been working so that I could arrive in the United States in good shape. I could not know then that during the ocean voyage I would need all of the stored up energy I could get.

People at work were wonderful. I had always been very quiet and minded my own business in addition to being isolated by the fact that I was the secretary of the "big boss" and worked in the same room with him. We had quite a few employees by now because of the bottling of some of the products at our facility. I had no idea that anybody cared whether or not I was there, or even knew that I was there. Now, people who knew anything about America stopped into my office to visit, and to offer help with information I might need.

The most helpful person was Dr. Burmester. He kept asking me questions about where I was going to live, and what I was going to do to make a living. When I told him of my plan, he did not seem to be happy with my idea of working in a factory. Upon questioning me, he

JMPORT   c. M. B. H.   **GROSSHANDEL**

TO WHOM IT MAY CONCERN!

Reference: **Miss Inge Stanneck**
　　　　　　born: 13.Sept.1934
　　　　　　Berlin-Lichterfelde
　　　　　　Germany.(US Sector)

BERLIN-WILMERSDORF
HOHENZOLLERNDAMM 204
TELEFON 91 52 49

Auslieferungslager:

HAMBURG 39

Hudtwalcker Straße 25c
TELEFON 48 22 22

Ihr Zeichen　　　Ihre Nachricht vom　　　Unser Zeichen **IV/S** BERLIN-WILMERSDORF 20.May 1954.

　　Miss Inge Stanneck started to work for us on 18.August 1951, on
her first position after leaving Commercial College, and remained with
us until 30.April 1954 when she left our services to join her relatives
in US. In the course of these almost 3 years Miss Stanneck has worked
her way from simple and routine office work to first secretarial position. This she achieved through her exceptional qualities of character
and intelligence which have made her our most valued employee.

　　From the first unto the last day of her employment Miss Stanneck
has untiringly devoted herself to whatever tasks were given her and
she has never once failed us, even under the most trying conditions
and during a time when this firm rose from comparatively modest begin-
nings to it's present position in the trade. Her capacity for work and
the precision with which she performed it were equally admirable; with
a sweet temper and a nice sense of humour she has endeared herself to
all her co-workers.

　　A thoroughly nice person, decent and modest, we hate to have her
leave our services; whenever she chooses to return she will find her
place waiting for her.

　　We wish Miss Stanneck the very best of luck for the new phase of
her life and are certain that she will prove herself wherever she is
placed.

　　　　　　　　　　　PARFUMERIE ROYALE G.m.b.H.

　　　　　　　　　　　(Alfred Heyn)
　　　　　　　　　　　Managing Director.

Postscheckkonto: Berlin-West 13 05. · Bankverbindung: Bankhaus Neumann & v. Massenbach, Berlin W 15

Letter of recommendation written by Dr. Burmester for Herr Heyn's signature.
Actually I never needed this letter because Dr. Burmester arranged for me to meet
Bill Mennen when he was visiting Herr Heyn in Berlin, and I had a job promised at
The Mennen Company before I left for the United States.

found out that my relatives lived in New Jersey, in the town of Cranford. He then made it his business to check with The Mennen Company to find out where Cranford is located in relation to Morristown, New Jersey. It turned out that the two towns were only about twenty miles apart. This pleased Dr. Burmester, and he immediately went to work on getting me a job with The Mennen Company. He told me that he would feel better if he knew I was going to be in good hands, which he certainly arranged, as I was to find out.

Soon Dr. Burmester received word from The Mennen Company that I would be hired there. He was relieved to know that someone would be looking out for me, and seemed to have been concerned about my journey into a strange country all by myself. How lucky could I get? Without my doing a thing the job question was resolved, and Aunt Martha was pleased when she received my letter telling her that she need not get involved in helping me find work.

Not only did Dr. Burmester arrange for me to be hired by The Mennen Company, but in addition he wrote a nice recommendation "To Whom it May Concern," in English, just in case I ever needed it. I don't know what I had done to deserve so much caring help, and in my mind I apologized to Dr. Burmester for feeling angry about his sneezing all over my typewriter at times when I was away from the office and he used my desk and typewriter.

During my last three months at the office we hired three girls, but Herr Heyn did not choose any of the three to be his secretary. He kept one girl for the general office, as the workload there had increased, and eventually let the other two go.

I was training each one of them, but then ran out of time. The training process was time consuming for me, and once again I stayed at work until late in the evenings to keep caught up. After I had left Germany, I found out that Herr Heyn eventually hired two other girls to work for him, replacing me. The reason for needing two was clear. As Berlin's economy recovered, jobs became more plentiful and nobody had to work the long hours that I did. Salaries had increased quite a bit, also.

My Days in Berlin are Numbered

After I left Parfumerie Royale at the end of April, I started a whirlwind of sightseeing in Berlin, visiting relatives, and getting ready for the trip. I had to sort out my stuff, sell my bicycle, and dispose of things I would not take. I also went to every dance that I could, with Mom as my chaperon. Ever since I knew that I would be leaving Germany, I had not been accepting any dates.

Along with the sorting of my belongings arose the question of toys. Yes, I was nineteen years old—but a familiar toy, a favorite doll perhaps, would be comforting to have. I never owned a teddy bear. The war must have started before I ever received one. At this point I remembered toys of the past. What happened to my doll house which Papa had built for me, my doll carriage and certain dolls, or even my favorite books? Abandoned? Left behind in the various moves? Toys had not been important during our fight for survival!

Rosemarie, my favorite doll, was still there, far in the back of the cabinet. It was the smallest one who always had more clothes than the others. Most leftover scraps of fabric which Mom could spare had been small ones. I loved to sew clothes for my dolls. Rosemarie, only about twelve inches tall, had been named for one of my two favorite little cousins who were killed in the last battle of Berlin. Rosemarie had been nearly five years old at the time and her sister, Hannelore was three and a half. Rosemarie had always been my favorite name when I was a child, and Hannelore my second favorite. Now Rosemarie was going to the United States with me.

Mom gave me a big farewell party to which she invited relatives and all of my friends. It surprised me that I had so many friends among the young police officers, who all wanted to come when Mom mentioned that she was having a party for me. I knew some of them from the police balls, but I had only danced and never dated anyone. Some of the men who wanted to come to our party were married, anyway. It was a great party with dancing and lots of good food, conversation, and fun. Papa's old gramophone which he had bought with some of his first paychecks, was playing the dance music.

Rosemarie on the bed in our first home. Unfortunately her head shattered from falling on the floor and she is no longer with us.

Something very touching happened at the end of this party. My close friend Gerda from next door and her boyfriend Gerhard were the last ones to leave. Gerhard, staying back for a moment to wish me well, said: "Inge, things may not work out the way you expect them to. It is possible that you will not like this faraway country, or that you are unhappy about being so far away from Berlin and your family. If that turns out to be the case, I want you to come home. I will help your mother get you back. I know she does not have the money, and neither do I, but we will find a way. She will not be alone. I promise you that I will help her get you back." Gerhard's words of reassurance gave me the courage to leave, and to stay in the United States even during some bouts with homesickness.

All of my friends liked my Mom, and several of them stopped by for visits during the next three years while she still lived in Berlin. Gerda and Gerhard married, and they still talk about Mom when I visit them in Berlin. A few days ago on the telephone—March 2002—Gerda told me that they walked past the old apartment house a few days earlier, and Gerhard said: "Let's stop in and visit Mother Stanneck."

Is Matchmaking a Custom in the USA?

About this time Aunt Martha wrote and, among other things, mentioned that German friends of theirs had a son who was about my age, and that they were anxious for me to meet him. I was shocked, surmising that matchmaking was a common practice in the United States. It scared me. I did not like the idea of well meaning people trying to find a prospective marriage partner for me. This was to become quite an issue in the years ahead. Furthermore, I was not going to get married at all. My parents' divorce had been hurting me to the point of thinking "what's the use."

In any case, I had no interest in getting tied down so soon, if at all. At this time I was only interested in seeing the world. I would go to America, work there, and eventually travel. Dreams of a nineteen–year–old!

Meeting Mr. Mennen

In 1878, the German immigrant Gerhard Mennen, a pharmacist, worked at a drugstore in Newark, New Jersey. He started his own business after buying the drugstore upon the owner's retirement. To start with, Mennen sold his own make of talcum powder and corn killer. He later manufactured men's toiletries, and eventually baby products which developed into a booming business. Two generations later in 1953, The Mennen Company had outgrown its quarters in the city of Newark and built a manufacturing plant in rural Morristown, New Jersey, employing three hundred fifty people. It was still a totally family–owned business, and William Gerhard Mennen, son of the founder, was in command as president. His two sons, William G. Mennen, Jr. and George S. Mennen, were vice presidents.

With Parfumerie Royale distributing the Mennen line in Germany and bottling Skin Bracer in Berlin, Mr. William G. Mennen, Jr. came to visit our facility in Berlin in 1954. One late morning in May, about ten days before I was to leave for the United States, the driver from the office stopped by our apartment—we had no telephone—and told me that Dr. Burmester had sent him to get me. I was to meet Mr. Mennen. Hastily I dressed up with a nice suit which I had made, and was ready to go within fifteen minutes. I was very nervous and hoped that I would make a good impression.

When I entered my familiar old office I was introduced to Mr. Mennen. He was a handsome man with a warm smile, a sense of humor, and a way of making people feel comfortable. Through Dr. Burmester's translation I was assured that I would have a job waiting for me. Mr. Mennen had asked me what kind of work I wanted to do. I told him about wanting to work on the production line until I learned adequate English and could do office work in the future. Mr. Mennen gave me his office telephone number and told me to phone him after my arrival in the United States, whenever I was ready to start working.

In the coming years Bill Mennen was to play an important role in my life.

Leaving Berlin

On Friday, May 21, 1954, I said "farewell" to my beloved Berlin. Mom was accompanying me to the port city of Hamburg, about one hundred and seventy miles northwest of Berlin. We were flying to Hamburg with Pan American Airlines, and it was to be the first airplane flight for both of us. Mom did not want me to travel through the Russian occupation zone with an American visa in my passport. Knowing how unpredictable the Soviets were, she was afraid to take any chances on their getting nasty to someone who was "escaping" to America, and possibly delaying me so that I would miss the departure of my ship. We had had enough experience with Soviet harassment to justify our mistrust.

I enjoyed my first airplane flight and was relieved that we did not have to sweat it out with fear at the East German border crossings. This immigration adventure started out great. Back came my memories of being a six–year–old, and how fascinated I was after learning from a friend that houses seen from an airplane look as small as matchboxes. Now my wish to see the matchbox size houses came true. I did see "matchboxes" down below. There were also little silver ribbons, which were rivers. It was wonderful to fly! The flight to Hamburg was much too short for me. Mom had enjoyed it as well.

Peter did not come with us. We could not afford the expenses for the three of us to travel to Hamburg. Mom had arranged for Peter to go to Tante Lotte's after work for the two nights that she would be away.

Not until a couple of years later did I find out what an awful time it was for Peter. It never occurred to me that my little brother would take my departure so hard. He went to pieces after I had left, and was devastated because we had not taken him to Hamburg with us to see me off. While at Tante Lotte's, Peter was also starting to suffer from terrifying nightmares in which he thought he was dying. This was a result of his having watched Papa die just nine months earlier. Peter's nightmares were to continue for years to come.

Auf Wiedersehen (Farewell)

Saturday, May 22 was departure day. We were at the pier hours ahead of time, along with many other people. Finally it was time to start the emigration process and the boarding. Mom was permitted to come on board and stay until a certain time before the ship sailed.

We were both shocked at how crowded and Spartan my accommodation was. We had noticed that the carpeting in the corridor stopped a ways back, and it looked as though the passenger area had already ended at that point. A sailor told us that the cabin I was in used to be crew quarters, housing two crew members. It had recently been modified to accommodate four passengers. Mom and I said to ourselves that we had booked the cheapest passage—other than a bunk in a dormitory for twenty—and that it would have to be my "home" for only eleven days. Except for sleeping, I would not spend any time in the room.

Mom and I enjoyed exploring the ship's facilities. It was luxurious, as ships have a reputation to be. I could not wait to get underway. Mom held up very well when the time came to say farewell. She pointed out to me where on the pier she would stand—underneath a certain sign on the building where I could easily spot her in the crowd. Also, since everybody would wave with a handkerchief—and it would be difficult to see who was who—she would wave with a newspaper instead. That way I would be able to identify her. It worked. Mom always had the best ideas. I would miss her so much.

Mom and I walking up the gangway of the M.S. Italia.

The M.S. Italia plying the North Atlantic.

Punctually at four o'clock, as the ship slowly moved out of the harbor, the band played *Auf Wiedersehen*, and a number of the other tear–jerkers. While it was meant to be festive, we immigrants did not appreciate it. Ours was not a cruise to be followed by a happy return, but rather it marked a separation for an unknown period of time, and the start of life in a strange country.

It was also the start of the greatest adventure of my life.

Epilogue

I immigrated to the United States in June 1954, thanks to the offer of Aunt Martha who herself had immigrated in 1929. The Timmanns had no children and generously allowed me to live with them. Two years later I was able to arrange for my brother, Peter, to join me. The following April 1957, Mom joined Peter and me. By that time Peter and I had moved out of the Timmanns' home into a garden apartment in Morristown, New Jersey.

The Mennen Company was located in Morristown. Readers will remember that I had met Bill Mennen in Berlin shortly before I immigrated, and I had a job at Mennen when I arrived in the United States. I was delighted when he placed me in the typing pool; I had expected to work on a production line until I had mastered English. That gave me an unusual opportunity to learn English quickly. In fact, Bill Mennen watched out for me, and later Peter, who was also offered a job before he arrived in this country. After Mom immigrated Bill Mennen was able to help her get a job and housing at Morristown Memorial Hospital where he served as a board member.

In late 1957 I met my future husband, Malvern Gross, an accountant with the international accounting firm of Price Waterhouse & Company. We were married in June 1958 and will celebrate forty–seven years of marriage in 2005. Mal rose through the ranks and became a partner of Price Waterhouse in 1968. He is a nationally recognized expert in the field of nonprofit accounting, having written the definitive work on the subject in 1972. This book is still in print thirty–three years later although others at Price Waterhouse have kept it up–to–date.

We have two children, Randolph Eric and Michele Andrea, both wonderful additions to our lives. Randy chose nursing for his career, and is a widely recognized expert on breast cancer at Memorial Sloan Kettering Cancer Center in New York. As of February 2005 he is taking courses at Columbia University to become a Nurse Practitioner.

Michele married John Siderius and has three beautiful children, Meagen, Johnny and Justin. A wonderful family, they are residing on Long Island in New York State where the Siderius family has deep roots.

Mom adjusted rapidly to her new country, becoming a citizen in 1962. For nearly fifteen years she lived in her own home in Daytona Beach, Florida. Unfortunately in the mid–nineteen seventies she was diagnosed with Alzheimer's Disease, and succumbed to this terrible disease in 1987 at the age of seventy–eight.

Peter married Jean Coviello in 1962 and they have three wonderful children and eight grandchildren, all living in New Jersey.

Private aviation has been an important part of our lives and we have owned a small plane most of our married life. I obtained a pilots license in 1963 although I had to give up flying when I got too busy raising children. Mal took early retirement in 1989 at age fifty–five to become President of the National Aeronautic Association, and we traveled widely in connection with those responsibilities. We have largely lived on the East Coast, first New Jersey and then the Washington DC area. Today we are retired and live on Orcas Island, in the beautiful San Juan Islands of Washington State.

* * * * *

I have included in this epilogue excerpts from a second book I have written, *Memories of Opportunities, Family and Adventures*. This volume covers the last fifty years of my life, beginning with my immigration to the United States on the M.S. Italia in 1954. These excerpts cover events affecting Berlin, the Cold War, and my heroes—those involved with the Berlin Airlift. Although these events took place after I had become a citizen of this great country, in fact they emanated from World War II and the years immediately afterwards.

1962
Berlin and the Cold War

My 1962 Trip to Berlin

In the fall of 1962, still childless, I went back to Germany for two months visiting relatives and friends, and listening to their reactions about the latest Soviet harassment measure—the infamous Berlin Wall, which had been built a year earlier.

The Infamous Berlin Wall

On Sunday morning, August 13, 1961, Berliners had awakened to construction in progress. Under the protection of heavy tanks and armed police and soldiers, concrete barriers and barbed wire fences were being put into place to seal off the borders of the Soviet–controlled sector of Berlin and the Soviet occupation zone, that is East Germany. The monstrous construction project, which was continuously reinforced over the following years, became known as the infamous Berlin Wall. This ugly wall was to stand for more than twenty–eight years and caused hundreds of deaths among those who tried to escape. It encircled, and therefore isolated, West Berlin, and cut it off from the eastern part of the city as well as from surrounding East Germany.

Berliners in both East and West Berlin went into shock. West Berliners who were visiting family or friends in East Berlin on that fateful weekend—including my cousin, Horst—were not allowed to return home. East Berlin residents who worked in West Berlin were cut off from their jobs. Any human contacts between families and friends that had still existed in the divided city were now totally cut. The *S–Bahn* (city train) and subway through–traffic was interrupted. Anyone who tried to escape in the years to come was ruthlessly shot.

Direct telephone service had been cut during the Blockade in 1948, but phone calls had been possible afterwards by routing a call through West Germany and East Germany, back to the other part of Berlin. Now even this circuitous way was no longer possible.

On this visit to Berlin a year after the construction of The Wall, I found that people had still not recovered from the shock. If anything, they were more disheartened than ever. The Wall affected their every-

This picture captures The Wall being constructed. East Berlin is on the right side, West Berlin on the left.

day lives. People could not attend weddings, births, and funerals on the "other side." There were sad scenes, where a bride and groom would stand on one side of The Wall on their wedding day and the parents or grandparents on the other, straining to get a glimpse of the happy couple.

Aunt Lotte and Uncle Martin had lost the sales personnel in their butcher shop. Help was extremely hard to find in West Berlin. At that particular time there were more jobs available than there were people to fill them. This led to the importation of guest workers from Turkey which, years later, turned into a migration, and some areas of West Berlin became wholly Turkish.

I also found a number of Berliners who were quite disappointed, and even angry, that the Americans had watched this happen and had done nothing to stop The Wall from being built.

The soldier is standing in East Berlin. The Wall is on the left, and anyone walking in the open area in the center would be shot. Note the buildings on the left are in West Berlin, and ahead and on the right is East Berlin. The Wall cuts right through the center of residential areas of Berlin.

In addition to the countless heart–wrenching experiences which befell the battle–weary Berliners, there were many tragedies. The Museum at Checkpoint Charlie tells some of the stories of the many people who tried to escape under, over, and through the fortified "wall system." It tells of the lucky ones who made it, and of the many who died trying to reach precious freedom. The museum has numerous ingenious inventions on display with which people tried to escape, such as inconceivably small and hidden spaces in cars, homemade flying machines, underground tunnels, and many more.

My term "wall system" means the following: The wall or barbed wire fence was not just a wall of concrete, or posts between which barbed wire had been strung. The fifteen foot high reinforced wall with rolled barbed wire on top which was visible from the West Berlin side,

The Wall is in the process of construction here. This picture gives a good view of the obstacles that someone would have to overcome when trying to escape.

was not all there was to it. On the East Berlin side there was the "death strip" which consisted of alternating barbed wire fences with strips of loose, raked sand to see footprints. There were mine fields, deep trenches, tank traps, and another reinforced barricade on the east side. In addition, there were spotlights every three hundred feet as well as watchtowers, each manned by two military men with binoculars. In some areas there were dog runs—each about half a mile long. Dog runs were fenced in strips of land in which trained vicious dogs were kept.

Not all of the above–mentioned reinforcements were in place in the beginning, so that a number of people did manage to escape during the very early days and months. Eventually, however, it became just about impossible to penetrate this barrier which in time had been reinforced to the highest degree.

A few words about the reason for building The Wall. At the end of World War II, Germany as well as Berlin, the capital city of the former Third Reich, were divided among the four Allies. While the three Western Allies jointly treated their sectors of Germany and Berlin as democracies, the Soviets forced their respective sectors into Communism. In the years following the war, quite a few people from both East Berlin and East Germany who were against Communism, fled to the West. As the years went by refugees arrived in West Berlin and West Germany by the thousands as the East German people became so dissatisfied with the Communist system that they preferred to leave all belongings behind in favor of freedom. Their numbers increased steadily and dramatically until by August 1961, refugees streamed into West Berlin by the thousands each day. The Wall was built by the communist government to stop this mass migration.

The easiest escape route was from East Berlin into West Berlin.

This section of The Wall was less than a mile from Uncle Martin's house. Note the wide "death zone" area between The Wall and the barrier beyond which were dog runs. There were spotlights on posts (right side and center) that were lit all night long.

One just had to get on the subway or city train in East Berlin and then, a few stops later, get off in West Berlin. People who were escaping from East Germany would come through Berlin because there was no passport check on the city trains.

The hardest part for the refugees was that they had to leave everything behind in order not to arouse suspicion with cumbersome baggage. It was also necessary for all family members to leave at the same time, as anyone left behind would encounter the punishment of the Communist system. Still, to gain precious freedom people left everything they owned and came to live in refugee camps in the West where they received help with starting a new life. This help initially consisted of shelter, food, and clothing, and then jobs and aid in finding housing. Shortage of housing was, and still is, one of the biggest problems in Germany.

With the building of The Wall, the "door to freedom" had been shut mercilessly.

Escape from East Berlin

While I was visiting Berlin in the fall of 1962 and staying with Uncle Rudolf and Aunt Hilda, Mom's oldest sister, I had a most interesting experience. Two of my cousins (nephews of Uncle Rudolf) showed up at the door one day. The boys had just risked their lives by escaping from East Berlin two or three days before. The following is the detailed story of their escape as the older cousin, Horst, told it to me. I wrote down his words in a letter to Mal just days after it happened. The account is unedited but it paints a very vivid picture of life in Berlin then.

October, 1962

Horst is my cousin and we lived in the same apartment building in Berlin–Lichterfelde until we were bombed and the buildings destroyed in 1943. His family moved in with his mother's parents in Niederschöneweide which today is in East Berlin. Horst has a younger brother and a sister. His father was killed in the war.

When Horst had finished school, he became a stonemason. He took a job in West Berlin and worked and lived in an apartment there for four and a half years. Almost every night he went to East Berlin to see his mother and have supper with the family. After work on Friday, August 11, 1961 Horst went home for the weekend to attend his sister's wedding. That was the fateful weekend of August 13 when the borders were closed and a wall was built to separate East and West Berlin. Horst could not return to his apartment or his job in West Berlin on Sunday night.

It was not so easy for him to just stay in East Berlin, either. The East German government gave him trouble because of his working and living in West Berlin, and they wanted to put him in jail. However, he told the police that he came as a refugee from West Berlin and would like to stay in the East now. They believed him, and he avoided jail, got a job, and earned a lot of money.

All of the time, however, he kept thinking about ways to escape.   But as each day passed, The Wall kept getting reinforced and escape became more and more difficult. Most people also thought that The Wall could not possibly stay up very long. The Americans surely would do something about it!

In the meantime, Horst married a girl he had known for a long time. He was still thinking of escaping and was making all kinds of plans. When he told his wife about wanting to escape, he found out that she wanted to stay in East Berlin. So he stayed.

One day while playing soccer, Horst broke his leg and had to stay off his feet for many weeks. It altogether took about six months before his leg was in good enough shape to risk a possible escape, and by that time it was almost impossible to break through a barrier which was being constantly reinforced. Many young men were shot to death while trying. However, Horst was now more determined to leave than before, especially since his marriage was not working out. All kinds of ideas came to his mind. For a while he thought of having a tunnel built (his brother Jürgen and a friend also wanted to escape), but it is very expensive to build a tunnel and they could not raise the money.

Horst had a friend who lived on Harzer Strasse where the wall goes down the middle of the street. He thought of getting a rope out of the window (fourth floor) and sliding down on it into the West side of the street, but on checking it out he found there is one of the guard houses a little ways down the street and there would not be much of a chance to even get the rope out of the window without being discovered.

Another friend lived in a house which is a part of the border. The first four floors have all windows bricked up and no one lives there now. The friend lives on the fifth floor, is a Vopo (East Berlin Police) and often works night shifts. Horst planned to get friendly with his wife, also a Vopo, to have a chance to be in her apartment some night when her husband is gone, and then he wanted to knock her out (since she as Vopo would not have approved of his escape) and jump out of the window. However, it turned out to be impossible to communicate with West Berlin to have a net put up into which he could jump from the fifth floor. When he could not get a definite commitment as to time and date, this plan had to be dropped. Most of the mail between East and West Berlin gets read so that communications in a case like that have to be done very skillfully. Of course, no telephone connections have existed since the Blockade in 1948.

One day, Horst received orders that he was to report to the recruiting station to become a member of the East German army. That was the day. In the evening, he took his brother, Jürgen, and his friend out to have some drinks so they would relax and not be so scared, and perhaps try to chicken out at the last minute. He needed their help as well as they needed his. At that point he told them that they had to leave that night. They went home to their mother to say good–bye, but their sister and her husband were there and Horst did not want them to know about the planned escape under any circumstances. When his mother made sandwiches for the boys, Horst wrote with a knife on the butter of his sandwich that he wanted to see his mother alone. Horst and Jürgen went into the other room, but they were unable to tell their mother. Instead, they got out sweaters and jackets and put them on, and their mother knew what was going to happen. Horst says, she really pulled herself together and did not even cry when they kissed her good–bye. She never gave anything away, even though there was such a very small chance that the boys would make it across, and a big chance that they would be killed. Next they told their mother to whom she should give their clothes and other belongings since they could not take anything; and at 10 p.m. Horst, Jürgen, and their friend were on their way.

They had picked one of the most dangerous spots to get across, thinking that no one would expect anybody to risk it there. At the last moment, Jürgen and the friend, both only 19 years old, got scared and wanted to back out, but Horst needed them and talked them into it.

Horst carried the binoculars, Jürgen the wire cutters, and the friend a shovel which they might need. Their approach was a deserted airport in the southeast of Berlin. They crawled on their stomachs for almost three hours before they reached the first fence of barbed wire. It was very important not to be seen when approaching the border as the guards would know immediately what they were up to. Once before, Horst and Jürgen had started out elsewhere on a spur of the moment and were noticed already on the approach. Fortunately, they were able to act as though they were just out for a walk and got a little too close to the border by mistake.

Cutting the first fence was easy, said Horst. The barbed wire was an East German product which was quite soft, and easy to cut. They now had to watch out for the guards who patrol the section in between the first and the second fence, an area of about two hundred feet consisting of a strip of very loose raked sand (to show footprints) and ending with a ditch, inside which more guards would be walking. When crawling across the airfield, the boys noticed with the help of the binoculars that it usually took about twenty minutes before the guards returned. There are always two guards walking about half a mile before they turn around and come back. The whole border is lit up at night with floodlights which are about three hundred feet apart, and there are guard houses on observation towers from which they watch with binoculars.

The boys got through the loose sand all right. Here they needed the shovel to smooth it out again after they had been sinking in nearly up to their knees. They now had to hurry and get across before the guards returned. The moment when all three of them looked at each other and hesitated was when they had to jump into the ditch on the chance that the guards might just be walking in there. However, there was no question that they had to go on because they would be shot turning back, too. So they jumped into the ditch—and were lucky. Next they had to get through the second fence of barbed wire which actually consists of three fences of barbed wire held up by concrete posts with barbed wire rolls in between each fence. This time they found that the wire was made of good steel which was hard to cut. Horst told me this was the barbed wire that Krupp, a West German industry, sold to the East. The two younger boys were so scared and exhausted by then that Horst had to go first and cut the wire himself. Presently he was in this mess of barbed wire and his clothes were ripping when the two boys behind him started to giggle because his pants were torn. He could not understand how they could be so silly all of a sudden and disregard the need for total silence.

Now the worst part was to come—swimming through the Teltow Kanal in the icy water. Horst wanted the youngest to go first, so it was Jürgen's turn. Jürgen was scared, but there was no turning back. Horst told him exactly how to swim—about half way and then to the right. There was a bridge across the canal on the left and this bridge was Russian zone and had guards on it, so they actually had the East on two sides. On the other side of the canal was a factory and there was a freight ship in the water. Horst wanted them to end up on the right side of the ship so that they would have protection in case there was any shooting. When the friend was ready to go into the water, Horst noticed that he no longer had the shovel. He had left it behind somewhere, and Horst was mad because it would give them away if the guards found the shovel.

The boys had expected the swimming to be the worst part of the escape, and it turned out to be even worse than they had thought. The difficulty they had was in trying to swim with all the clothes and heavy shoes. For a while they did not feel how cold the water really was, but they had trouble keep-

This is where my cousins swam across the Teltow Kanal. East Berlin is on the left and you can barely see some of the obstacles they came through. The factory they swam to is on the right. Horst brought me here several days after the boys escaped.

ing above water. Because of the factory, the water was quite oily and smelly right there.

It took them ten minutes to swim across the canal. There was no shooting, and once they got out of the water they started to run as fast as they could, for nothing would keep the guards from shooting into West Berlin. In the frigid air of the night they started to feel the cold as they walked along in their wet clothes. They were extremely lucky that a truck passed them on the street. It was nearly 3 a.m. by then, and unlikely that they would find anyone in this deserted industrial area. The truck passed by them, then stopped and backed up, apparently realizing what had happened. The boys were so cold and exhausted that they needed help getting into the truck. The truck driver took them back to the nearby factory and the boys took off their wet clothes. Then the ambulance came and took them to the hospital where they were kept overnight.

Jürgen (left) and Horst just before they went to Tempelhof Airport for their flight out of Berlin.

It did not take long for newspaper reporters to show up, wanting stories, but Horst had them thrown out. The boys were not going to give details of their escape so as not to spoil a chance for others. In the morning they received clothes from the refugee camp, and the clothes they had worn the night before had already been washed and patched up as well as possible. Horst said they could not sleep all night wondering what would happen to their mother. She waited nineteen hours before they were able to get a message through to her that they had made it.

In the morning, the boys were picked up by people from the Marienfelde Refugee Camp where they had to go through all the formalities. It was like clearing into another country, said Horst. They also got jobs and had to wait to be flown to West Germany.

Horst said they had to write to their mother and act as though they did not plan an escape. They told her in the letter that they went out for a walk and discovered a chance to get across easily and that they are willing to try the West and don't know yet whether they made the right decision. The letter also had to state that their mother did not know the boys were planning to leave, otherwise they would put her into jail.

By now, East Berlin has put up an additional barbed–wire fence where the three boys came across, and they are talking about putting mine fields in between the fences.

The foregoing description is hard to imagine for someone living in the United States. These words do not adequately convey the emotions, fear and risks my two cousins took. Certainly I felt it to a large extent because only a few years earlier Berlin and the Communist system had been a dominant part of Mom's, Peter's and my lives. The fact that my two cousins had "made it" when so many others had not, was really just a matter of chance.

After my return from Berlin, I kept up a correspondence with Horst for awhile. The boys had lived in a refugee camp in West Germany for a couple of months, found work and then an apartment. Their friend remained in Berlin where he had family. Jürgen, the younger brother who was only 19 years old, missed his mother very much and eventually went back to East Berlin. He had not been sure about wanting to leave in the first place, but had done it more because his brother and friend needed his help. I never heard what happened to him.

Horst and I corresponded for perhaps a year. The last I heard from him was that he was moving, either within the city in which he lived or to another location. I do not remember, and I never heard from him again.

1990
After the Wall Fell

My visit to Berlin in 1990 was a most interesting one. The Berlin Wall had fallen the year before. Uncle Martin and Aunt Lotte lived within walking distance of The Wall and the southeastern city limits, and while I was staying with them, I could easily observe what was going on at that time.

Return to Straupitz

One day during my stay, my cousin Klaus took me to the Spreewald in former East Germany to visit the little village of Straupitz, where we

After Germany's reunification, two friends from childhood days came back into my life—my friend Marga (right) and an over 1,000–year–old oak tree (behind us). Marga's husband, Werner, is in the center.

had lived for more than three years, from 1943 until late 1946. Many times over the years I had longed to see Straupitz again, it having been a tranquil part of my childhood and a respite from the air raids and destruction of Berlin until near the end of the war.

Not too much had changed in the village. It is a bit larger than it used to be. I went to the house where my best friend from those times, Marga Konzack, had lived (see Chapter 4). There were two women and a man standing at the gate talking. I went up to them and asked if the Konzack family was still living in this house.

The man turned to me and said: "I am Manfred Konzack." I looked at him in surprise and exclaimed with excitement: "Marga's little brother—one brown eye and one blue eye!"

The man turned his face, looked at me in incredible surprise, and I could see that he still had one brown eye and one blue eye! No one had uttered those words to him since childhood. I don't know whether he remembered me or not; he was several years younger, but he certainly knew I must have lived in Straupitz. It was an emotional moment for both of us.

Manfred gave me Marga's address. She lived in the nearby city of Lübben. Eventually we had a happy reunion, and we have kept in contact since then. Two lives had been lived in totally opposite circumstances, and it was challenging to compare notes. If Mom had not gotten Peter and me out of Straupitz when she did—on the very last day and at the last hour the Russians had permitted families to return to Berlin from Staupitz— my life would have paralleled Marga's.

Marga's picture is on the jacket of this book, the second girl from the left.

Remembering the Airlift

As the years went by and I was living a good life in the United States, memories of the very difficult times during and after World War II returned often. One memory in particular was that of the incredible feat of the Berlin Airlift, which saved 2.2 million West Berliners from being forced to become Communists by trying to starve them into submission. Without West Berlin's freedom, it would have been impossible for me to ever have come to the United States. The lives of Mom, Peter, and me would have taken quite a different course, and who knows if my brother and I would even be alive today.

It has always been a burning desire of mine to be able to thank personally just one of those brave pilots for what he and the Airlift did for us West Berliners. Seeing and hearing the airplanes fly into Berlin was reassuring because we knew they were bringing in food to keep us alive. But those planes were flown by "anonymous" people with whom we had no contact.

The first time I met a former Airlift pilot was in 1978, quite unexpectedly. We lived in the Washington, DC area and Mal was involved with the National Aviation Club. One evening we had dinner with Colonel Everett Langworthy. As he and I tried to get acquainted and I said I was from Berlin, he casually mentioned that he had been to

Ev Langworthy, the first Airlift pilot whom I had a chance to personally thank for his part in keeping us alive.

Sam Burgess at the controls during the Airlift. I never met Sam, but he honored me by giving me his Airlift scrapbook.

Berlin many times. In answer to my question of "when," he told me that he flew in the Berlin Airlift. The next thing I knew was that I was in tears and hugging him. Ev has been a very special person to me. He was the first Airlift pilot whom I was able to thank personally for my freedom.

Years later while living on Orcas Island, Mal met Colonel Sam Burgess at an aviation meeting. In the course of discussion Sam mentioned he had been an Airlift pilot, and Mal, of course, told him I was one of those saved by

Colonel Gail Halvorsen at Kitty Hawk December 17, 2003.

that gallant effort. Subsequently I talked with Sam by telephone and thanked him for his part. Several years later he sent me his scrapbook on the Airlift, saying that he wanted to leave it to someone who would appreciate it. He had no family. I was deeply moved by this, and his scrapbook is a treasured memento. Sam has since passed on.

One of the things Sam urged was that I join BAVA, the Berlin Airlift Veterans Association. Not being a veteran, I did not think I qualified, but he assured me that I was because I had been there, in Berlin, during the Airlift.

I attended my first BAVA Reunion in Washington DC in September 1998. It was an incredible experience as I walked into a roomful of pilots, mechanics, air traffic controllers and other airlift personnel who—50 years earlier—had risked their lives to keep me alive and free. I did not know whom to hug and thank first. They were all precious.

At the Hill Air Force Museum in Utah in 1998, I am seeing one of the Airlift aircraft up close for the first time. This plane had been flown by Col. Gail S. Halvorsen, "The Berlin Candy Bomber."

The most special one of the pilots whom I met that day was Colonel Gail Halvorsen, the legendary "Berlin Candy Bomber." He became famous by putting the "Heart into the Airlift" and candy into the children's hands. When I met him, I saw *love* and *caring* in his eyes, and I knew that only he could have thought up such a daring idea as to make parachutes out of handkerchiefs, tie candy bars and gum to them, and throw them out of his airplane to the waiting Berlin children below.

I feel fortunate that fifty years later I had the opportunity to meet Colonel Halvorsen and to be able to thank him personally for his love and kindness towards the little Berliners, and for the HOPE that he and his comrades gave to all of the people in West Berlin. Today Mal and I consider the Halvorsens among our most precious friends.

Quite a few times I was surprised that, when thanking one of these men for helping to keep Berlin free, I was being thanked by him instead. "We had orders and were just doing our job," I was told, "but we thank the Berliners for being willing to get along on the smallest amounts of food in exchange for freedom." "The Berliners were the real heroes" one airlift pilot told me.

The Airlift pilots could fly in only limited supplies of food, just enough for us to survive, but they brought us *hope*. It was the hope we needed more than the calories in order to survive; the hope to keep our freedom, and because of it to have a better life.

Without the Airlift to keep West Berlin free, I would not be here as a free person in the United States. My special, personal thanks go to all who were involved in making the Berlin Airlift a success, and to one unique person in particular, Colonel Gail Halvorsen, who put the personal touch of love on the operation.

Auf Wiedersehen
"Farewell," until we meet again in Volume II

Also by Inge Gross

**Memories
of Opportunities,
Family and Adventures
1954-2004
An Autobiography**
Volume Two

(Hard cover, 384 pages, 200 pictures, $23.95)

At the age of nineteen Inge managed to find her way to America from Berlin to start the greatest adventure of her life. Volume II is the story of that adventure.

She was told on her first day of work by one of her mentors at The Mennen Company: "The door of opportunity is open. We are not going to serve anything to you on a silver platter, but you can have whatever you want here, if you work for it." She did, and she quickly integrated herself into her new country.

She married Malvern Gross in 1958. Her life became a celebration of freedom as she and her husband traveled widely, including many return trips to Berlin, a pioneering automobile trip to the U.S.S.R. at the height of the Cold War, and more recently a trip to the winter huts of Antarctic explorers Shackleton and Scott just 850 miles from the South Pole. In between her many adventures she and her husband raised two fine children.

Inge's story above all else expresses her love of this country and the freedom and opportunities that we enjoy, which too often so many of us seem to take for granted.

Both Volume One and Volume Two are available directly from the publisher, Island In The Sky Publishing Co., PO Box 139, Eastsound, WA 98245. The price of each book including shipping via media mail is $23.95 if ordered directly from the publisher and paid by check. Readers preferring the use of priority mail or the use of a credit card should go on–line at: *www.MemoriesOfWWII.com, or Amazon.com.*